Understanding Movement Parties Through their Communication

In many countries, movement parties have swayed large tracts of the electorate. Contributions to this edited book reflect on the place of movement parties in democratic politics through analyses of their communication. Reviewing evidence from several countries including cases from Europe, Australia and India where movement parties have gained ground in politics, this book illuminates the important role that communication has played in their rise as well as the issues surrounding it. Movement parties have expressed greater sensitivity to neglected issues, a commitment to renewing links with marginalized social groups through more direct—chiefly online—communication with them as well as an ambition to overhaul both the party organization and the political system. In doing so, they have signalled a desire to disrupt and reimagine politics. Yet, the critical examination of their efforts—and of the communication environment in which they operate—against questions regarding the quality of democracy—throws into relief a mismatch between a participation-oriented rhetoric and concrete democratic practices. Accordingly, contributions draw attention to disconnections between a professed need for more immediate and greater participation in movement party organization and policy-making, on the one hand, their organizational practices and the communication of parties, leaders, and supporters, on the other. This book was originally published as a special issue of the journal, *Information, Communication & Society*.

Dan Mercea is Reader in Digital and Social Change at City, University of London, UK.

Lorenzo Mosca is Professor of Digital Media and Datafied Society at the University of Milan, Italy.

Understanding Movement Parties Through their Communication

Edited by
Dan Mercea and Lorenzo Mosca

NEW YORK AND LONDON

First published 2023
by Routledge
605 Third Avenue, New York, NY 10158

and by Routledge
4 Park Square, Milton Park, Abingdon, Oxon OX14 4RN

Routledge is an imprint of the Taylor & Francis Group, an informa business

Chapters 1–10 © 2023 Taylor & Francis

All rights reserved. No part of this book may be reprinted or reproduced or utilised in any form or by any electronic, mechanical, or other means, now known or hereafter invented, including photocopying and recording, or in any information storage or retrieval system, without permission in writing from the publishers.

Trademark notice: Product or corporate names may be trademarks or registered trademarks, and are used only for identification and explanation without intent to infringe.

British Library Cataloguing in Publication Data
A catalogue record for this book is available from the British Library

ISBN13: 978-1-032-43910-5 (hbk)
ISBN13: 978-1-032-43911-2 (pbk)
ISBN13: 978-1-003-36936-3 (ebk)

DOI: 10.4324/9781003369363

Typeset in Minion Pro
by Newgen Publishing UK

Publisher's Note
The publisher accepts responsibility for any inconsistencies that may have arisen during the conversion of this book from journal articles to book chapters, namely the inclusion of journal terminology.

Disclaimer
Every effort has been made to contact copyright holders for their permission to reprint material in this book. The publishers would be grateful to hear from any copyright holder who is not here acknowledged and will undertake to rectify any errors or omissions in future editions of this book.

Contents

Citation Information vii
Notes on Contributors ix

1 Introduction: Understanding movement parties through their communication 1
 Dan Mercea and Lorenzo Mosca

2 Communication in progressive movement parties: against populism and beyond digitalism 18
 Donatella della Porta

3 'We do politics so we can change politics': communication strategies and practices in the Aam Aadmi Party's institutionalization process 35
 Divya Siddarth, Roshan Shankar and Joyojeet Pal

4 Reverting trajectories? UKIP's organisational and discursive change after the Brexit referendum 56
 Ofra Klein and Andrea L. P. Pirro

5 Social networks and digital organisation: far right parties at the 2019 Australian federal election 75
 Jordan McSwiney

6 Decentralizing electoral campaigns? New-old parties, grassroots and digital activism 93
 Josep Lobera and Martín Portos

7 Are digital platforms potential drivers of the populist vote? A comparative analysis of France, Germany and Italy 115
 Lorenzo Mosca and Mario Quaranta

8 Still 'fire in the (full) belly'? Anti-establishment rhetoric before and after government participation 134
 Andrea Ceron, Alessandro Gandini and Patrizio Lodetti

9 Does populism go viral? How Italian leaders engage citizens
   through social media   151
   Roberta Bracciale, Massimiliano Andretta and Antonio Martella

10 Why study media ecosystems?   169
   Ethan Zuckerman

   Index   188

Citation Information

The chapters in this book were originally published in the journal *Information, Communication and Society*, volume 24, issue 10 (2021). When citing this material, please use the original page numbering for each article, as follows:

Chapter 1
Understanding movement parties through their communication
Dan Mercea and Lorenzo Mosca
Information, Communication and Society, volume 24, issue 10 (2021), pp. 1327–1343

Chapter 2
Communication in progressive movement parties: against populism and beyond digitalism
Donatella della Porta
Information, Communication and Society, volume 24, issue 10 (2021), pp. 1344–1360

Chapter 3
'We do politics so we can change politics': communication strategies and practices in the Aam Aadmi Party's institutionalization process
Divya Siddarth, Roshan Shankar and Joyojeet Pal
Information, Communication and Society, volume 24, issue 10 (2021), pp. 1361–1381

Chapter 4
Reverting trajectories? UKIP's organisational and discursive change after the Brexit referendum
Ofra Klein and Andrea L. P. Pirro
Information, Communication and Society, volume 24, issue 10 (2021), pp. 1382–1400

Chapter 5
Social networks and digital organisation: far right parties at the 2019 Australian federal election
Jordan McSwiney
Information, Communication and Society, volume 24, issue 10 (2021), pp. 1401–1418

Chapter 6
Decentralizing electoral campaigns? New-old parties, grassroots and digital activism
Josep Lobera and Martín Portos
Information, Communication and Society, volume 24, issue 10 (2021), pp. 1419–1440

Chapter 7
Are digital platforms potential drivers of the populist vote? A comparative analysis of France, Germany and Italy
Lorenzo Mosca and Mario Quaranta
Information, Communication and Society, volume 24, issue 10 (2021), pp. 1441–1459

Chapter 8
Still 'fire in the (full) belly'? Anti-establishment rhetoric before and after government participation
Andrea Ceron, Alessandro Gandini and Patrizio Lodetti
Information, Communication and Society, volume 24, issue 10 (2021), pp. 1460–1476

Chapter 9
Does populism go viral? How Italian leaders engage citizens through social media
Roberta Bracciale, Massimiliano Andretta and Antonio Martella
Information, Communication and Society, volume 24, issue 10 (2021), pp. 1477–1494

Chapter 10
Why study media ecosystems?
Ethan Zuckerman
Information, Communication and Society, volume 24, issue 10 (2021), pp. 1495–1513

For any permission-related enquiries please visit:
www.tandfonline.com/page/help/permissions

Notes on Contributors

Massimiliano Andretta, Department of Political Science, University of Pisa, Pisa, Italy.

Roberta Bracciale, Department of Political Science, University of Pisa, Pisa, Italy.

Andrea Ceron, Department of Social and Political Sciences, State University of Milan, Milano, Italy.

Donatella della Porta, Faculty of Political and Social Sciences, Scuola Normale Superiore, Firenze, Italy.

Alessandro Gandini, Department of Social and Political Sciences, State University of Milan, Milano, Italy.

Ofra Klein, Erasmus School of History, Culture and Communication, Erasmus University Rotterdam, Rotterdam, The Netherlands.

Josep Lobera, Department of Sociology, Autonomous University of Madrid, Madrid, Spain.

Patrizio Lodetti, Statistics, Informatics and Applications Department, University of Florence, Firenze, Italy.

Antonio Martella, Department of Cultures, Politics and Society, University of Turin, Torino, Italy.

Jordan McSwiney, Centre for Deliberative Democracy and Global Governance, University of Canberra, Australia.

Dan Mercea, Department of Sociology and Criminology, City, University of London, London, UK.

Lorenzo Mosca, Department of Social and Political Sciences, State University of Milan, Milano, Italy.

Joyojeet Pal, Microsoft Research, Bengaluru, India.

Andrea L. P. Pirro, Department of Political and Social Sciences, University of Bologna, Bologna, Italy.

Martín Portos, Department of Social Sciences, Universidad Carlos III de Madrid, Madrid, Spain.

Mario Quaranta, Department of Sociology and Social Research, University of Trento, Trento, Italy.

Roshan Shankar, Freelance Researcher, Delhi, India.

Divya Siddarth, Microsoft Research, Bengaluru, India.

Ethan Zuckerman, University of Massachusetts Amherst, Amherst, MA, USA.

Introduction: Understanding movement parties through their communication

Dan Mercea ⓘ and Lorenzo Mosca ⓘ

ABSTRACT
In many countries, movement parties have gained traction among the electorate. This special issue spotlights the communication of movement parties as an avenue for researching their purchase on democratic politics. Through a combination of empirical studies and commentaries, the issue covers multiple countries where movement parties have established a foothold in politics. The introduction makes the case that communication has played a vital part in their rise. Movement parties have expressed greater sensitivity to neglected issues, a drive to renew links with marginalized social groups through more direct – chiefly online – communication with them as well as an ambition to overhaul both the party organization and the political system. While movement parties have signalled a desire to disrupt and reimagine politics, we argue for their critical examination against questions regarding the quality of democracy. Specifically, we problematize the mismatch between a populist rhetoric emphasizing the need for more immediate and greater participation in the party organization as well as policymaking and movement party practices.

Introduction

As countries across the world face the daunting task of making policy choices in rushed attempts to mitigate another severe economic downturn in little over a decade, this time at the hand of the global Covid-19 pandemic, the stage seems set again for new political realignments. In this article, we consider a primary indicator of political realignment – the surge of movement parties – whose multiple causes manifest conspicuously as a shift, on the one hand, of voter allegiances away from established and towards challenger parties; and, on the other hand, of party positions on the dominant issues of the time (Kriesi & Frey, 2008).

Popular mobilisations may long precede electoral contests as a more immediate vehicle for the articulation of collective grievances (McAdam & Tarrow, 2010). The social movements arising to champion them can act as a hotbed for new parties vying to weave fresh links with society, to maximize opportunities for realignment (della Porta et al.,

2017; Mosca, 2014). As we introduce this special issue, we propose a research agenda for the study of movement parties that concentrates on their communication as a multi-pronged avenue – for reimagining party membership, nurturing engagement with the electorate as well as for building innovative types of organization – that invites fresh reflections on the opportunities for participation offered by these political actors, as links with society are reformulated.

Communication can be a vital expedient for resource-poor political challengers hamstrung by precarious and weak organizational structures (della Porta et al., 2017). We discuss the relationship of communication to organization, particularly as movement parties seek renewed and wider ties with their base, extending over and above electoral support. We review evidence of movement parties adopting a populist rhetoric and discuss it against the literature on populist communication that has been shown to be predicated on the disintermediation of links with society through a bypassing of traditional media and journalism in favour of social media and network connectivity (Deseriis, 2020; Engesser et al., 2017). We then consider participation in movement parties stressing the mismatch between their democratic conceptions and the quality of democratic practices they have introduced. We conclude by presenting the articles in this special issue, underscoring their contribution to understanding movement parties through their communication.

An amalgamation of movements, parties and networked communication

An expanding domain of scholarly investigation, the relation between social movements and political parties has been retraced back to an interest in the capacity of the latter to sustain *linkages* with society that feed into their policies (Luttbeg, 1974), organization or electoral strategies (McAdam & Tarrow, 2010); or to questions regarding the capacity of social movements to maximize cultural and structural opportunities for mobilization, collective action and for them to gain political traction (Pirro, 2019, p. 787). Multiple possible entanglements of movements with parties have been explored under the conceptual umbrella of the term movement parties. Succinctly, they have been defined as 'political parties that have particularly strong organizational and external links with social movements' (della Porta et al., 2017, p. 5). At the same time, movements encompass multiple groups – of which one may be parties – into variable networks espousing a common identity (Diani, 1992). A prominent distinction between movements and parties flows from the modalities whereby they seek to effect social change, i.e., by institutional means in the case of parties putting forward candidates competing in elections and extra-institutional actions such as protests, by movements (Kitschelt, 2006).

The point of any neat analytical distinction is to allow observers to outline a phenomenon they investigate by specifying the categorical boundaries that separate it from other phenomena (Wang et al., 2019). However, teasing out categorical boundaries need not obviate movement-party intersections. Movements can feed ideas into party policy; they can bolster the numbers of party cadres or supporters, mobilizing the latter in the course of electoral campaigns or at the polling booth (McAdam & Tarrow, 2010; Vann, 2018). Parties can embrace and champion movement issues, providing previously inaccessible avenues for social change (Tormey & Feenstra, 2015, p. 599). They can introduce movement claims directly into the electoral and later policy arenas, disrupting these through a critique of favourable bias towards the preferences of the political establishment (Pirro, 2018). In turn, party members are particularly likely to become involved in movement activities, regardless of their ideological leanings (Giugni & Grasso, 2021). Parties can thus shore up movement numbers. Equally, electoral success of a party can dampen movement mobilization (Minkenberg, 2019).

Movement-party alliances may take a local, contextual flavour accounting for the strength of electoral competition, political cleavages, prevalent socio-economic conditions or the participation by the latter in government (Giugni & Grasso, 2021; Kriesi, 1989; Piven & Cloward, 1977). Indeed, the literature on movement parties has highlighted their volatile and temporary nature. As della Porta et al. (2017, p. 24) argue, the term expresses a drive to shed light on 'complex and contingent dynamics developed when the field of party politics meets with protest politics with unexpected outcomes during critical junctures'. As such, they contend, the movement party has been a useful heuristic for social scientists who may otherwise be ill-equipped to bridge political party and social movement studies when observing what may be transient arrangements that nevertheless appear to encapsulate wider social change.

The seminal delineation of movement parties by Kitschelt (2006) has emphasized that the direction in which they develop is from movements to parties. Movement parties are a project undertaken by movement entrepreneurs seeking to move a limited set of neglected or new issues into the electoral and policy arenas with a new political vehicle organizationally more akin to a porous movement than a party with formalized rules and procedures. In his analysis, Kitschelt (2006) mapped out key organizational itineraries of movement parties as they navigate the electoral terrain and later negotiate institutional incentives. Of late, however, examples of movements taking root within established parties in majoritarian democracies – e.g., the Tea Party in the US Republican Party, Momentum in the UK Labour Party – conversely reveal movements as a vehicle for party renewal; for the revitalization and expansion of party links with society (Dennis, 2020; Klein & Pirro, 2020; Klug et al., 2016). They testify to a growing appeal of the movement-party nexus bridging protest and electoral politics over longer cycles of organization alternating between electoral competition, institutionalization and policymaking.

While electoral success can and has spelled the demise of the movement – as in the case of some far-right movements in Western Europe (Kitschelt, 2006; Minkenberg, 2019, p. 2) – the extent to which issues central to a movement endure or expand, can influence the viability of the movement-party as it alternates between periods in and out of legislatures or governments. The communication of such issues is therefore particularly salient to the relationship between movement-parties, movements and their support base. To grapple with this notion more widely, it may help to briefly turn to organizational communication studies. Communication Constitutive of Organization (or CCO) is a meta-theory rather than an explanatory theory that casts communication as the medium for the development and reproduction of organization; for the articulation of organizational boundaries, of its membership, of relationships among members and of the organization with its wider 'social reality' (Schoeneborn et al., 2014, p. 303). Accordingly, the development, transformation, adaptation or impact of movement party relations with supporting movements, their membership as well as political rivals or democratic institutions can be garnered through an examination of their communication.

The generation of movement parties that has emerged after the 2007–2008 financial crisis has stoked scholarly interest for their choice to marry the technological affordances for networked communication of information and communication technologies (ICTs) with an ethos of direct participation by their membership in both party affairs and the political system (Anduiza et al., 2019; Tormey & Feenstra, 2015). A low entry threshold, conceived of as 'an entitlement to participation' (Kitschelt, 2006, p. 202), has led to movement party membership being granted to anyone proactively seeking involvement, albeit not only in a party meeting or activity but also in their online networks of social and policy platforms (for insights into the Italian 5 Star Movement or M5S see Deseriis, 2020; Mosca, 2020). This conception of membership has been rooted in a critique of established, mass parties characterized by a delineation of the ordinary membership from the party leadership and activists (Tormey & Feenstra, 2015, p. 598).

Attention paid to this transformation of organizational communication was informed by observations that predominant parties in modern democracies had seen their traditional electoral base erode as socio-economic transformations diluted ideological bonds rooted chiefly in materialist values (Inglehart & Norris, 2017). As a result, parties started to compete in the centre-ground of the electoral field by courting voters using market research tools (Lees-Marshment & Lilleker, 2001) and permanent campaign communication strategies offline (Sparrow & Turner, 2001) as well as online (Larsson, 2016). Accordingly, their organizations became bureaucratic, centralized around the leadership and cultivating a top-down mode of communication from the party to the electorate (Bennett et al., 2018, p. 1658). Displacing it, in the case of movement parties, has been a *connective* modality of engagement. It complements and extends longer-running modes of participation such as attendance at physical gatherings (Bennett et al., 2018; Deseriis, 2020; Mosca, 2014; Tormey & Feenstra, 2015) and is predicated on 'technology platforms and affordances [that] are indistinguishable from, and replace, key components of brick and mortar organization and intra-party functions' (Bennett et al., 2018, p. 1666).

Accounts of movement parties as diverse as the Pirate parties in various European countries, the Italian *M5S*, the Danish *Alternativet*, the French *La France Insoumise* or *Podemos* in Spain, paint them as innovators seeking to revitalize participation by making networked communication central to their operation (Bennett et al., 2018; Gerbaudo, 2019). The renewal of the party organizational form that they beckon has hinged on direct access for the membership to the political agenda, to policy deliberations, candidate selection and voting in primary elections. Instrumental to such involvement, digital platforms have embodied a programmatic goal to enable a bottom-up input by the membership into the workings of the party.

The extent to which this communication modality realized with digital technologies has translated into meaningful participation in party decision or policy-making has been empirically shown to be limited and to become restricted over time (Rodríguez-Teruel et al., 2016, p. 572). Examples of the narrowing scope for input are candidate or policy choices that are predefined by small cadres of party activists before they are presented to the membership (Deseriis, 2020). Such strictures to participation have been described as an upshot of organizational adaptation, for example to administrative and territorial specificities of states where movement parties operate (Rodríguez-Teruel et al., 2016, p. 580). The technologies themselves have contributed to these challenges, as parties have struggled with expanding their digital infrastructures, with moderating deliberations among the membership (Bennett et al., 2018, p. 1671), as well as with assembling new voter coalitions around unified online messaging (Siddarth et al., 2021). Conversely, those very technologies have helped reproduce the dominance of extant party hierarchies over a social media base gesturing their support without any prospect of a seat at the decision or policy-making table (as exemplified by the Australian far-right, McSwiney, 2020). In sum, in several countries, movement parties have been at the forefront of a recent shake up of party politics through a combination of experiments – not always successful – with networked communication with their support base, scaled with ICTs.

Populist communication by movement parties

The narrowing scope for supporter or member participation does not seem to have been strictly matched with a change in rhetoric. Movement parties have continued to extol the merits of direct democratic participation (Bennett et al., 2018, p. 1668; Deseriis, 2020; Mosca, 2014). This, in part, may be attributed to the populist communication (Engesser et al., 2017) embraced by some of them. As discussed below, movement parties mirror the main features of the dominant party model of the historical period in which they emerged, which – for those we discuss in this contribution – is the neoliberal populist party (della Porta et al., 2017).

Populism is a concept at the heart of a large body of literature straddling political science and communication studies (Albertazzi & Mueller, 2013; Anduiza et al., 2019; Mudde & Rovira Kaltwasser, 2012; Pirro, 2018). Described as an 'empty signifier' (Laclau, 2005), populism has been conceptually grafted onto political projects predicated on anti-elitism and a discursive claim to restore the 'supremacy of popular sovereignty' usurped by elites (Aslanidis, 2016, p. 96).

A singularity of logic, style and strategy characterizes populist communication (Engesser et al., 2017, pp. 1280, 1286). Logic pertains to the 'norms, routines and procedures' underpinning political messaging that, in the case of populist communication, circumvents media organizations to build a more immediate relationship with the public. This is achieved by dint of a distinct 'mode of presentation' which is used strategically to leverage 'power, legitimacy and [opportunities for] mobilization'. To take these in turn, a populist logic foregrounds unmediated communication with the people, envisaged as a homogenous entity defined along ideological lines as the nation (in right-wing populism) or the subordinate classes (in left-wing populism, Engesser et al., 2017, p. 1283). In that way, populism de facto embraces distinction and finds utility in associative yet insulated forms of online communication generically designated as echo-chambers (Bastos et al., 2018) that notably now span multiple platforms and national borders (Zuckerman, 2021).

Second, its messaging simplifies complex policy choices, which are painted in emotional and often negative (Engesser et al., 2017, p. 1285), individualized, personalized and even aggressive language (Bracciale et al., 2021). Third, populist communication can be harnessed strategically to accrue power and legitimacy – including through the evasion of public scrutiny on grounds that populists derive their support directly from the people. Populist communication can thus serve to mobilize 'the people' in rallies, at the ballot box or in other shows of approval enhancing the power of the populists (Engesser et al., 2017, p. 1286). Online, especially, it may find fertile ground. Comparative evidence points to a tendency to vote for populist parties – including movement parties such as M5S and La France Insoumise – among politically active users of social media and mobile instant messaging services (Mosca & Quaranta, 2021).

In Italy, the epitomal movement party, M5S, espoused anti-elitism in both its left and right-wing guises by marrying calls for progressive and inclusive politics to tackle postmaterialist concerns with the environment, identity as well as inequality with nativism, i.e., adversity towards immigrants and ethnic minorities, and Euroscepticism. It has done so with recourse to emotive language regarding immigration and a dichotomous approach to complex policy choices such as membership of the Eurozone, so as to mobilize a broad ideological coalition and maximize its share of the vote (Pirro, 2018, pp. 445, 452).

M5S additionally provides an illuminating indication of how a movement party embracing populist communication evolves once in government. It first formed a coalition government with the far-right Lega (2018–2019), which was followed by an alliance with the centre-left Democratic party, from 2019 and by a remarkably broad coalition including all parliamentary forces but the far-right Fratelli d'Italia, since 2020. Despite an overt post-election moderation of its language reflecting this change and its institutionalization as it entered into government (Ceron et al., 2020), M5S' anti-establishment claims lingered in the party's rhetoric. The online communication of its 'eclectic' or 'polyvalent populism' has been programmatically associated with the party's aforementioned drive to harness digital technologies for renewed citizen participation in party affairs and the legislative process alike (Mosca & Tronconi, 2019; Pirro, 2018, p. 451).

In Spain, drawing roots from the 15M movement and inspiration from Latin America, Podemos has been an exponent of the left-leaning variant of anti-elitism (della Porta et al., 2017). It has decried the plight of working people in the wake of the economic crisis and fiscal austerity, clamouring an aloofness of corruption-prone democratic representatives bent on structural adjustments that heightened rising inequalities (Casero-Ripollés et al., 2017, p. 988). Yet, similarly to M5S, it imbued its campaign communication with a syncretic populism eschewing erstwhile distinctions between the ideological left and the right. Its bifurcated media strategy appealed directly to supporters online while seizing on mainstream media news values to challenge the political establishment on the airwaves (Casero-Ripollés et al., 2016, pp. 384–385). Electorally successful soon after its creation in early 2014, it has used emotive language to turn its intellectual critique into a rallying cry (Casero-Ripollés et al., 2016, p. 386) but has displayed less of an appetite than M5S for nativist tropes (Casero-Ripollés et al., 2017, p. 997; Font et al., 2021). The intentional and explicit use of populist rhetoric was in part rolled back after the second Podemos Citizen Assembly in 2017. That forum delivered a more definitive turn to the left and the marginalization of the former political secretary, Íñigo Errejón, who left the party in 2019. Most recently, Podemos became a key partner in the first coalition government in the history of democratic Spain that took office in January 2020.

A third vignette, from Germany, is of right-wing populism reinforced discursively by the Pegida movement and the Alternative für Deutschland (AfD) party (Stier et al., 2017).

The former emerged in 2014 as a nativist reaction to the perceived composite threats of islamization, immigration, trade liberalization, Europeanization and gender politics (Kemper, 2015; Stier et al., 2017, p. 1366). It soon drew the sympathies of the AfD, a Eurosceptic party formed in 2013 to protest the European Stabilisation Mechanism (Kemper, 2015) created by the European Union in response to the sovereign debt crisis that afflicted Greece and other member states. Within a few years, the AfD 'veered to the radical right' (Arzheimer & Berning, 2019; see also Schwörer, 2019) thanks in part to the xenophobic opinion climate seeded by Pegida.

The movement-party nexus became manifest in the autumn of 2015, in the midst of the refugee crisis, when a prominent AfD politician helped organize anti-migrant demonstrations in the East-German city of Erfurt (Kemper, 2015, p. 47). Their confluence was further evidenced by research revealing a substantial overlap – of up to one third – among their supporters on Facebook. Between late 2014 and the summer of 2016, such support was expressed with likes to posts on their public pages (Stier et al., 2017, p. 1373). On Facebook – an outlet favoured by both movement and party – both articulated an anti-elitism directed at the media and Europhile elites welcoming of refugees alongside an exclusionary outlook depicting immigrants as an outgroup threatening the community of the nation (Stier et al., 2017, p. 1378). Together, elites and outgroup carried the blame for an alleged demise of the German nation state (Kemper, 2015), acting as a rhetorical enemy against which movement and party bases were mobilized.

Fourth, in Hungary, Jobbik transitioned from a Christian right student movement to a political party which entered into Parliament within little over a decade (Pirro, 2019, p. 791). It pitched itself in opposition to a gallery of parties whose hitherto key shortcoming had been a failure to 'represent national values and interests'; it drew a direct connection between criminality and a minority group, the Roma ethnic community; it devised a varied portfolio of means to circumvent hostile media so as to nurture its support base on social media as well as through concerts and festivals appealing to the young (Pirro, 2019, pp. 792–793). As a counterweight to those purported ills, Jobbik championed an anti-capitalist, anti-globalist agenda. It lamented elite corruption and the dissolution of the ethno-national community in the face of the threat of criminality and immigration.

Lastly, in the United Kingdom, and especially under the leadership of Nigel Farage, UKIP embraced a populist communication style that made many among the British to regard it as 'the people's party' (Block & Negrine, 2017). As the party lost its main *raison d'etre* after the Brexit referendum (Usherwood, 2019), it had to reckon with a series of dilemmas as it struggled to reposition itself. It thus shifted from 'single issue populism' into being a more conventionally exclusionary European populist party (Usherwood, 2019, p. 1210). UKIP consequently took an organizational and discursive turn into movement politics (Hanna & Busher, 2019) with the Brexit referendum opening the party up to attempts by far-right movements and activists to transition it into the movement party form (Davidson & Berezin, 2018; Klein & Pirro, 2020).

These five examples of populist communication among movement parties on the left and the right illustrate how divergent ideological orientations are married to communication styles distinctly emphasizing either inclusivity or exclusivity. Notwithstanding evidence that regardless of ideology, extra-institutional activists among party ranks are one of the most active online contingents who may be responsible for more polarized party messaging on social media (Lobera & Portos, 2020), we can imagine the two extremes of far-right movement parties magnifying exclusion (see for example McSwiney, 2020) and left-wing movement parties championing inclusion (della Porta, 2021). In-between the two poles, we can find ideologically eclectic, vote-maximizing movement parties.

Ideological positioning of movement parties additionally seems linked to their relationship with traditional media. On the one hand, leftist movement parties such as Podemos embraced alternative media as a tried and tested means to circumvent the mass media but not its penchant for infotainment, which in the end paved the way to a reinforcing relationship with the media that had been previously enjoyed by other political populists (Casero-Ripollés et al., 2016). On the other, far-right movement parties have similarly tended to see legacy media as part of the corrupt establishment while expediently banking on the spread of online misinformation and conspiracy theories aligning with their political agenda (Bergmann, 2018). Ultimately, the ideological stance of a movement party seems likely to colour its communication in as far as 'populists on the left and the right interpret complex socio-economic and socio-cultural processes as favouring 'the elite' and going against the interests of 'the people', but they focus on different processes and evaluate them differently' (De Cleen et al., 2018). The same applies to democratic participation. While populist parties are often critical of representative democracy and strive for the introduction of elements of direct democracy (Mudde, 2004), when compared to far-right parties such as Jobbik, AfD and UKIP, the M5S and Podemos display a greater sensitivity to direct democracy. Indeed, as shown in the next section, the latter deeply informs their political programmes as well as the relationship with their members and the electorate. However, a mismatch has emerged between democratic ideas and practices as M5s and Podemos themselves became members of the political establishment by joining government coalitions.

Quality of democratic participation in movement parties

The standing of movement parties among the electorate and in relation to other parties has had discernible ramifications for voter turnout (e.g., by mobilizing apathetic voters, Passarelli & Tuorto, 2018), policy-making (e.g., through the plebiscitarian use of online fora to engage the membership in policy choices, Deseriis, 2020; Gerbaudo, 2019) or party systems (e.g., through the remodelling of party organizations and a renewed representation of ideological cleavages, della Porta et al., 2017). As such, movement parties have become primary exponents of alternative organizational and communicational approaches. Yet, there is variance in the degree to which membership renewal and its digital extension alongside the disintermediation of party communication with social media and other online platforms is associated with greater participation and a revival of bonds between the electorate and representatives. For this reason, we believe it is instructive to ponder the relation of movement parties to quality of democracy and specifically citizen participation as a key dimension of this concept.

Quality of democracy is a sprawling area of enquiry, which we reference here as a body of literature that has sought to map and evaluate the breadth of the relationship between the citizenry and their representatives. To maintain their legitimacy, the latter are normatively disposed to satisfy free and equal citizens who are able to participate in the affairs of the polity through various forms of association that keep governments accountable and willing to attend to their citizens (Morlino, 2012). Citizen participation is a fundamental component of the concept pertaining to

> the entire set of behaviours, be they conventional or unconventional (…) that allows women and men, as individuals or groups, to create, revive, or strengthen group identification or to try to influence the recruitment of, and decisions by, political authorities. (Morlino, 2012, p. 204)

The extent to which movement parties have been innovators in respect to participation is a determination one might make against the backdrop of existing party models (della Porta et al., 2017), i.e., the dominant party type during a certain period in the course of the historical evolution of a party system. Accordingly, it has been proposed that a neoliberal party model that preceded the surge of movement parties over the last decade has impressed on them certain characteristics despite their best efforts to challenge that very model (della Porta et al., 2017, p. 2). Neoliberal policy eroded the capacity of parties for representation through market-orientated reforms and trade liberalization – a failing thrown into relief by the 2007–08 global financial crisis – creating the conditions for new parties to step into the void (della Porta et al., 2017, p. 18). Yet, a hegemonic neoliberal populist party model that is 'organizationally thin, highly personalized, post-ideological and mediatized' has, at the same time, lent some of these features to movement parties.

As described, movement parties offered multiple remediations to the crisis of representation galvanized by neoliberalism – a more immediate and direct relationship with the membership, the importation of neglected or new issues into the representative arena and a robust critique of the status quo embodied by political and media institutions. As they have charted this path, movement parties have made strategic choices, of which we have discussed those pertaining to relations with reimagined memberships that are in turn tied to broader conceptions of democratic participation, public communication and political legitimation. Evidence to date suggests that the M5S in Italy and Podemos in Spain succeeded in channelling the votes of disaffected protestors rising against the establishment and austerity, respectively (Mosca & Quaranta, 2017). These are notable achievements attesting to the electoral appeal of populist communication among aggrieved social groups harbouring a sense of abandonment by the political elite (Aslanidis, 2017). They arguably add to the quality of democratic participation in those countries by affording hitherto politically disengaged citizens new opportunities to associate, select representatives and influence policymaking. They, however, have to be juxtaposed with the evolving adaptations of the party organization – which have restricted participation – and with any damage to participation likewise flowing from populist communication (e.g., a continued erosion of general trust, institutional trust or outgroup exclusion in the specific case of right-wing populism).

While digital platforms may ease access to party organizations – now more readily accessible at the click of a button – we would again note that diverse efforts by movement parties to broaden their membership have yielded disparate results. Podemos and M5S have succeeded in enrolling half a million subscribers (see Podemos, 2020b) and two hundred thousand, respectively, on their online platforms (see M5S, 2021). The level of enrolment on Rousseau, the M5S platform, was a rather disappointing result given that the party's stated goal was to reach one million subscribers by the end of 2018

(Gerbaudo, 2019). In terms of *quantity*, then, the experiment set up by Podemos seems comparatively more successful. However, it is worth stressing that just a tiny portion of those registered on the platform are active members (ibid.). Thus, in terms of the *quality* of member's engagement, the platform did not seem to have radically transformed the decision-making processes within the party. Additionally, as Gomez and Ramiro explain, 'the radically new notion of membership implemented by Podemos has not been able to remedy the voters-members gap' (2019, p. 544). Being male, highly educated, with a better employment status, active in voluntary associations and ideologically radical still distinguishes members and voters.

M5S has further differentiated members' involvement in party life extending it beyond online ballots to also engage them in the discussion of draft laws and in the proposal of law initiatives. Nonetheless, the multiplication and fragmentation of procedures did not generate greater participation as members perceived that 'who decides on the other side of the screen is generally not listening, not responding and that inputs from users are not making a difference' (Mosca, 2020, p. 16). Moreover, the Rousseau platform denies members any horizontal interaction and rules out any possibility to control the agenda from below (Deseriis, 2020). Democratic participation through digital platforms seems then to level off at the point where it involves significant numbers of citizens in cut-and-dried activities.

In the end, despite gaining government positions and resources, neither M5S nor Podemos were able to implement innovative participatory practices. In its first experience in government, together with the Lega, M5S created a ministry for direct democracy. Notwithstanding successful efforts to reduce the number of MPs through constitutional reform, it failed to introduce binding popular law initiatives and promises to involve citizens in the law-making process through the creation of a single portal for government consultations have remained unattained. As for Podemos, 'more effective bottom-up decision-making processes – such as citizens' initiatives, recall or extraordinary congresses – have never been implemented for lack of support' while a great deal of local structures – círculos or circles – have been deemed 'zombie circles' because of their inactivity and the absence of real citizen participation (Lisi, 2019, p. 254 and 256). Moreover, Podemos stopped using online ballots ('consultas ciudadanas') as a means to involve its supporters in party decisions after it became a member of the left-wing executive with the socialist PSOE. The last one was called in November 2019, concerning its participation in the coalition government (Podemos, 2020a).

Lastly, the disruption caused by the Covid-19 pandemic to the organization of work and everyday life arguably presented an opportunity to put to the test alternative modes of citizen participation. In this respect, movement parties seemed better positioned and able than traditional parties to leverage digital media as engines of civic engagement. Nevertheless, as the pandemic compressed democratic freedoms reducing spaces for more or less conventional forms of participation, efforts to imagine and propose innovative modes of democratic participation did not originate with movement parties. Instead, local grassroots citizens' initiatives have arisen to meet this latest challenge (e.g., Frena la curva – Stop the curve – in Spain, which spread internationally in Europe and Latin America, see Falanga, 2020). Consequently, a rejuvenation of citizen participation wrought by movement parties seems to have been constrained by observed similarities with the neoliberal party model as well as by a limited capacity to attract and retain supporters on online platforms and to use these to widen involvement in party affairs or policymaking, especially once in government.

Issue outline and conclusion

The articles in this special issue contribute to the systematic examination of movement party communication as an avenue for illuminating these parties' purchase on democratic politics. In her article, della Porta makes the case for a wider interrogation of movement party communication that steps outside their online platforms so as to approach their use as one of potentially multiple communication practices and underpinning party strategies. Failing to do so, della Porta argues, can lead to a partial treatment of movement parties that does not fully account for either relations within the party that are not manifest online – thus only offering a 'partial vision of the qualities of democracy in the parties as such' (2021, p. 5); or for prevalent understandings of ICTs within party systems. Both of these contentions are very welcome as they alert observers to a necessary, longer perspective one may now take on movement parties, their development and, most notably, any treatment of their communication as expressive of relations within such parties and party systems more widely. In this issue, Siddarth and her colleagues take up this very task in their analysis of the institutionalization of the Indian Aam Aadmi Party (AAD).

As indicated above, movement parties emerged as a reaction to perceived failings of retrenched established parties. The extent to which they have managed to maintain distinctly participatory relations with either membership or electorate has varied. In the case of the AAD, its meteoric electoral trajectory – repeatedly winning regional elections between 2013 and 2020 – was paralleled by its transformation from 'a movement party, to a political party with social movement origins, to an uneasy mix of political institution, personalistic political party and self-identified political "outsider"' (2021, p. 2). Siddarth et al.'s case study reveals a long-standing tension in the AAD between a drive to consolidate the party leadership – inter-alia through its structure and not unlike Podemos (Casero-Ripollés et al., 2016) messaging concentrated around the leader – and renewed efforts to maintain the core anti-corruption ideology of the movement wherefrom it originated. AAD thus adopted a split communication strategy emphasizing both aspects to carefully segmented audiences on social media, where the anti-corruption movement had initially made headway.

A similarly bifurcated communication strategy was embraced by the UK Independence Party (UKIP) in the wake of the Brexit referendum, Klein and Pirro highlight also in this issue. Its activists founded War Plan Purple (WPP), a spin-off group catering to the cultural agenda of the party's radical right flank, on social media. The WPP created an opening for UKIP 'to venture down a social movement route' (2020, p. 14) as the party reorganized following the 2016 referendum. UKIP moved in the opposite direction to the AAD, namely further away from the institutional arena and closer to the grassroots movement, reverting to a more familiar position of movement parties. Similarly, links to the grassroots have been cultivated by Australian far-right parties, who, as McSwiney (2020) explains, have used social media chiefly to reinforce exclusionary identities and discourse.

In their article, Lobera and Portos stress that, online, grassroots activists can play a pivotal role in the emergence of political challengers – such as Gerard Batten, UKIP's president during the period examined by Klein and Pirro – when they are co-opted into digital campaigns for office. Grassroots activism may both energize and radicalize campaigns. As the authors put it, 'activists may be favouring messages of more radical candidates, polarizing the discourse of their own parties' (2020, p. 13). Lobera and Portos argue that activists' extra-institutional participation drives online political engagement irrespectively of their party affiliation. In turn, this supports the hypothesis that movement parties can maximize their online campaigning by mobilizing greater pools of grassroots activists.

Examining the relationship between movement parties and their support base, Mosca and Quaranta (2021) importantly likewise indicate that a penchant among politically active social media users to vote for parties such as M5S may be owed not just to the populist communication of the latter online but also to their push to rejuvenate political participation and party decision-making. Evidence that, in Germany, the AfD did not benefit from a similar tendency is put forward by the authors as a basis for further scrutiny of the link between technological innovation by movement parties and their electoral gains. Likewise, varying institutional features, web regulations and constellations of media systems are shown by the two authors to matter in the relation between the political use of digital media and the vote for populist movement parties.

In their comparative analysis of speeches by leaders of M5S, Podemos, Lega Nord and the Austrian Freedom Party (FPÖ), Ceron et al. additionally paint a contrast between right-wing and 'non-right-wing' populist communication styles. The authors unpick differences between them to reveal a persistence of the right-wing style during periods in and out of government. Ceron and his colleagues argue that contrary to some expectations, right-wing populists may not moderate their criticism of the political establishment and institutions once in government or in a supporting coalition, something that M5S and Podemos leaders seemed more amenable to doing.

Yet, in a study resonating with della Porta's call for research on movement party communication to be observed in context, Bracciale et al. (2021) evince that a populist communication style was adopted across the board by party leaders during the 2018 Italian elections, on social media. They emphasize (p.12) that while 'the leaders employed and mixed populist style elements in different ways and at different intensities … the overall differences were slight'. Their investigation thus points to a normalization of the populist communication style, in recent Italian elections, that was nevertheless more prevalent among the messages of the M5S and the Lega leaders.

Finally, the implications of these empirical findings are thrown into relief by Ethan Zuckerman's contribution to this issue. In his commentary, Zuckerman paints a dynamic media ecosystem and advocates for cross-platform, transnational, and multi-media approaches to recent 'flows of attention' – e.g., to social and climate justice or far-right ideas – that scale and spill over, are driven by ideology, monetized by multiple platforms and advertisers, and are amplified or dampened by media organizations and social media users alike. To understand how strategic actors such as political parties or social movements negotiate those flows, scholars require new and improved tools, methods and data.

To conclude, we want to stress the importance of examining the communicative dimension of movement parties. As conceived by CCO proponents (Schoeneborn et al., 2014, p. 305), organization and communication are interlocking constitutive processes whereby movement parties form and transform. Studying movement party communication can provide important insights into their relationships, originally weak and evolving structures, workings, and also their identity as a collective actor (Block & Negrine, 2017). Second, the 'elective affinity' between populists and social media (Gerbaudo, 2018) and a common recourse to populist rhetoric by movement parties should not obscure differences among them or their contexts and the need for continued, discerning analyses of their communication and media ecosystem. Third, democratic innovations pushed by movement parties should be critically inspected as evidence so far implies that increases in the number of members are often achieved at the expense of the quality of democratic participation, and that reaching government positions further distances movement parties from ordinary citizens.

Disclosure statement

No potential conflict of interest was reported by the author(s).

Funding

This work was supported by Scuola Normale Superiore; Volkswagen Foundation.

ORCID

Dan Mercea http://orcid.org/0000-0003-3762-2404
Lorenzo Mosca http://orcid.org/0000-0002-3248-0489

References

Albertazzi, D., & Mueller, S. (2013). Populism and liberal democracy: Populists in government in Austria, Italy, Poland and Switzerland. *Government and Opposition, 48*(Special Issue 03), 343–371. https://doi.org/10.1017/gov.2013.12
Anduiza, E., Guinjoan, M., & Rico, G. (2019). Populism, participation, and political equality. *European Political Science Review, 11*(1), 109–124. https://doi.org/10.1017/S1755773918000243
Arzheimer, K., & Berning, C. C. (2019). How the Alternative for Germany (AfD) and their voters veered to the radical right, 2013–2017. *Electoral Studies, 60*, 102040. https://doi.org/10.1016/j.electstud.2019.04.004
Aslanidis, P. (2016). Is populism an ideology? A refutation and a new perspective. *Political Studies, 64*(1_suppl.), 88–104. https://doi.org/10.1111/1467-9248.12224
Aslanidis, P. (2017). Populism and social movements. In C. Rovira Kaltwasser, P. Taggart, P. Ochoa Espejo, & P. Ostiguy (Eds.), *The Oxford handbook of populism*. Oxford University Press. https://doi.org/10.1093/oxfordhb/9780198803560.013.23

Bastos, M., Mercea, D., & Baronchelli, A. (2018). The geographic embedding of online echo chambers: Evidence from the Brexit campaign. *PLoS ONE, 13*(11), e0206841. https://doi.org/10.1371/journal.pone.0206841

Bennett, W. L., Segerberg, A., & Knüpfer, C. B. (2018). The democratic interface: Technology, political organization, and diverging patterns of electoral representation. *Information, Communication & Society, 21*(11), 1655–1680. https://doi.org/10.1080/1369118X.2017.1348533

Bergmann, E. (2018). *Conspiracy & populism: The politics of misinformation*. Palgrave.

Block, E., & Negrine, R. (2017). *The populist communication style: Toward a critical framework* (Vol. 11). [populism, populist communication style, Chávez, Farage, Trump]. https://ijoc.org/index.php/ijoc/article/view/5820

Bracciale, R., Andretta, M., & Martella, A. (2021). Does populism go viral? How Italian leaders engage citizens through social media. *Information, Communication & Society*, 1–18. https://doi.org/10.1080/1369118X.2021.1874472

Casero-Ripollés, A., Feenstra, R. A., & Tormey, S. (2016). Old and new media logics in an electoral campaign: The case of Podemos and the two-way street mediatization of politics. *The International Journal of Press/Politics, 21*(3), 378–397. https://doi.org/10.1177/1940161216645340

Casero-Ripollés, A., Sintes-Olivella, M., & Franch, P. (2017). The populist political communication style in action: Podemos's issues and functions on Twitter during the 2016 Spanish general election. *American Behavioral Scientist, 61*(9), 986–1001. https://doi.org/10.1177/0002764217707624

Ceron, A., Gandini, A., & Lodetti, P. (2020). Still 'fire in the (full) belly'? Anti-establishment rhetoric before and after government participation. *Information, Communication & Society*, 1–17. https://doi.org/10.1080/1369118X.2020.1776373

Davidson, T., & Berezin, M. (2018). Britain first and the UK Independence Party: Social media and movement-party dynamics. *Mobilization: An International Quarterly, 23*(4), 485–510. https://doi.org/10.17813/1086-671X-23-4-485

De Cleen, B., Glynos, J., & Mondon, A. (2018). Critical research on populism: Nine rules of engagement. *Organization, 25*(5), 649–661. https://doi.org/10.1177/1350508418768053

della Porta, D. (2021). Communication in progressive movement parties: Against populism and beyond digitalism. *Information, Communication & Society*, 1–17. https://doi.org/10.1080/1369118X.2021.1894212

della Porta, D., Fernández, J., Kouki, H., & Mosca, L. (2017). *Movement parties against austerity*. Polity Press. http://ebookcentral.proquest.com/lib/city/detail.action?docID=4850324

Dennis, J. (2020). A party within a party posing as a movement? Momentum as a movement faction. *Journal of Information Technology & Politics, 17*(2), 97–113. https://doi.org/10.1080/19331681.2019.1702608

Deseriis, M. (2020). Digital movement parties: A comparative analysis of the technopolitical cultures and the participation platforms of the Movimento 5 Stelle and the Piratenpartei. *Information, Communication & Society, 23*(12), 1770–1786. https://doi.org/10.1080/1369118X.2019.1631375

Diani, M. (1992). The concept of social movement. *The Sociological Review, 40*(1), 1–25. https://doi.org/10.1111/j.1467-954X.1992.tb02943.x

Engesser, S., Fawzi, N., & Larsson, A. O. (2017). Populist online communication: Introduction to the special issue. *Information, Communication & Society, 20*(9), 1279–1292. https://doi.org/10.1080/1369118X.2017.1328525

Falanga, R. (2020). *Citizen participation during the Covid-19 pandemic. Insights from local practices in European cities*. Friedrich-Ebert-Stiftung.

Font, N., Graziano, P., & Tsakatika, M. (2021). Varieties of inclusionary populism? SYRIZA, Podemos and the Five Star Movement. *Government and Opposition, 56*(1), 163–183. https://doi.org/10.1017/gov.2019.17

Gerbaudo, P. (2018). Social media and populism: An elective affinity? *Media, Culture & Society, 40*(5), 745–753. https://doi.org/10.1177/0163443718772192

Gerbaudo, P. (2019). *The digital party. Political organisation and online democracy*. Pluto Press.

Giugni, M., & Grasso, M. (2021). Party membership and social movement activism: A macro-micro analysis. *Party Politics*, *27*(1), 92–102. https://doi.org/10.1177/1354068818823446

Gomez, R., & Ramiro, L. (2019). The limits of organizational innovation and multi-speed membership: Podemos and its new forms of party membership. *Party Politics*, *25*(4), 534–546. https://doi.org/10.1177/1354068817742844

Hanna, J., & Busher, J. (2019). UKIP and the UK's radical right: A tale of movement party success? In M. Caiani, & O. Císař (Eds.), *Radical right movement parties in Europe* (pp. 46–62). Routledge.

Inglehart, R., & Norris, P. (2017). Trump and the Populist Authoritarian Parties: The Silent Revolution in Reverse. *Perspectives on Politics*, *15*(2). https://doi.org/10.1017/S1537592717000111

Kemper, A. (2015). Afd, Pegida and the new right in Germany. In G. Charalambous (Ed.), *The European far right: Historical and contemporary perspectives* (pp. 43–48). Friedrich-Ebert-Stiftung and Peace Research Institute Oslo.

Kitschelt, H. (2006). Movement parties. In R. S. Katz & W. Crotty (Eds.), *Handbook of party politics* (pp. 278–290). Sage. https://doi.org/10.4135/9781848608047

Klein, O., & Pirro, A. L. P. (2020). Reverting trajectories? UKIP's organisational and discursive change after the Brexit referendum. *Information, Communication & Society*, 1–19. https://doi.org/10.1080/1369118X.2020.1792532

Klug, A., Rees, E., & Schneider, J. (2016). Momentum: A new kind of politics. *Renewal: A Journal of Social Democracy*, *24*(2), 36–44.

Kriesi, H. (1989). New social movements and the new class in the Netherlands. *American Journal of Sociology*, *94*(5), 1078–1116. https://doi.org/10.1086/229112

Kriesi, H., & Frey, T. (2008). The United Kingdom: Moving parties in a stable configuration. In E. Grande, H. Kriesi, M. Dolezal, R. Lachat, S. Bornschier, & T. Frey (Eds.), *West European politics in the age of globalization* (pp. 183–207). Cambridge University Press. https://doi.org/10.1017/CBO9780511790720.009

Laclau, E. (2005). *On populist reason*. Verso.

Larsson, A. O. (2016). Online, all the time? A quantitative assessment of the permanent campaign on Facebook. *New Media & Society*, *18*(2), 274–292. https://doi.org/10.1177/1461444814538798

Lees-Marshment, J., & Lilleker, D. (2001). Political marketing and traditional values: 'Old labour' for 'new times'? *Contemporary Politics*, *7*(3), 205–216. https://doi.org/10.1080/13569770127543

Lisi, M. (2019). Party innovation, hybridization and the crisis: The case of podemos. *Italian Political Science Review/Rivista Italiana di Scienza Politica*, *49*(3), 245–262. https://doi.org/10.1017/ipo.2018.20

Lobera, J., & Portos, M. (2020). Decentralizing electoral campaigns? New-old parties, grassroots and digital activism. *Information, Communication & Society*, 1–22. https://doi.org/10.1080/1369118X.2020.1749697

Luttbeg, N. R. (1974). *Public opinion and public policy; models of political linkage*. Dorsey Press.

M5S. (2021). *Rousseau: A platform for participatory democracy and active citizenship*. https://rousseau.movimento5stelle.it/

McAdam, D., & Tarrow, S. (2010). Ballots and barricades: On the reciprocal relationship between elections and social movements. *Perspectives on Politics*, *8*(2), 529–542. https://doi.org/10.1017/S1537592710001234

McSwiney, J. (2020). Social networks and digital organisation: Far right parties at the 2019 Australian federal election. *Information, Communication & Society*, 1–18. https://doi.org/10.1080/1369118X.2020.1757132

Minkenberg, M. (2019). Between party and movement: Conceptual and empirical considerations of the radical right's organizational boundaries and mobilization processes. *European Societies*, *21*(4), 463–486. https://doi.org/10.1080/14616696.2018.1494296

Morlino, L. (2012). *Changes for democracy: Actors, structures, processes*. Oxford University Press. https://doi.org/10.1093/acprof:oso/9780199572533.001.0001

Mosca, L. (2014). The Five Star Movement: Exception or Vanguard in Europe? *The International Spectator*, *49*(1), 36–52. https://doi.org/10.1080/03932729.2013.875821

Mosca, L. (2020). Democratic vision and online participatory spaces in the Italian Movimento 5 Stelle. *Acta Politica, 55*(1), 1–18. https://doi.org/10.1057/s41269-018-0096-y

Mosca, L., & Quaranta, M. (2017). Voting for movement parties in Southern Europe: The role of protest and digital information. *South European Society and Politics, 22*(4), 427–446. https://doi.org/10.1080/13608746.2017.1411980

Mosca, L., & Quaranta, M. (2021). Are digital platforms potential drivers of the populist vote? A comparative analysis of France, Germany and Italy. *Information, Communication & Society*, 1–19. https://doi.org/10.1080/1369118X.2021.1894211

Mosca, L., & Tronconi, F. (2019). Beyond left and right: The eclectic populism of the Five Star Movement. *West European Politics, 42*(6), 1258–1283. https://doi.org/10.1080/01402382.2019.1596691

Mudde, C. (2004). The populist zeitgeist. *Government and Opposition, 39*(4), 541–563. https://doi.org/10.1111/j.1477-7053.2004.00135.x

Mudde, C., & Rovira Kaltwasser, C. (2012). *Populism in Europe and the Americas*. Cambridge University Press. https://doi.org/10.1017/CBO9781139152365

Passarelli, G., & Tuorto, D. (2018). The Five Star Movement: Purely a matter of protest? The rise of a new party between political discontent and reasoned voting. *Party Politics, 24*(2), 129–140. https://doi.org/10.1177/1354068816642809

Pirro, A. L. P. (2018). The polyvalent populism of the 5 Star Movement. *Journal of Contemporary European Studies, 26*(4), 443–458. https://doi.org/10.1080/14782804.2018.1519484

Pirro, A. L. P. (2019). Ballots and barricades enhanced: Far-right 'movement parties' and movement-electoral interactions. *Nations and Nationalism, 25*(3), 782–802. https://doi.org/10.1111/nana.12483

Piven, F. F., & Cloward, R. A. (1977). *Poor people's movements: Why they succeed, how they fail*. Vintage Books.

Podemos. (2020a). *Consultas Ciudadanas*. https://podemos.info/consultasciudadanas/

Podemos. (2020b). *Portal de Participación de Podemos*. https://participa.podemos.info/es

Rodríguez-Teruel, J., Barrio, A., & Barberà, O. (2016). Fast and furious: Podemos' Quest for power in multi-level Spain. *South European Society and Politics, 21*(4), 561–585. https://doi.org/10.1080/13608746.2016.1250397

Schoeneborn, D., Blaschke, S., Cooren, F., McPhee, R. D., Seidl, D., & Taylor, J. R. (2014). The three schools of CCO thinking: Interactive dialogue and systematic comparison. *Management Communication Quarterly, 28*(2), 285–316. https://doi.org/10.1177/0893318914527000

Schwörer, J. (2019). Alternative für Deutschland: from the streets to the Parliament? In M. Caiani & O. Císař (Eds.), *Radical Right Movement Parties in Europe* (pp. 29–45). Routledge.

Siddarth, D., Shankar, R., & Pal, J. (2021). 'We do politics so we can change politics': Communication strategies and practices in the Aam Aadmi Party's institutionalization process. *Information, Communication & Society*, 1–21. https://doi.org/10.1080/1369118X.2020.1856910

Sparrow, N., & Turner, J. (2001). The permanent campaign - The integration of market research techniques in developing strategies in a more uncertain political climate. *European Journal of Marketing, 35*(9/10), 984–1002. https://doi.org/10.1108/03090560110400605

Stier, S., Posch, L., Bleier, A., & Strohmaier, M. (2017). When populists become popular: Comparing Facebook use by the right-wing movement Pegida and German political parties. *Information, Communication & Society, 20*(9), 1365–1388. https://doi.org/10.1080/1369118X.2017.1328519

Tormey, S., & Feenstra, R. A. (2015). Reinventing the political party in Spain: The case of 15M and the Spanish mobilisations. *Policy Studies, 36*(6), 590–606. https://doi.org/10.1080/01442872.2015.1073243

Usherwood, S. (2019). Shooting the fox? UKIP's populism in the post-Brexit era. *West European Politics, 42*(6), 1209–1229. https://doi.org/10.1080/01402382.2019.1596692

Vann, B., Jr. (2018). Movement-countermovement dynamics and mobilizing the electorate. *Mobilization: An International Quarterly, 23*(3), 285–305. https://doi.org/10.17813/1086-671X-23-3-285

Wang, D. J., Rao, H., & Soule, S. A. (2019). Crossing categorical boundaries: A study of diversification by social movement organizations. *American Sociological Review*, *84*(3), 420–458. https://doi.org/10.1177/0003122419846111

Zuckerman, E. (2021). Why Study Media Ecosystems?. *Information, Communication & Society*, 1–19. https://doi.org/10.1080/1369118X.2021.1942513

Communication in progressive movement parties: against populism and beyond digitalism

Donatella della Porta

ABSTRACT
In this article, I discuss the conceptualization of movement parties and bridge it with that of communication practices. In particular, I show how the analysis of communication practices within movement parties allows going beyond the technological determinism implicit in concepts such as online populism or digital parties. At different moments in history, social movements entered institutions by forming political parties. When this happened with progressive movements, movement parties were characterized by an appeal to broaden participation through the inclusion of new groups among the population within representative institutions. This general trend is to be kept in mind when addressing the latest wave of movement parties, in particular, the progressive ones, that build upon the history of left-wing party families. Based on these reflections, I critique analyses that, with a specific focus on the core subject of this special issue, have addressed communication strategies, depicting movement parties – including those on the Left – as online populist parties or digital parties. Considering alternative (less technological and more political) explanations, I suggest instead that the effects of the technology are filtered through activists' agency, the movement parties' evolution being influenced by movements' dynamics and competition in the party system. In particular, the concept of communication practices, as developed in social movement studies, will be referred to in order to move beyond some stereotypes coming from either mass media or digital media studies, and so allowing for an historical account of the evolution of movement parties' communication.

Movement parties and communication: an introduction

At different moments in history, social movements entered institutions by forming political parties. When this happened with progressive movements, movement parties were characterized by an appeal to broaden participation through the inclusion of new groups among the population within representative institutions (della Porta, 2020). In doing this, they resonated with claims made by the social movements from which they originated, proposing participatory visions of democracy. While attempts to practice them in political parties (or even social movement organizations) have never been fully successful, they have nevertheless produced long-lasting innovations in party models as well as in collective framing, accompanied also by transformations in communication practices that have become more participatory themselves. If evaluated against an ideal-type of participatory democracy, but also against the hope of their activists, the functioning of these innovations has never been satisfactory. They nevertheless often improved upon existing party organizational and communication models by opening them up to the grassroots, with apparent consequences on the organizational structure, but also on the communication strategies of political parties. Additionally, left-wing parties have often seen internal movements periodically opposing oligarchic tendencies and calling for a return to the participatory spirit of their origins.

This general trend is to be kept in mind when addressing the latest wave of movement parties, in particular, the progressive ones, that build upon the above-sketched history of left-wing party families. Based on these reflections, in what follows, I will discuss analyses that, with a specific focus on the core subject of this special issue, have addressed communication strategies, depicting movement parties – including those on the Left – as online populist parties or digital parties. In doing this, I will counter notions that risk promoting a partial view, or which reify some specific aspects in these parties' rhetoric, or their use of specific communication technologies that minimizes their complex evolution, including in respect to political communication. In addition, such analyses tend to support a technologically driven explanation attributing an erosion of democratic qualities to an over-reliance on online technology.

Considering alternative (less technological and more political) explanations, I will suggest that the effects of the technology are filtered through activists' agency, the movement parties' evolution being influenced by movements' dynamics and competition in the party system. Visions of online populism or digital parties are insufficient to address a complex system of communication in which (a) a multiplicity of online and offline technologies, (b) are used by a multiplicity of players; (c) within multiple arenas; (d) with frequent dilemmas and (e) adaptation through trial-and-error. This conceptualization of movement parties is not designed to deny existing limits within their organizational models and communication strategies, but to point instead at their hybrid location within party systems and social movement sectors. It is a counterweight to their assumed populist views or their use of digital technologies as the main sources of tension between proclaimed aims and real achievements.

In particular, the concept of communication practices, as developed in social movement studies, will be referred to in order to move beyond some stereotypes coming from either mass media or digital media studies, and so allowing for an historical account of the evolution of movement parties' communication. In fact, the more traditional approaches focusing on alternative media or those which have cast mass media as brokers of protest messages would not be sufficient in order to capture the richness of the communicative activities in and around social movements and movement parties. The reference to practices could instead help bridge the focus on structures present in social movement studies on mass media selectivity with the interest in agency developed in research on alternative media. To this end, attention has to be afforded not only to the effects of the use of some media technologies but also to the complex process of the production, distribution and consumptions of information, in which various actors (professionals and not) express their agency (Couldry, 2003, p. 44).

In short, I will use this article to develop a theoretical proposition about how the analysis of communication practices within movement parties allows one to go beyond the technological determinism implicit in concepts such as online populism or digital parties. References to my and others' work on progressive movement parties in recent times will be made as an illustration of alternative explanations vis-à-vis the technological one, to reflect on potentials and challenges for progressive movement parties, the democratic developments and the quality of the communication in which they partake.

Movement parties: beyond online populism and digital parties

Given the spreading of digital technologies in party communication, attention has been paid to the connections between the use of platforms and the democratic qualities of political parties (De Blasio & Viviani, 2020). Without pretense of completeness, I will look at some of these contributions and their focus, advocating for the need to combine the analysis of these channels to that of much broader and more complex communication practices.

If the term populism has been used with such a broad range of meanings that it often obfuscates more than it clarifies, the same can be said about the definition of populist online communication. In an introduction to a special issue of 'Information, Communication and Society', Engesser et al. (2017) bring together four different meaning of populism:

> The approach of populism as ideology defines populism as a set of ideas and focuses, within the context of the special issue at hand, on the content of populist communication (What?). The approach of populism as style conceives of populism as mode of presentation and is interested in the form of populist communication (How?). The approach of populism as strategy refers to populism as a means to an end and focuses on the motives and aims of populist communication (Why?). Beside these three aspects of populism in the media, scholarship has also been interested in the populist actor or messenger of populist communication (Who?). (Engesser et al., 2017, p. 1280)

These four elements are said to come together in a populist communication logic, as a sum of norms, routines and procedures (Engesser et al., 2017). In this view, the content is inspired by the populists' belief in popular sovereignty and 'direct democracy optimism'; the style is based upon simplification, emotionalization and negativity; the actors are charismatic leaders; the strategy aims at achieving power, legitimacy and mobilization. In particular, the populist style of communication, referring to the ways in which ideas are communicated, is said to be characterized by 'extensive dramatization, polarization, moralization, directness, ordinariness, colloquial and vulgar language', with a tendency 'to reduce complexity', relying mainly on negative emotions (such as anger, fear and resentment). Populist actors 'prefer to paint in black' (Engesser et al., 2017, p. 1285).

The reference to the online dimension points to the importance of technological affordances. As on the internet attention is a scarce resource, 'the populist style of simplification, emotionalization and negativity increases our attention by addressing fundamental perceptual patterns and news values' (Engesser et al., 2017, p. 1286). Moreover, the 'Internet might provide the populist actors with exactly those non-institutionalized masses they seek' (Engesser et al., 2017). The necessary connection between the four elements however remains largely to be proved empirically. Furthermore, progressive actors, let alone left-wing movement parties, were not considered in the studies included in that special issue. The focus of attention on the impact of online technology also risks simplifying complex communication practices, involving various techniques, used by various players in various arenas.

Similarly, potentially misleading is the definition of some movement parties as digital parties. The conceptualization of digital parties proposed by Paolo Gerbaudo (2019a) includes three dimensions: their large use of digital technology (Gerbaudo, 2019a, p. 4), their platform-like structure as data driven (Gerbaudo, 2019a, p. 15), and a confidence in dis-intermediated democracy. While giving power to hyper-leaders and their close circles, these parties would discourage activists, focusing instead on a super-base of lowly committed members. The main consideration is, here as well, the poor performance of the digital parties' platforms. The ethos of open participation (Gerbaudo, 2019a, p. 77) is so considered as misplaced as digital parties create re-intermediation trough personalized leadership and a cloud, light party (Gerbaudo, 2019a, 79), following a forum logic and working as a start-up. Techno-optimism is considered as responsible for this failure. Digital technologies would drive the trend towards this type of parties as they facilitate appeals to broad and individualized masses (the 'people of the web', Gerbaudo, 2019a, p. 14). Selecting on the dependent variable, this research does not systematically contrast digital with non-digital parties in their democratic performances. Without measuring the democratic qualities of the other contemporary parties, this conceptualization contrasts digital parties with the idealtype of ideological mass parties. Additionally, focusing exclusively on the use of the online platform as a mean of communication introduces a selection bias that obscures interactions with collective actors (i.e., social movements and the party system) while also simplifying much more complex communication practices that bridge on- and off-line forms of communication, involving various types of party activists and sympathizers. Comparatively assessing the forms of 'disintermediation' in communication would be important as agency-oriented, participatory forms of communication aim at developing channels of direct intervention which are aimed at a 'reintermediation' from below, rather than from above.

Further elaborations around the concept of digital parties have in fact singled out their different forms, so nuancing some claims about their characteristics. Recently, Deseriis (2020) has distinguished between two types of digital party: the platform one and the networked one. In the latter, the use of digital technology allows for the participation of activists, a decentralized structure, a diffused leadership, a horizontal organization and hybrid conceptions of participation. Platform parties, on the other hand, have been seen as 'a space for the emergence of authoritarian tendencies (hyper-leadership) but also as an organizational opportunity for the development of new forms of digital activism' (De Blasio & Viviani, 2020, p. 16; see also De Blasio & Sorice, 2020). Other research also pointed to the challenges of controlling interactivity in decentralized structures (see Dennis, 2020 on Momentum) and the quickly changing conceptions of the leadership role in movements and parties (on Podemos, see de Nadal, 2020). Especially, as Marco Deseriis (2019) noted in a comparison of the Pirate Party and the Five Star Movement, the specific use of platforms is in fact strongly influenced by the widespread conceptions of technology and, especially, of democracy.

While this literature has the merit of analysing the specific use of platform by different organizations, and their (de)merit vis-à-vis the claim of participatory democracy (e.g., Gerbaudo, 2019b), in some cases it risks too easily extending that assessment to the entire party. This means overlooking the fact that as no party has an 'only-digital' life, and as anyhow digital activities require offline ones, looking at platforms offers an important but partial vision of the qualities of democracy in the parties as such. If digital technologies are used by most parties, as with other technologies, their specific use is in fact influenced to a large extent by norms and experiences of the different specific players that are active within a party.

Going beyond online populism and digital parties, the concept of *movement parties'* points at the role of particularly intense relations with social movements (della Porta, Fernandez et al., 2017). In a broadly accepted definition, social movements are conceptualized as networks of groups and individuals, endowed with some collective identification, that pursue goals of social transformation mainly through unconventional forms of participation (della Porta & Diani, 2020). Political parties are free associations built with the aim of achieving institutional change, mainly through participation in elections. Movement parties emerge as a sort of hybrid between the two. In Kitschelt's (2006, p. 280) definition, 'movement parties are coalitions of political activists who emanate from social movements and try to apply the organization and strategic practice of social movements in the arena of party competition.' As social movements are networks of organizations and individuals, movement parties can be part of them, as testified by overlapping memberships as well as organizational networks and action links. Movement parties aim in fact at integrating the movement constituencies within their organizations, by representing movement claims.

While the definition of movement parties can be equally partial as the ones of online populism or digital parties, I suggest that it alludes to a very important explanation of complex communication strategies. A relational and dynamic view of movement parties, as I adopt below, might, in fact, help understand their formation and transformation as they are caught between the legacy of previous movement parties of the Left (i.e., socialist mass parties and left-libertarian Green parties) and the influence of their kindred social movements, with however also need to adapt to the actual electoral context and party system. In this sense, social movement studies allow moving beyond technological determinism, looking at movement parties' communication strategies as influenced by the tensions between interactions in the movement arena and in the party system. In these relations, we can locate explanations for both the innovative potentials of digital technologies as well as the successes and failures in implementing them. The use of communication technologies in a very dense communicative environment is influenced by the specific movement a party is rooted in. Accordingly, rather than assuming a homogeneous effect of the use of platforms, we have to consider the characteristics of communication practices as influenced by existing conceptions of democracy in the social movement families. Over time, experiences within institutions can be expected to create tensions within a movement party which is pressured towards adapting, at least in part, to the mode of communication that is dominant in the party system. Rather than being derived from the use of specific technologies or a generic reference to the people (populism as a thin ideology), the party's conception of democracy is therefore expected to vary and impact upon the specific disposition towards the available technological affordances.

A relational and dynamic perspective on movement parties and their communication practices

The adoption of specific conceptions of democracy, that drives the use of various technologies for knowledge production, distribution and consumption, is embedded in complex transformations in the movement as well as party arenas. While progressive movement parties have usually promoted participatory visions of democracy, the specific characteristics of the participatory visions have changed over time, being embedded in a sort of repertoire, historically defined, of party models.

The emergence, particularly of progressive movement parties, is facilitated by certain conditions: the transformation in the cleavage structures as new parties tend to appear when there are neglected issues; conduciveness in the electoral field (especially a proportional electoral system and contingent electoral volatility); the de-legitimation of mainstream political parties, in particular of the party family to which social movements traditionally referred to, perceived as compromising with austerity policies. Especially, since movement parties tend to develop during massive movement mobilizations their emergence and, even more so, their success are influenced by the characteristics of the social movements to which they are connected.

Progressive movement parties can be located as actors of democratic innovation within a broad trend of party transformations, characterized by parties drawing continuously closer to state institutions and a growing detachment from society. In nineteenth-century Europe, following *parties of the notables* that represented elite constituencies in pre-democratic societies, the *ideological mass parties* emerged, endowed with a stable bureaucracy designed to represent the collective interests of those who had hitherto been excluded. Various concepts were then proposed to describe the later autonomization of parties from their linkages with a specific social base (*catch-all parties*), a focus on getting votes (*electoral parties*), or an interpenetration of party and state based on inter-party collusion (*cartel party*) (della Porta, 2015a). These tendencies seem to peak in what I have named *neoliberal populist parties* – organizationally light, heavily personalized, split into non-ideological factions, characterized by heavily manipulative use of mass media but also by a power rooted in the occupation of institutional positions, often used for clientelistic or corrupt exchanges (della Porta, Fernandez, et al., 2017). As relations between parties and civil society organizations are further weakened and membership declines, party activists are substituted by the mass media as channels of communication with potential voters. In sum, the current model of mainstream neoliberal populist parties is shallow, weak, and opportunistic; ideological appeals are (at best) vague, with an overwhelmingly electoral orientation.

In parallel to the evolution of the mainstream party types, specific movement parties have been singled out that at the same time opposed some aspect of the mainstream parties, but also adapted to some characteristics of the dominant party types in different historical periods (della Porta, Fernandez, et al., 2017). First of all, the party of the notables can be contrasted by parties of (left-wing) *cadres* that, in conditions of limited representation, tended to defend the interests of the excluded, within a conception of the party as a vanguard of the proletariat. Labour, organized, class-based, ideological parties emerged and were characterized by a hierarchical relationship with the labour movement. They exemplified an integrated interaction of parties and unions, with leadership and membership overlapping and interchanging (Allern 2010, p. 37). Born in Europe in the nineteenth century, from within the labour movement, these parties advocated new political and social rights, contributing to the development of the very conception of democracy (della Porta, 2013, chap. 2). Especially since the 1950s, with a clear acceleration since the early 1980s, class-mass parties have, however, dramatically transformed themselves, due in particular to a decline in party linkages with workers' organizations (Kitschelt, 1994, p. 3).

It was from the critique of the bureaucratization of the ideological class party that a new form of movement party emerged with the development of new social movements: the left-libertarian party family, often identified with the Greens. As new social movements called for a more horizontal relationship, left-libertarian parties have reflected this mood, with attempts to implement participatory conceptions of politics (Kitschelt, 1989, p. 3). Their renewed stress on internal democracy can be read within a dialectic process, in which 'each new party type generates a reaction that stimulates further development, thus leading to yet another party type, and to another set of reactions, and so on.' Born long before the invention of online platforms, left-libertarian movement parties were, in fact, characterized by open membership, loose networks of grassroots support, a call for social solidarity, and participatory structures (Frankland et al., 2008). At their origins, these parties adopted a non-conventional repertoire of action, including forms of protest (Poguntke, 1993, p. 81). Green parties were more likely to form within strong environmental movements, from problem push (Rüdig, 1990) but also opportunity pull, being, however, perceived as just one node in a (tendentially) horizontal network (Rootes, 1995). Linkages between Green parties and new social movements remained mostly informal, unstable and influenced by cycles of protest (Poguntke, 2002, p. 22). Moving in the direction of a professional-electoral party, Green parties had even looser ties to movements.

A new wave of movement parties has developed in the year 2010, as the legitimacy crisis of late neoliberalism fuelled anti-austerity protests denouncing the corruption of an entire political class (della Porta, 2015b). In opposition to corrupt elites, protestors defined themselves as part of the large majority of those suffering from social and political inequalities. While these attitudes reflected a drop-in trust in existing parties, which was widespread in the electorate, social movement activists became however convinced of the need for political intervention to control the market, campaigning for a return of the public. This brought about the choice to create new movement parties, whose electoral affirmation was then favoured by the widespread mistrust in the existing political parties. During the economic crisis, the PASOK in Greece, the Democratic Party in Italy and the PSOE in Spain all turned toward neoliberal policies based on structural reforms and privatization programs. Syriza, the Five Star Movement and Podemos emerged and grew from the dissatisfaction with mainstream parties in particular (but not only) of the centre-left (della Porta, Fernandez, et al., 2017).

Communication practices in movement parties

Examining movement parties' communication strategies circumvents technological determinism to instead untangle complex communication practices. A central approach in previous research on communication in social movement studies has paralleled the attention to political opportunities with one to media (or discursive) opportunities pointing at the selectivity of mass media towards movement actors; limitations on media freedoms and pluralism that discourage the coverage of contentious politics and deny access to new actors (Cammaerts, 2012; della Porta & Mattoni, 2015; Della Porta & Pavan, 2018). In recent times, tendencies towards concentration, commercialization and deregulation in the mass media system (Bennett & Pfetsch, 2018) made access for progressive movement parties all the more difficult.

If the analysis of media opportunities tended to consider especially structural constraints, agency emerges in research that, in the tradition of the resource mobilization approach, has looked at alternative media as strategic instruments for mobilization and, a fortiori, arenas for the prefiguration of horizontal and participatory visions of production and communication (Downing 2001; Atkinson, 2010). These accounts emphasized the capacity of alternative media to involve not only (or mainly) professional journalists, but also normal citizens in news production, thanks to their horizontal links with their audience. Even before the availability of online communication, alternative media had long overcome the distinction between audience and producers, the readers and writers.

Going beyond discursive opportunities and alternative media, analyses of social movements and their communication, attention on media practices as 'practices of resistance in their own right' (Cammaerts, 2012; Mattoni & Treré, 2014) addresses the ways in which 'people exercise their agency in relation to media flows' (Couldry, 2003, p. 27). While digital technologies might have facilitated a blurring of the borders between news production and news consumption, producers and the public, the very logic of communication in progressive social movements has always aimed (even if with various results) at producing alternative public spheres, giving citizens a right to speak that also means a right to communicate and 'be the media'.

The concept of media practices points therefore at the importance of the agency of various actors. In this vein, it allows one to understand not only the growing blurring of borders between production, distribution and consumption in the activist milieus but also the innovation in the layering out of different means of communication (production, distribution and consumption) in movements and movement parties.

Media practices are certainly influenced by available technologies for communication. Digital media have by their very limited costs, immediate time and global spread deeply transformed the media opportunities for communications in movements and movement parties. Digital media so shape the modes in which individuals can express and present themselves in public (Gerbaudo & Treré, 2015). As social movement activists are however critical users, they tend to single out the strengths as well as the weaknesses of the different technologies. Movement parties as well develop attempts at innovating in the use of some communication technologies, trying (even if at times unsuccessfully) to adapt them for their aims. So, movement and movement parties actors 'purposively and strategically create, select, juxtapose, and publicly display digital contents of all types (photos, video, texts, animated gifs etc.) that, altogether, define their public presence' (della Porta & Pavan, 2018, p. 33).

Beyond the materiality of the media, movements' communication practices are, as other repertoires of action, led by norms. New technologies are used in as far as they resonate with social movements' vision of democracy at the normative level. Fast and inexpensive communication allows for flexible organizational and more participatory structures. Research on movement parties has in fact confirmed the importance of normative visions of democracy in leading the use of new technologies (Deseriis, 2019). Conceptions of democracy inside and outside the groups tend to filter the technological potentials of technological innovations so pointing at different styles in the political use of the web. So, different social movement organizations tend to exploit different technological opportunities, producing communication endowed with different qualities that apparently reflect different organizational models. Different types of governance of the interactions between platform providers and online creative communities are related to different conceptions of democratic decision-making (Fuster, 2010). Activists of community radio and radical internet projects use differently old and new technologies as their repertoires of action, networking strategies and organizational forms are filtered through the activists' motivations and ideological/cultural backgrounds with particular attention paid to the normative meanings of internal democracy as well as relations with the users (Milan, 2013). Thus, 'accounting more systematically for the knowledge that movements produce in the current digital mediascape appears to be a necessary step to comprehend how fluid and ever-evolving communication networks can become *agents of democratization*' (Della Porta & Pavan, 2018, p. 35). Practices are, in fact, permanently rethought and changed.

Communication practices in contemporary progressive movement parties

Drawing on these theoretical and conceptual tools, as well as existing research on the progressive side of the recent generation of movement parties, I will argue in what follows that their organizational and communication modes are: (a) influenced by the democratic conceptions of related social movements and party families' traditions, rather than by a blind faith in digital technology; (b) based on a complex bridging of on – but especially off-line forms of participation that are not underpinned by a data-driven platform logic but rather by a deep-rooted attempt to open the party structure to external sympathizers; (c) not driven by attempts at disintermediation but rather by attempts at empowering the grassroots, typical of alternative movement media; and (d) characterized by positive sentiments (such as hope) rather than by a negative and exclusive style.

Contemporary movement parties on the Left reflect an evolution in the organizational structures, identity frames, and repertoires of action of progressive social movements. However, this adaptation is not without its tensions, as movement parties have to balance the different logics and pressures present within party systems and social movement networks as main fields of intervention. Looking at movement parties, as with social movement organizations, we can therefore observe complex media ecologies, in which activists, not just media specialists, communicate. The communication is driven by opportunities but also normative concerns. Beyond the biased mass media and the internally oriented alternative media, movement parties develop complex practices which are alternative, activist, radical, and autonomous (Mattoni, 2012).

Movement parties vary with the specific characteristics of the movements they refer to, but also the type of relations they establish with them. So, the MAS in Bolivia developed different strategies towards the peasants' movement it originated in, the Cocaleros, and the urban movements, it entered in contact with (Anria, 2019). Similarly, Podemos and its local allies had more intense interactions with some core movements, such as the housing movement in Barcelona (della Porta, 2020; Flesher Fominaya, 2020).

Moreover, research has shown that communication practices changed in time, alternating moments of cooperation with moments of competition. As movement parties need to adapt to the communication practices considered as more effective during electoral campaigns, social movement organizations criticized the personalization of leaders as well as the simplification of messaging (again on Podemos, e.g., della Porta, 2020). Since, however, movement parties need also to rely on movements to mobilize support, channels of communication tend to remain open and activists with double membership can bring within the parties themselves the pressures for more participatory forms. Not by chance, the history of old generations of movement parties – from the socialist ones to the green ones – is characterized by moves and countermoves, professionalization of communication and pressure from more horizontal forms, adaptation with moderation and 'return to the origins', as exemplified by the recent vicissitudes of the Labour party in the UK.

What is more, tensions between different visions and strategies – including on communication forms and contents – become all the more dramatic when movement parties access power, entering in governments at local but also national level. The development of Syriza in Greece but also of the Five Star Movement in Italy testify to sudden shifts, especially when accessing the national governments. As former movement activists become party leaders and then access high level institutional positions, their style of communication becomes more mainstream and, especially, the claims and policy choices become more moderate (della Porta, Fernandez, et al., 2017).

In addressing these tensions, movement parties build, however, upon and found media outlets that to a certain degree reflect a desire, but also a need for innovation. First of all, as social movements tend to innovate through the experimentation of alternative media,[1] also movement parties build upon these attempts, adapting them to new circumstances through the hybridization of innovative and mainstream practices. So, movement parties participate in complex media environments which are 'open, unpredictable and controversial spaces of mediatization and communication, made up of different layers which continuously combine with one another due to the information flows circulating within the media environment itself' (Mattoni, 2012, p. 33). Different persons intervene and different types of media interact as 'individuals simultaneously play different roles, especially in particular situations of protest, mobilization and claims-making' (Mattoni, 2012, p. 34).

While adapting to (some) rules of communication dominating the party system – generally top down and professionalized – movement parties still have to deal with a reference base of supporters often endowed with high capacity for agency as well as high critical propensity towards any vertical structure. In the social movement arena, movement parties are an illustration of how 'the media audience is transformed into a communicative subject increasingly able to redefine the process by which societal communication frames the culture of society' (Castells, 2009, p. 116), Activists are said to adopt a 'dialectical, mutual-shaping, or co-production perspective, where artefacts and social action are seen as mutually constitutive and determining' (Lievrouw, 2014, p. 23). So, movement parties have to search for ways to strike a balance between top-down and bottom-up forms of communication.

While certainly also oriented to power, movement parties are deeply affected by their core reference to social movements as they build upon the hybrid and multifarious infrastructures for communication in the movements in which they originated. As movement parties evolve, moving towards institutions, tensions with social movements are reflected in the building of parties' more autonomous means of communication. So, research on communication in movement parties, as the articles presented in this special issue, reports of their frequent (even if often unsuccessful) attempts at innovating with media practices in order to overcome the bias of the mainstream media towards them and exploit the potential for alternative forms of communication in their privileged basis of reference within social movements.

So, while some analyses have explained the participatory ethos of progressive movement parties by their 'platformization', to which a logic of 'distributing organizing' and disintermediation of politics' is linked (e.g., Gerbaudo, 2019a, pp. 14–15), I suggest that it is not an effect of their use of online platforms, but one that long predates the very emergence of the technologies. Rather, the participatory ethos reflects the social movements' visions and practices of democracy: their achievements but also their limitations. This is well visible if we look at the history of Podemos. As in Spain the financial crisis hit fast and deep, dramatically affecting the everyday life of citizens, on 15 May 2011 the occupation of Puerta del Sol in Madrid started a long and massive wave of contention that came to be known as the 15M movement (the movement of the 15 May). The collective framing included a defence of citizenship rights, but also proactive visions of progressive transformations of the welfare system towards conceptions and practices of the commons. Values of equality, inclusiveness and dialogue were practised within deliberative and participatory conceptions of democracy (della Porta et al., 2016). These frames were present in Podemos from the very beginning, with some tensions between mistrust in mainstream parties and the decision to form a party (della Porta, Fernandez, et al., 2017). So, Podemos was a deliberate choice by movement actors to create an electoral tool that could eventually exploit the new energies which emerged during the peak of the protest cycle, channelling them into institutional politics (della Porta, Fernandez, et al., 2017, p. 49). The 15M movement contributed to preparing the terrain for Podemos through a critique of the parties and the party system that were identified with the Spanish democratic transition (Sampedro & Lobera, 2014). Interactions between the party and progressive social movements continue to be facilitated also by personal experiences and overlapping membership (della Porta, Fernandez, et al., 2017, p. 122).

Important to consider is also that the reliance on communication via online platforms – which is however always combined with a prevalent off-line communication – varies a lot from movement parties to movement parties, being more relevant for the Pirate Party in Germany or the Five Stars Movement in Italy than in Podemos in Spain and even less in Syriza in Greece or the MAS in Bolivia (della Porta, Fernandez, et al., 2017). While progressive movement parties have always tended to exploit new communication technologies in order to reduce the cost of communication and overcome the mainstream media bias against them, they have never focused on just one technology, rather stratifying all of them in their internal and external communication. Being themselves critical media users, movement parties have, in fact, hybrid organizational models, blending innovative and traditional characteristics. What is more, in time they have tended to become more conventional in their organization and communication, given the growing role of electoral politics and (often) declining mobilization of social movements of reference. To remain with the example of Podemos, the organizational choices and evolution in the party testifies to the influence of the 15M, but also of some tensions between party and movements, between a grassroots participatory structure and a personalized style of decision-making (della Porta, Fernandez, et al., 2017, p. 98; Font et al., 2019). Eventually, going well beyond the platform, the organizational structure of Podemos mixes traditional elements of the left-wing party model with some participatory innovations, generating tensions between horizontal networking and centralization as well as personalization of the leadership (Galindo et al., 2015; Rendueles & Sola, 2015). Rather than one based on a substitution of party branches with a platform (Gerbaudo, 2019a, p. 16), a quite traditional party structure was put in place (della Porta, Fernandez, et al., 2017).

Also, the presence of blurred boundaries between the inside and the outside of the party have characterized progressive movement parties for a long time. Historically, not only the socialist parties developed ancillary associations open to sympathizers, but even more so the Green parties. From the outset, they opened the decision-making process to non-members, privileging open assemblies and horizontal forms of communication to delegation and vertical forms of communication. More recently, progressive movement parties have built upon these previous attempts, also experimenting with digital technologies.

Among the new generation of progressive movement parties, participatory tools have been looked for, also in the use of digital media. Inspired by the 15M movement to increase participation, Podemos has for instance experimented with existing commercial online platforms that have seldom been used by social movements (Romanos & Sádaba, 2016). In particular, Plaza Podemos has been defined as a digital square, 'with collective life which thinks, debates and cooperates socializing information and generating debates and processes of collective intelligence' (Toret, 2015, p. 132); a forum online for internal party discussion self-described as 'a most complete citizens' participation tool for an open, transparent and democratic government' (Toret, 2015, p. 120) supported by the Consul Software, that is used also by several municipalities. It allows for propositions to be developed through thread discussions, as in the collaborative drafting of the party program for the national election of 2015 on axes such as democracy, economy, justice and culture in which more than 15,000 people took part (Gerbaudo, 2019a, p. 131). In addition, Participa is a section on the party's website that allows discussing and voting on various issues. More ambitious but less successful was the Iniciativa Ciudadanas Podemos. Launched in order to allow for the development of motions on the party statute or policy decision, it has never been fully operational (Gerbaudo, 2019a, p. 133). Appgree is used for the organization of mass protests as it allows for rapid participant polling (Romanos & Sádaba, 2016).

While all these instruments have shown their limitations, they have however at times increased participation in the movement parties as well as allowing for multiplying the arenas for debate. Additionally, rather than being limited to a specific party, these instruments have been developed and applied both by the social movements and at the institutional level. Moreover, they have been combined with off-line open structures. So, Podemos also launched (offline) the Area of Civil Society, led by an ex-lawyer for the *Plataforma de Afectados por la Hipoteca* (PAH), which in July 2015 organized the 'Forum for Change,' with the participation of more than 2500 activists.

In sum, Podemos, as other movement parties attempted to develop an organizational structure that addresses in part the critique of representative democracy that was widespread in 15M, with particular emphasis on grassroots participation. The party 'generated a great social effervescence: hundreds of circles were created in the first months, an intense public scrutiny of the different programs and projects of the organization took place, and tens of thousands periodically participated in votes through the Internet' (Rendueles & Sola, 2018, p. 37). The frequent elections in 2015 and 2016 pushed however towards a rapid institutionalization oriented toward capturing the opening of electoral opportunities (Rendueles & Sola, 2018). In time, the leadership chose to strengthen its control at the expense of a greater plurality, in order to maximize its chances of success in the upcoming elections. As electoral politics pushed the privileging of efficacy over internal pluralism, tensions emerged inside the party.

Finally, if we look at the content of the message and the style of communication, the norms and practices of social movements seem more influential than the use of online technology. Progressive movement parties share, first of all, inclusive frames with the reference movements as well as the attempt at a grassroot communication style defying definition as populist. In the same direction, the appeal to the people is mainly framed in the traditional language of the Left, with some innovation that is resonant with the anti-austerity protests. Research on Podemos or the MAS has pointed to their counter-hegemonic strategy toward transforming the political status quo through a radical change in discourse. As for its communication style, Podemos presents itself as a movement for a political renewal of the symbols and identities of the traditional left. Resonant with the 15M discourse, the critique of the Old Left is expressed in the choice of the party name, its colour and its logo. The very name Podemos (We can) 'signals the willingness to capitalize on the sense of popular empowerment emerging from virtual and physical *plazas* as a way to promote action into the Spanish parliamentary system' (Agustin & Briziarelli, 2018, p. 7). Here as well, transformations were noted with the increasing focus on electoral politics that brought about a growing need to attract voters located on the centre-left, as well as to find party allies on the centre-left.

In conclusion

In conclusion, movement parties – as movement organizations and political parties – use complex communication practices with a stratification of various modes and means of communication in which different internal and external actors intervene. Movement parties coming from progressive movements have historically promoted innovations in the party structures, strategies and communication as well as in their framing. The stress on participation dates from well before the internet, having been at the root of the socialist ideological mass party as well as the left-libertarian Green parties. The latest wave of movement parties emerged from the anti-austerity protests has built upon those previous experiences, developing hybrid models between democratic centralism and open party structures.

The specific types of democratic innovations and their use of available communication technologies are then deeply influenced by the conceptions and practices of democracy in the social movement family from which they originate. While the assessment of the democratic qualities of the *platform/s* used by a party is certainly relevant, the assessment of the democratic qualities of a *party* is much more complex and cannot be done by isolating a fraction, however important, of its activities. In the case of the contemporary wave of progressive movement parties, the experience of the Global Justice Movement first and the anti-austerity protests, later on, pushed for a combination of deliberative forums and direct democracy. Open membership as well as instruments for consensual decision making and open debate are not determined by the invention of online platforms, but instead long precede them (Polletta, 2002). They build upon the experiences of Green parties mixed with the inspiration drawn from contemporary social movements.

As for the use of digital technologies, social movement organizations and movement parties have been inspired by critical users to develop alternatives to the more and more close discursive opportunities they face. Offline and online alternative media traditions have been innovated within new movements and adapted by movement parties – as it has happened with the press, the radio, the TV and then the internet and, most recently, social media. By necessity and predisposition, social movements have been innovators in communication strategies, but usually far from acritical ones. In fact, social movement and movement party activists still use all of these media, for internal and external communication, blending them in order to adapt to participatory conceptions of democracy.

Activists have however always been aware of the limits of specific technologies, experimenting with them but also trying to correct their shortcoming. Even if not always successfully, they have innovated in their search for solutions to communication challenges. As research on communication practices clearly indicates, online communication is embedded in offline relations, being often produced by groupings of activists. As studies of referendums from below testify, informal networks and the rank-and-file participate in the production and distribution of messages (della Porta, O'Connor, et al., 2017). All these experiences have migrated from movements to movement parties.

In terms of communication styles, while emotions are always part of political communication, progressive social movements and movement parties have been building upon principles of civicness and inclusiveness that are far removed from the fake news and aggressive framing observed in rightwing online populism (Engesser et al., 2017). As for progressive movements, an inclusive attitude as well as the need to mobilize on hope for change has characterized also related party movements, since at least the origins of the socialist party family.

In sum, the participatory ethos does not come from digital platforms. Rather, participative and deliberative democracy as an aspiration is a value coming from social movements, as well as previous generations of movement parties. The organizational format, while using also digital technologies as instruments of communication, bridges old with new models as well as new and old media. Digital technologies are, in fact, mainly seen in a critical way, far away from techno-enthusiasm. Far from disappearing, the movement parties tend however to adapt in time to the party system, electoral competition and institutional logics.

A final remark refers to the perspective of these progressive movement parties of the last wave. While experiencing ups and downs, successes and failures, hope and disillusionment vis-à-vis the most optimistic expectations, they do not seem to be transient parties. Rather, occupying the space the socialist party family left empty, the most recent generation of progressive movement parties have built long-lasting organizations.

Even when maintaining competitive relations with the old left, they have contributed to a revival of the radical Left that had been proclaimed dead, entering not only parliaments but also governments, and not only at local but also at national level. Their innovative potential, even if far from being fully materialized, has contributed not only to their positive electoral results but also to the emergence of new frames and strategies that might affect also other, more mainstream, parties.

Note

1. In Downing's definition (2001, p. 3), 'radical alternative media constitute the most active form of the active audience and express oppositional strands, overt and covert, within popular cultures'. They are 'media, generally small scale and in many different forms, that express an alternative vision to hegemonic policies, priorities and perspectives' (2001, p. v).

Disclosure statement

No potential conflict of interest was reported by the author(s).

ORCID

Donatella della Porta http://orcid.org/0000-0002-5239-8773

References

Agustin, O. G., & Briziarelli, M. (2018). Wind of change: Podemos, its dreams and politics. In O. G. Agustin & M. Briziarelli (Eds.), *Podemos and the new political cycle: Left-wing populism and anti-establishment politics* (pp. 1–25). Palgrave.
Allern, E. H. (2010). *Political parties and interest groups in Norway*. ECPR Press.
Anria, S. (2019). *When movements become parties: The bolivian MAS in comparative perspective*. Cambridge University Press.
Atkinson, J. D. (2010). *Alternative media and politics of resistance*. Peter Lang.
Bennett, L. W., & Pfetsch, B. (2018). Rethinking political communication in a time of disrupted public spheres. *Journal of Communication, 68*(2), 243–253. https://doi.org/10.1093/joc/jqx017
Cammaerts, B. (2012). Protest logics and the mediation opportunity structure. *European Journal of Communication, 27*(2), 117–134. https://doi.org/10.1177/0267323112441007
Castells, M. (2009). *Communication power*. Oxford University Press.
Couldry, N. (2003). Beyond the hall of mirrors? Some theoretical reflections on the global contestation of media power. In N. Couldry & J. Curran (Eds.), *Contesting media power. Alternative media in a networked world* (pp. 39–55). Rowman & Littlefield.

De Blasio, E., & Sorice, M. (2020). 'Spaces of struggle: Socialism and neoliberalism with a human face among digital parties and online movements in Europe'. *tripleC: Communication, Capitalism & Critique, 18*(1), 84–100.

De Blasio, E., & Viviani, L. (2020). Platform party between digital activism and hyper-leadership: The reshaping of the public sphere. *Media and Communication, 8*(4), 16–27. https://doi.org/10.17645/mac.v8i4.3230

della Porta, D. (2013). *Can democracy be saved? Participation, deliberation and social movements*. Polity Press.

della Porta, D. (2015a). *I partiti politici*. Il Mulino.

della Porta, D. (2015b). *Social movements in times of austerity: Bringing capitalism back into protest analysis*. Polity Press.

della Porta, D. (2020). *How social movements can save democracy*. Polity Press.

della Porta, D., Andretta, M., Fernandes, T., O'Connor, F., Romanos, E., & Vogiatzoglou, M. (2016). *Late neoliberalism and its discontents in the economic crisis: Comparing social movements in the European periphery*. Palgrave Macmillan.

della Porta, D., & Diani, M. (2020). *Social movements: An introduction* (3rd ed). Blackwell.

della Porta, D., Fernandez, J., Kouki, H., & Mosca, L. (2017). *Movement parties in times of austerity*. Polity.

della Porta, D., & A. Mattoni (2015), Social movements, in *the international encyclopedia of political communication*. Malden: John Wiley and Sons, pp. 1496-1503

della Porta, D., O'Connor, F., Portos, M., & Subirats, A. (2017). *Referendums from below*. Policy Press/Chicago University Press.

Della Porta, D.-, & Pavan, E. E. (2018). The nexus between media, communication and social movements. In G. Meikle (Ed.), *The Routledge companion to media and activism* (pp. 29–37). Routledge.

de Nadal, L. (2020). On populism and social movements: From the Indignados to Podemos. *Social Movement Studies*. https://doi.org/10.1080/14742837.2020.1722626

Dennis, J. (2020). A party within a party posing as a movement? Momentum as a movement faction. *Journal of Information Technology & Politics, 17*(2), 97–113. https://doi.org/10.1080/19331681.2019.1702608

Deseriis, M. (2019). Digital movement parties: A comparative analysis of the technopolitical cultures and the participation platforms of the Movimento 5 Stelle and the piratenpartei, information. *Communication & Society*, https://doi.org/10.1080/1369118X.2019.1631375Downing

Deseriis, M. (2020). Two variants of the digital party: The platform party and the networked party. *Partecipazione e Conflitto, 13*(1), 896–917.

Downing, J. D. H., Villareal Ford, T., Gil, G., & Stein, L. (2001). *Radical media. Rebellious communication and social movements*. Sage.

Engesser, S., Fawzi, N., & Larsson, A. O. (2017). Populist online communication: Introduction to the special issue. *Information, Communication & Society, 20*(9), 1279–1292. https://doi.org/10.1080/1369118X.2017.1328525

Flesher Fominaya, C. (2020). *Democracy reloaded*. Oxford University Press.

Font, N., Graziano, P., & Tsakatika, M. (2019). Varieties of inclusionary populism? SYRIZA, podemos and the five star movement. *Government and Opposition*, 1–21.

Frankland, E. G., Lucardie, P., & Rihoux, B. (Eds.) (2008). *Green parties in transition: The end of grass-roots democracy?* Ashgate.

Fuster, M. (2010). *Governance of online creation communities* [unpublished PhD Thesis]. European University Institute, Florence.

Galindo, J., Llaneras, K., Medina, O., San Miguel, J., Senserrich, R., & Simón, P. (2015). *Podemos: La cuadratura del círculo*. Madrid, Debate.

Gerbaudo, P. (2019a). *The digital party*. Verso.

Gerbaudo, P. (2019b). 'Are digital parties more democratic than traditional parties? Evaluating Podemos and Movimento 5 stelle's online decision-making platforms,'. *Party Politics*, 1–13. https://doi.org/10.1177/1354068819884878

Gerbaudo, P., & Treré, E. (2015). In search of the 'we' of social media activism: Introduction to the special issue on social media and protest identities. *Information, Communication & Society, 18*(8), 865–871. https://doi.org/10.1080/1369118X.2015.1043319

Kitschelt, H. (1989). *The logicss of party formation: Ecological parties in Belgium and west Germany.* Cornell University Press.

Kitschelt, H. (1994). *The transformation of European social democracy.* Cambridge University Press.

Kitschelt, H. (2006). 'Movement parties'. In R. Katz & W. Crotty (Eds.), *Handbook of party politics* (pp. 278–291). Sage.

Lievrouw, L. (2014). Materiality and media in communication and technology studies: An unfinished project. In T. Gillespie, P. J. Boczkowski, & K. A. Foot (Eds.), *Media technologies. Essays on communication, materiality, and society* (pp. 21–51). MIT Press.

Mattoni, A. (2012). *Media practices and protest politics.* Ashgate.

Mattoni, A., & Treré, E. (2014). Media practices, mediation processes, and mediatization in the study of social movements. *Communication Theory, 24*(3), 252–271. https://doi.org/10.1111/comt.12038

Milan, S. (2013). *Social movements and their technologies: Wiring social change.* Palgrave Macmillan.

Poguntke, T. (1993). *Alternative politics: The German green party.* Edinburgh University Press.

Poguntke, T. (2002). Party organizational linkage: Parties without firm social roots?. In K. R. Luther & F. Müller-Rommel (Eds.), *Political parties in the New Europe: Political and analytical challenges* (pp. 43–62). Oxford University Press.

Polletta, F. (2002). *Freedom is an endless meeting.* Chicago University Press.

Rendueles, C., & Sola, J. (2015, April 13). Podemos and the paradigm shift. *Jacobin Magazine: A Magazine of Culture and Polemic.* https://www.jacobinmag.com/2015/04/podemos-spain-pablo-iglesias-european-left/

Rendueles, C., & Sola, J. (2018). Podemos and the overturn of Spanish politics. In O. G. Agustin & M. Briziarelli (Eds.), *Podemos and the new political cycle: Left-wing populism and anti-establishment politics* (pp. 25–47). Palgrave.

Romanos, E., & Sádaba, I. (2016). From the street to institutions through the App: Digitally enabled political outcomes of the Spanish indignados movement. *Revista Internacional de Sociología, 74*(4), e048. https://doi.org/10.3989/ris.2016.74.4.048

Rootes, C. (1995). 'A new class? The higher educated and the new politics'. In L. Maheu (Ed.), *Social movements and social classes* (pp. 220–235). Sage.

Rüdig, W. (1990). Explaining green party development: Reflections on a theoretical framework. Strathclyde papers on government and politics 71. Department of Government, University of Strathclyde.

Sampedro, V., & Lobera, J. (2014). The Spanish 15-m movement: A consensual dissent? *Journal of Spanish Cultural Studies, 15*(1-2), 61–80. https://doi.org/10.1080/14636204.2014.938466

Toret, J. (2015). Una mirada tecnopolítica al primer año de Podemos. Seis hipótesis. *Revista Teknokultura, 12*(1), 121–135.

'We do politics so we can change politics': communication strategies and practices in the Aam Aadmi Party's institutionalization process

Divya Siddarth, Roshan Shankar and Joyojeet Pal

ABSTRACT
This decade has marked a rise in social movement-originating political parties, many of which have gained considerable political power and achieved surprising electoral success. In doing so, these parties have challenged traditional definitions and conceptualizations of party institutionalization. One such party is the Aam Aadmi Party in India, formed in the wake of the massively viral 2011 India Against Corruption (IAC) movement. Through interviews and observations, as well as digital artefact analysis, we trace the process of the Aam Aadmi Party's institutionalization through an analysis of its media and communication practices. We argue that party workers' drive to institutionalize into a durable electoral force has pushed AAP into projecting contradictory images and embracing conflicting narratives, both online and offline. However, the durability of the party and recent electoral successes point to the ways AAP can nonetheless inform conceptions of institutionalization.

Introduction

In 2013, Arvind Kejriwal, the head of the nascent Aam Aadmi Party (AAP), spoke to a reporter at the *New Yorker* about transitioning from being one of the leaders of a mass movement in India to being the leader of an upstart political party in the nation's capital. He maintained that the two roles were, at their core, the same. 'The next election,' he said, 'will be a revolution'. And indeed, the following elections did mark a turning point for Indian politics, both in the national capital of Delhi and around the country.

The meteoric rise and subsequent mixed fortunes of AAP provides a rich case study for understanding the process, framing, and context of movement party institutionalization. The party was formed in the wake of the 2011 India Against Corruption (IAC) movement, which brought hundreds of thousands of Indians to the streets in urban centers around the country, to raise their voices in a campaign against government corruption. Driven by a massively viral social media campaign, the movement saw significant spontaneous mobilization, particularly in the national capital of Delhi (Eipe et al., 2012). Yet, it failed to achieve its stated aim of establishing a *jan lokpal* (people's ombudsman) to investigate state corruption. Amid skepticism, a group of leaders from the thus far loosely organized movement formed a political party – the Aam Aadmi Party, or Common Man's Party.

AAP ran in the Delhi elections on an anti-corruption platform in 2013. The party shocked the political system by forming a minority government after its very first poll contest, and by almost as dramatically resigning from that government in less than two months, a decision that was widely criticized and led to major losses in the 2014 general elections. However, this seemingly catastrophic resignation would eventually be vindicated, as AAP won a re-election by landslide in 2015, capturing 67 out of 70 seats in the nation's capital. This marked a stunning upset, particularly given that the opposition campaign was spearheaded by Narendra Modi, the hugely popular, recently elected prime minister (Bornstein & Sharma, 2016; Jaffrelot, 2015). Since then, the party has had stops and starts in its momentum, winning just one seat across the 40 it contested in the 2019 national elections, but again sweeping the Delhi elections in 2020, with 62 seats out of 70 – indicating a persistent split between its strength in the capital city and its performance across the rest of the country. Further, all of this has occurred during a particularly tumultuous decade in Indian politics, seeing both the unprecedented rise of the Hindu nationalist Bharatiya Janata Party (BJP) and the steep decline of the traditionally dominant Indian National Congress (INC).

From its victory in 2013, which was heralded as a 'new era in Indian politics', to its national losses in 2019 and Delhi success in 2020, AAP has evolved, both ideologically, in terms of its positioning in the political spectrum, and structurally, as an organization seeking its place in the political system of India. In this process of institutionalization, the party's internal and external narratives, particularly in the digital sphere, has morphed from that of a social movement party, to a political party with social movement origins, to an uneasy mix of political institution, personalistic political party, and self-identified political 'outsider'.

In this paper, we analyze aspects of those changes, examining the institutionalization of AAP from its social movement origins to its current place in the Indian political system. First, we examine and define party institutionalization, particularly with regards to movement parties and personalistic parties. Then, we apply this definition to a case study of AAP, focusing on the strategies used to construct and communicate the party's institutionalization. We draw from 23 interviews with activists, journalists, party workers, and party leaders, supplemented with an analysis of party documents.

This piece first serves to complicate the current understanding of social movements and movement parties in the Indian context, where existing literature currently focuses either on India's two main national parties or on caste – or religion-based regional parties (DeSouza, 2006; Ziegfeld, 2012). Secondly, we qualitatively map the practices and processes that construct digitally mediated voter outreach in emerging democracies more generally. Lastly, this study deepens scholarly approaches to understanding institutionalization in the context of early-stage personalistic movement parties.

Understanding party institutionalization

Personalistic and movement party institutionalization

We ground our analysis in an understanding of the Aam Aadmi Party as a movement party with personalistic tendencies. *Movement parties* are coalitions of political activists who emanate from social movements and try to apply the strategic practice of social movements in the area of party competition (Kitschelt, 2006). AAP, which was formed by leaders of the 'India Against Corruption' movement in the wake of protests and mass mobilization, and carried forward movement tactics into electioneering, falls into this category (Leichty et al., 2016).

Personalistic parties are defined as 'strongly related to or even dependent on the figure of political leaders' (Musella, 2015). AAP is in an interesting position with regards to this definition. Often, personalistic movement parties will be led by the central figure of the movement (Mossige, 2009), which in this case would be Anna Hazare. However, Hazare was against the formation of a political party from the start, and actively distanced himself from AAP (Leichty et al., 2016). Instead, the current leader of the party and another major figure in the movement, Arvind Kejriwal, formed AAP, along with several prominent leaders, most of whom were well-known by the public and the media during the IAC movement (Sengupta, 2012). Over the next few years, Kejriwal, himself a charismatic figure and author of a bestselling book on governance, *Swaraj* (self-governance), slowly consolidated power and support within AAP. This process came to a head in 2015, when several of the other prominent leaders and party officials were ousted for 'anti-party activities' (Sriram, 2015). This left Kejriwal as the last major public figure associated with the party's movement origins and as the single head of AAP, crystallizing AAP as a personalistic party centered around his leadership (Subrahmaniam, 2015).

Approaches to institutionalization

Party institutionalization at large is crucial to understanding the development and success of political parties, party systems, and democracy at large (Kuenzi & Lambright, 2001; Mainwaring & Scully, 1995; Mainwaring & Torcal, 2006); as such, it has been theorized extensively. This paper does not provide an exhaustive summary of the literature; rather, we aim to present an operational definition of party institutionalization in the context of personalistic movement parties, considering institutionalization as a multidimensional and sequenced process (Weissenbach & Bukow, 2019).

One of the first conceptualizations of party institutionalization is in Panebianco's *Political Parties*, which states that a party is institutionalized 'when it becomes valuable in and of itself.' Panebianco provides two scales by which this can be measured: *autonomy* – the degree of autonomy in decision-making between a party and its external environment, and between a party and its own leader, and *systemness* – the internal organization and composition of the party (Panebianco, 1988).

There have been several critiques of this definition for being imprecise in general, and particularly lacking explanatory power in the cases of personalistic parties, movement parties, and other nontraditional political formations (Randall & Svåsand, 2002; Rose & Mackie, 1988). The necessary dimension of internal autonomy emerged as problematic: under this, personalistic, charismatic parties, which are not autonomous from their leader, cannot become institutionalized (Pedahzur & Brichta, 2002). For example, far-right charismatic parties, such as the National Front in France and the Freedom Party of Austria, have attained substantial electoral support and continuous legislative representation, despite decisions being very much leader-driven (Pedahzur & Brichta, 2002). In fact, even parties which score poorly on metrics of both autonomy and systemness, such as, the Justicialist Party in Argentina and the Party of the Democratic Revolution in Mexico, have proved remarkably resilient despite internal turmoil (Mossige, 2009).

Thus, initial extensions of Panebianco's definition focused on internal and external measures of reification, as well as adaptability and durability, holding that a party must have some measure of coherence, flexibility, and electoral success to be considered institutionalized (Harmel & Svåsand, 1993; Rose & Mackie, 1988). Our analysis is rooted in a review of these extensions, formalized in the theory of institutionalization laid out by Harmel et al. (2016), which considers institutionalization along three distinct (and not necessarily co-occurring) dimensions:

(a) internal, measured by internal decision-making routinization and ability to persist after current leadership;
(b) external, measured by external perception that the party is an established, lasting 'institution'; and
(c) objective, measured by adaptability and longevity.

However, we must adapt this framework to account for the current case of upstart 'technopopulist parties', such as AAP, which are a fairly new phenomenon and have not yet been fully theorized in the space (Bickerton, 2018). First, the focus on routinization and decision-making processes as internal measures and 'perceived lasting power' as an external measure does not adequately capture the need for narrative and communicative cohesion that is core to media-centric movement parties such as AAP (Udupa, 2014). Thus, we add measures of internal and external *reification*, measured by cohesion around narrative, purpose, and presence, in both internal party identity and in the mind of the public and external actors (Basedau & Stroh, 2008; Levitsky, 1998). Second, many of the objective measures of longevity that have been proposed, including participation in three national elections (Rose & Mackie, 1988), ability to transcend initial founding generation of leadership (Randall & Svåsand, 2002), electoral and legislative stability (Pedahzur & Brichta, 2002), and criteria around name changes and organizational discontinuities (Janda, 1980), do not form an instructive basis to evaluate recent parties such as AAP. We thus focus specifically on outlined aspects of adaptability to environmental change, as well as shorter-term electoral success and base-building (Arter & Kestilä-Kekkonen, 2014), as the appropriate objective measures.

Studies of movement parties

While the institutionalization process of movement parties has not been studied in depth, there have been significant contributions. For example, Deseriis investigated how the technopolitical cultures of the Pirate Party of Germany and the Italian 5-Star Movement (M5S), both digital movement parties, have influenced decision-making and routinization processes, finding that they often fall short of promises of radical democratic functioning (Deseriis, 2019). These organizational trends have also been studied in the context of Podemos and the 15M movement, with regards to the use of technology platforms as participatory, democratic spaces, and how this affects movement functioning (Bennett, 2012; Kouki & González, 2018; Micó & Casero-Ripollés, 2014).

M5S forms a particularly instructive comparative case study to AAP, as one of the most evident examples of how a digital movement party may seem to institutionalize quickly on the dimension of objective electoral success, despite potential contradictions, and then lose these gains due to failures on the internal and external measures. The party began as strongly leader-centric (Musella, 2015; Turner, 2013), but also pushed claims of internal democracy and non-hierarchical functioning on its digital and social platforms, operating initially as 'a pyramid truncated in the middle' (Vignati, 2015), with consistent tensions between grassroots participation and centralized control. The party has also promoted conflicting and confused policy proposals, and is still in search of a clear ideological definition (Manucci & Amsler, 2018). Despite this lack of internal and external reification, M5S was electorally successful in both the 2013 and 2018 elections, with support from a diverse set of voters (Corbetta et al., 2018). However, this success was short-lived, with major vote losses in the 2019 elections and the party currently in disarray (Horowitz, 2020). This shows not only the possibility of significant variation *between* the three described dimensions, particularly for upstart movement parties, but also highlights the need for cohesion *across* these three dimensions for successful institutionalization.

There has been considerable study of the social media use and communication practices of social movements and of political parties. Notably, Garrett diagrammed new ICT use in movements, providing a pre-social media framework for the study of digital and media-involved activism (Kelly Garrett, 2006). Extending this, Bennett put forth the theory of 'connective action', the light-touch, low-risk activist actions encouraged by social media (Bennett & Segerberg, 2012), and Coretti et. al. diagrammed the centralization and fragmentation that occurs due to the erosion of collective identity on social media (Coretti & Pica, 2015). On the other hand, it has also been shown that social media involvement in a movement is intertwined with on-ground action, even of unaffiliated audiences (Mercea, 2012), and can be used to forecast onsite protest (Bastos et al., 2015). However, the implications for these trends on digital movement parties requires more systematic analysis, particularly with regards to the external and communicative practices of these parties as they institutionalize, and situated in emerging democracies, in which voter coalitions are often more fluid (Mainwaring & Torcal, 2006).

The Aam Aadmi party: the internal narrative

Background

First, we briefly outline AAP's remarkable trajectory, from its beginnings in November 2012 to the present (Kumar, 2019; Leichty et al., 2016). In December 2013, one year after its formation, AAP won 28 out of 70 state legislature seats in the Delhi elections, forming a coalition government with INC, with Kejriwal as Chief Minister. However, Kejriwal resigned from government in February 2014, and soon after, in May, AAP won only four out of the 432 seats across India; Narendra Modi, and the BJP, were elected to the central government.

Then, in a huge upset, AAP won 67 out of 70 state legislature seats in the Delhi elections in February 2015, and formed the government. Soon after, Arvind Kejriwal expelled top AAP leaders for 'anti-party activities' and centralized power. However, this victory was not sustained nationwide, and in April 2017, AAP won zero seats in Goa and 20 seats in Punjab during assembly elections. This was followed by more major losses in June 2019, when AAP contested 40 seats in the Indian national election and lost 39. Finally, in February 2020, AAP again swept the Delhi election, winning 62 out of 70 contested seats.

Previous research on the party has examined AAP's election successes and failures, its policies, and its relationships to other parties (Diwakar, 2016; Gianolla, 2017). There has also been some study, largely quantitative, of AAP's digital media presence, with Leichty et. al. determining that AAP was able to appeal on Twitter to audience members' collective identities and grievances against corruption (Leichty et al., 2016; Udupa, 2014). Most of these studies investigate AAP's conceptual role in the Indian socio-political sphere or focus on quantitative analysis, rather than subjectively investigating the party's narrative and structural evolution. We address this lacuna in the present study.

Methods

Our aim was to understand the evolution of AAP as a movement party *through the experiences* of the flesh-and-blood party workers, leaders, and strategists who together constructed this evolution. Thus, data collection and analysis were targeted to highlight the various narrative intentions, strategies, and implementations that together constitute AAP's institutionalization process.

To this end, the primary researcher conducted 23 semi-structured interviews with a range of participants affiliated with or adjacent to the party and the IAC movement, as well as a total of 60 h of observation. Semi-structured interviews were chosen over unstructured interviews to enable us to understand how participants described their experiences of the party's evolution from a range of vantage points. Semi-structured interviews enable the researcher to explore a topics they believe are core to their investigation, ensuring some consistency across interviewees, whilst at the same time giving the interviewees freedom to highlight issues and experiences which are important to them (Silverman, 2005). In this case, participants were asked about when and why they joined AAP, the extent of their involvement in the IAC movement, online and offline communication strategies, their views on AAP's place in the political establishment, and their perspectives on AAP's trajectory. We further asked participants to evaluate the effectiveness of AAP's communication strategies and to discuss the criteria by which they determined this effectiveness, as in Rohlinger et al. (Rohlinger & Bunnage, 2015).

All interviews were conducted from September 2018 to February 2019 in batches, alongside the transcript analysis process. Of the total of 23 interviews conducted, 15 were in Delhi, 2 were in Chennai, and 6 were via telephone or Skype. Three journalists, five activists, three party canvassers, and twelve party leaders and strategists at a variety of levels were interviewed (Table 1). Interviewees were chosen based on proximity to party communication strategy and decisions, and to cover the range of party activities. Other than the party canvassers, who were interviewed as a group and spoke a combination of

Table 1. Interviewee information.

Interviewee category	Number of interviews	Interviewee roles
Journalists (J)	3	Journalists who covered AAP from 2013 to 2017
Activists (A)	5	IAC activists, three no longer involved with AAP, two in advisory roles
Party leadership (L)	3	AAP Delhi co-conveners (highest position in Delhi wing of the party), two from 2013 to 2017 and one from 2013-present
On-ground heads (H)	3	AAP Operational heads for district campaigns (each in charge of 1–4 of Delhi's eleven districts, two later in charge of districts in Punjab), two from 2013 to 2015, one from 2018
Party canvassers (C)	3	On-ground canvassers for AAP (lowest-level party operatives), all from 2014 to present
Digital strategy (S)	3	Two IAC and AAP social media heads from 2012 to present; one AAP digital messaging strategist from 2015 to 2018
Media strategy (M)	3	One AAP media strategy coordinator from 2013 to 2016; two media narrative strategists from IAC, one of whom also worked with AAP from 2013 to 2017

Hindi and English, all interviews were individual and in English. Interviews ranged in time from thirty minutes to three hours, with an average of 75 min. All interviews were translated when needed and transcribed verbatim. It was clear from the initial round of interviews that most stakeholders in the party clearly demarcated the party's progress around key electoral battles from 2013 to 2016, based on which we analyzed changes around these temporal lines.

Observation was conducted in Delhi, for one week each in September 2018, December 2018, and January 2019; data collected consisted of field notes and audio recordings. The aim was to inform the context of analysis, and develop a background understanding of the lived practices and processes of the party leaders and strategists (Silverman, 2005). The primary researcher shadowed two party strategists as they conducted internal meetings and events and discussed public-facing media and communication strategies, largely located in five different Delhi locations (two party-affiliated houses, three tea shops). This allowed the researcher to observe first-hand how party narratives were constructed, and how internal and external structures were navigated by various party affiliates. The process was coordinated by one of the paper authors, who was associated with the party and its functionaries through work with the Delhi government.

During the analysis process, the primary researcher assigned descriptive codes by hand, and thematic and descriptive discussions were held stepwise with the research team. Analyses were built on inductive methods of applied thematic analysis, designed for sensemaking in this semi-structured approach with both interviews and document-based artefacts (Guest et al., 2012). Specifically, we coded for aspects of electoral success, voter targeting and base construction, internal and external organizational structure, and internal and external narrative reification, all of which are associated with notions of institutionalization. We stopped conducting interviews once we confirmed that codes on these key themes had reached saturation and were being repeated consistently (Table 2).

Concurrently, we performed an in-depth discursive analysis of key internal and external-facing party documents, identifying and coding the patterns present (Guest et al., 2012). These documents were sampled based on their relevance to the themes that emerged from the interviews, and provided a second angle of inquiry regarding the

Table 2. Thematic distribution among interviews.

Theme	Interviewee mentions	Proportion mentioned
Theme 1: Desire to become an established political party	L1, L2, H1, H2, C1, C2, C3, S1, S2, S4, M1, M2	12 / 23
Theme 2: Personalization around Kejriwal / Kejriwal-centric messaging	J1, J3, A1, A2, A3, H1, S1, S2, M1, M2	10 / 23
Theme 3: Pulling together disparate voter bases into a coalition	A2, L1, L3, H1, H2, S1, S2, M1, M3	9 / 23
Theme 4: Anti-corruption centric messaging	A3, A4, L1, L2, H2, C1, C2, S2, S4, M1, M2	11 / 23

institutionalization process, allowing the research team to supplement subjective, post-hoc interview data with specific illustrative snapshots of the party's evolution.

Four main themes were identified: the desire to become established (e.g., the need for consistent electoral success, hopes and plans for national expansion), personalization (e.g., the primacy of Kejriwal-centric messaging and narratives), coalition-building (e.g., desire to remain outside of identity-based parties, group-targeted messaging), and the IAC / anti-corruption narrative (e.g., external messaging focused on IAC, internal discussions around party purpose and identity). In the remainder of the paper, we describe these main themes and illustrate them with quotations from the interviews and an analysis of party documents.

Findings

Our participants unilaterally described AAP's current goal as that of becoming an established, consistent, and stable political party, and the need to communicate this clearly. *'We are here to win elections, after all. That is how we can change things. We are not here to just say we are the good guys... We are here to win.' (L2)*, as one senior party official put it, echoing similar quotes heard in many interviews. This shows the move to an institutionalist standing, nested in which is a departure from the discourse and tone of AAP's social movement origins and *'activist heart' (C1)*, with electoral success and stability now the ultimate goal.

'No, Arvind is the party' (H1)

Participants were clear about the outsize role that AAP's leader, Arvind Kejriwal, played, particularly in being the face of external strategy and communication. As one-party strategist put it, *'See, people like me are triggered by Swaraj (self-rule, independence), ok. Then there are many others, voters, who are triggered by Arvind's face only.' (M1)*.

This points to a feeling, even within the party, that party members, volunteers, and voters support AAP in large part due to Kejriwal's charismatic leadership, rather than due to AAP's ideology, which was arguably crucial for the early electoral successes of the party. Many strategists pragmatically took advantage of this perception, creating digital artefacts with 'Arvind's face' prominently featured, making billboards that were centered on Kejriwal, and linking AAP's narrative to Kejriwal's at every opportunity.

Thus, when AAP was losing support, after resigning from the Delhi government in 2013 and a disastrous 2014 national and municipal election, actions that were viewed as the intransigence of Kejriwal, the natural solution proposed by workers was still to centralize messaging around their leader, and to subsume the party narrative under its leader's story and promises.

> In 2014 we had lost some credibility – two things were troubling the brand. One was ... that you leave government when we gave it to you ... Second thing, Arvind was more loved than the party. 15 points more. So instead of going with AAP messaging, we said no – Paanch saal Kejriwal (Kejriwal for 5 years). That's what people want. On social media, on ground, we even made a song, everywhere. And we won. – H2

The idea that the party would build credibility through this practice points to the role of Kejriwal in legitimizing AAP's electoral success in the political sphere. This party worker draws a comparison between two possible types of messaging – 'AAP' messaging and Kejriwal messaging and believes that the messaging that will resonate best with AAP's voters will be around the party leader. The slogan decided upon by the party – 5 years of Kejriwal! – flooded their digital properties as well as their on-ground rallies, becoming their rhetorical identity, and the worker credits this with the sweep victory in 2015. The fact that the nation had just experienced a successful, massively personality-centric digital campaign (from a party that is typically ideologically driven), in the election of Narendra Modi (Jaffrelot, 2015; Pal, 2015), signaled an important change in the way Indian voters were looking at elections, particularly online. This clearly influenced the decision to bring Kejriwal to the fore, with one strategist explaining that social media posts and volunteer rhetoric was targeted to potential voters by drawing a clear, personalistic distinction, '*We tried to say, subtly, you want Modi for PM, he won't solve your Delhi problems, so take Arvind for CM' (M2)*.

The strategic decisions made to centralize both communication and messaging around Kejriwal at this stage is very clearly seen in the progression of AAP's election manifesto, from 2013, 2014, and 2015.

The 2013 manifesto (Figure 1) distinctly characterizes AAP as a social movement-based party, immediately contextualizing it in the 'struggles of Ramlila Maidan and Jantar Mantar', the two main protest venues of the IAC movement in Delhi. The party is positioned as 'not just another party', but instead a transformative force, ready to bend the government to the will of the people. The first promise on this manifesto is the implementation of the Lokpal bill, which was the goal of the IAC movement. There is no mention of either Kejriwal or of any other party leaders, and the agency is given to AAP as an entity and to 'the people', who are consistently mentioned as the leaders of this movement.

Aesthetically, we see the change in the party's branding in 2014 (Figure 2), as messaging becomes more visually pleasing and professionalized. However, the background image, of a crowd of 'common people' holding up AAP's symbol (the broom), still evokes viral images and rhetoric shared during the IAC movement. The first page of the manifesto, which can be compared to the 2013 image, lists 'martyrs', who have 'sacrificed their lives to free the nation', including Gandhi, Bhagat Singh, and others who died during the Independence struggle. The manifesto then implies that these martyrs' dream of freedom can only continue if AAP is elected to power. While these sentiments are similar to the previous manifesto – the sentence on 'Ramlila Maidan and Jantar Mantar' is copied exactly – the drama and intensity of the language is heightened. This manifesto paints AAP as a crusading, revolutionary party, tying it to other revolutionaries in India's history.

> ### AAM AADMI PARTY
>
> DELHI ELECTION MANIFESTO 2013
> SUMMARY
>
> *1. WHY VOTE FOR THE 'AAM AADMI PARTY'?*
>
> Elections happen every five years, but a chance to change the country is a rare occurrence. The upcoming Delhi elections, to be held on the 4th of December, present one such unique opportunity. This is not merely an opportunity to change the party in power in Delhi, this is a moment to transform the politics of India. The possibility of Swaraj is knocking at doors of Delhi. If this electoral battle is won in Delhi, it would open the whole country to the winds of change. You hold the key to the future of this country…
>
> The announcement of elections is accompanied by the rituals that have come to define today's electoral politics. Ruling parties make untruthful and exaggerated claims. Election manifestoes are released, which are a collection of false promises; both the readers and the writers of these documents are aware of the untruthfulness and the insignificance of these promises. In these elections, there is not one, but two ruling parties. While Congress has been holding the reins of the Delhi government for 15 years, BJP has been in power in the MCD for the past 7 years. Both parties are hand-in-glove and share the fruits of power. The result lies before you/
>
> The Aam Aadmi Party is not just another party. It is a party that has arisen from the struggles of Ramlila Maidan and Jantar Mantar. It is a party that is not here merely to fight elections, it is here to change the rules of the game. It is here to rewrite the politics of this country, it is here to transform the relationship between the government and the people, it here to make the government truly 'of the people'. It is a party that brings with it the perspective of the common women and men of this country; it is a party that wants to bring power back into the hands of the people.
>
> *2. BRINGING AN END TO CORRUPTION IN DELHI*
>
> 2.1   Delhi Jan Lokpal Bill
>
> > The Aam Aadmi Party is committed to the passing the Delhi Jan Lokpal Bill within 15 days of coming to power. This would model the Lokayukta along the lines of the Jan Lokpal Bill. The provisions of this law include:
> > i.   All public officials (including the Chief Minister, Ministers and MLAs) shall fall within the purview of the investigation of the Lokayukta
> > ii. Any public official found guilty of corruption would be removed from their jobs, sent to prison and their property confiscated
> > iii. Time bound investigation and punishment in cases of corruption

Figure 1. AAP 2013 manifesto, first page.

In the 2015 manifesto (Figure 3), the cover is almost entirely taken over with a picture of Kejriwal. This reflects the strategist's perceptions that, after the 2014 losses, messaging should focus not on the social movement or policy aspect of AAP, but on its charismatic and popular leader. On the first page, the dramatic rhetoric of the 2014 manifesto has been replaced with a pragmatic summary of AAP's achievements in its 49 days in office in 2013, and an explanation of the Delhi Dialogues, a people-centric, partly online process through which AAP crowdsourced its manifesto. This process is painted in contrast to the opposition political parties, Congress and the BJP, rather than as evidence of a people's movement. Callbacks to AAP's origins

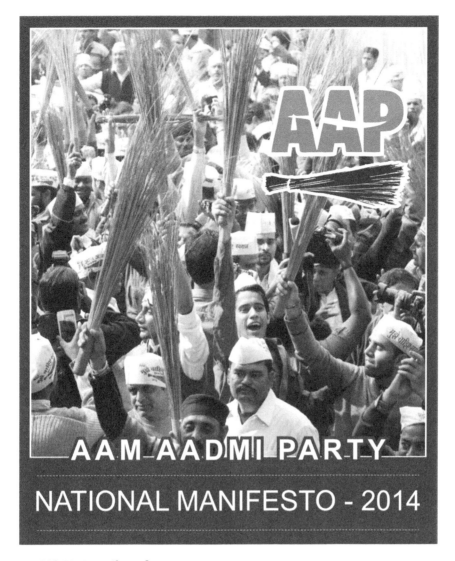

Figure 2. AAP 2014 manifesto, first page.

are far more subdued, and while Kejriwal is referred to as 'fearless, honest, and clean' in the first sentence of the manifesto, there is no direct mention of the IAC movement.

The 2013 and 2015 manifesto are for Delhi elections, whereas the 2014 manifesto was for national elections, possibly influencing the content and aesthetic choices. However, the clear progression in aesthetic, from the basic, text-only 2013 manifesto, to the energized crowd in the 2014 manifesto, to a smiling Kejriwal in the 2015 manifesto, as well as the transition in content, from that of a movement to a revolutionary political party to a more typical opposition party, mirrors AAP's trajectory in the electoral space, and tracks the increasing centrality of Kejriwal as leader, symbol, and preacher for the party.

Figure 3. AAP 2015 manifesto, first page.

'Different things for different people' (S2)

AAP's media strategists spoke about trying to create a new, winning coalition in the urban center of Delhi, bringing together groups into a nontraditional voter base. The India Against Corruption movement was, at its core, a middle-class movement (Sitapati, 2011), but AAP has attempted to buttress this core group of support with outreach to a range of other target groups without falling into the identity-based voting model employed by many other Indian political parties (Chhibber & Verma, 2019). During its first two campaigns, AAP was careful to avoid overt calls to caste or religion, and mentioned class only implicitly, through the broom-and-muffler branding as well as, of course, in the name of the party itself. However, the attempt to reach out to marginalized urban populations was clear in both its branding and its election promises in 2015, which, while never explicitly calling out to caste, aimed to balanced welfarist populism alongside a technocratic justification to power (Tripathy, 2017) (Figure 4).

> So, 70% of Delhi is Hindi speaking. But writing about WiFi in Hindi is something that no one understands. That content has to go out in English, has to have more beautiful graphics, on social media. That would not attract anyone from some unauthorized colony, it doesn't solve their problem … But … it looks futuristic. Similarly, with women … Specific promises for specific demographics, specific geographies … we are different things, for different people, that's the way we can win. – S1

This type of messaging is particularly common on AAP's social media pages. The promises in Figure 5 – degree, income, WiFi, governance via phone, support for women entrepreneurs – are atypical for Indian political parties, and highlight the piecemeal nature of AAP's coalition. In the quote above, the campaigner speaks about trying to appeal to these distinct sets of the population. He outlines the needs of each group, realizing that AAP's voting bloc requires a breadth and variety of campaign promises. Consequently, AAP has taken on causes such as ending the oppression faced by unauthorized slum colonies, offering cuts to electricity and water bills, and providing free transit and healthcare. Yet, at the same time, we see that the party will put conservative individualist Ayn Rand's quotes on messaging and create highly designed graphics promoting WiFi access, deftly signaling a tech-forward and entrepreneurial ethic to upper-class professionals (Figures 6 and 7).

Interviewees pointed to this breadth of promises, carried through to the 2019 and 2020 elections, as evidence of AAP's consistently inclusive platform. However, it must be noted that the party has been criticized for the under-representation of women and lack of caste diversity in its upper echelons (Rajesh Ramachandran, 2016). Unlike

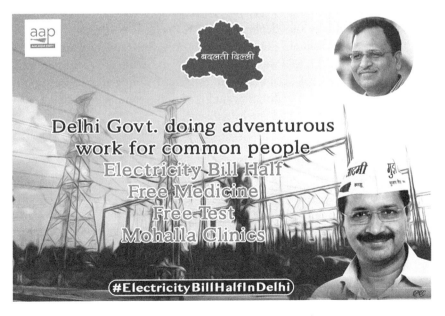

Figure 4. AAP 2015 Facebook post, promises to the common people.

Figure 5. AAP 2015 Facebook post, E-governance.

most other prominent Indian political parties, AAP did not have a Dalit or minority wing until 2018 (NDTV, 2018), and the induction of Dalit leaders Raj Kumar Anand and Surendra Kumar in the run up to the 2019 elections was largely seen as driven by electoral exigency.

Citing these criticisms, some original IAC activists felt that, unlike in a social movement, AAP and its supporters have not retained their ideological core. We spoke to one IAC activist who held this view, and who had never supported the formation of the political party:

> Arvind was successful because he won the first election. Without that, the whole organization would have fallen apart … If you look at his people – they were with Congress and BJP at some point in time. They are there for the winnability. But I don't know what will be the future if [AAP] loses an election … their coalition, all that won't exist then. – A2

This activist is suspicious of the ideological commitment of AAP's cadre and coalition, instead attributing the sweep elections in 2015 to pure strategy and winnability. In this activists' view, the moment AAP loses this winnability quotient, their coalition will crumble. To an extent, this view has been borne out, with AAP failing at coalition building at a national level, where it has suffered significant losses, but retaining votes and party cadres within Delhi, where they have had consistent success.

'Our brand is anti-corruption' (L2)

Despite spending significant time on both personalization and coalition-building, most participants still maintained that AAP's narrative would, or at least should, always be centered around anti-corruption. Multiple interviewees referred to their anti-corruption messaging and promises for clean, honest politics as *'the brand of the party' (L2)* and *'our party's USP (unique selling point)' (C2)*, particularly in their digital outreach. The party's social media head discusses how this manifest.

> [IAC] … and Anna, you could say they were created by the social media. Messaging has to be very, very simple. For us, the USP was, fighting against corruption. Too many messages, that central message is lost, especially on these platforms. – S2

Figure 6. AAP 2015 Facebook posts, degree, income, WiFi.

This campaigner found that clear, simple, familiar messaging was around anti-corruption was most successful online, partially attributing the reduction of the party to this single message to the specific affordances of social media, where more complex, involved messaging does not drive attention and engagement.

Another digital strategist explained how consistent callbacks to AAP's social movement origins, as well as to the story and mythology surrounding AAP's leader, helps establish this brand on social media.

> See – what do people recognize us for? Honesty. Anti-corruption, yes, and the ultimate deliverable is honesty, that's our brand. In 2018 … we still bind to the same thing, with every post … It ties to the same thread of honesty we have been talking to 2011, we tie it to Annaji,

"The question isn't who's going to let me; it's who is going to stop me." – Ayn Rand

AAP will support and empower women entrepreneurs.

Figure 7. AAP 2015 Facebook posts, women entrepreneurs.

> then to Arvind, the way he has lived his life, all that … .Somehow, we try to tie that in every post. – S4

Through the consistency of the messaging around this 'brand' of honesty, this campaigner hopes to create a clear association between this party and the issue of anti-corruption, solidified with every digital post. The emphasis on the timeline, and the continuity shown between the leader of the IAC movement, Anna, and the leader of AAP, Arvind, shows the intensity with which, despite contradictions with increasing personalization, AAP still campaigns on its social movement origins. For seven years, and through five local, state, and national-level campaigns, AAP's social media lead has tried to attach this narrative in some way to every message. Even Kejriwal's own life story is tied to this anti-corruption narrative, intertwining the personalistic and movement nature of the party around a single issue and brand.

An ex-party leader felt so strongly that anti-corruption should be the crux of AAP's messaging that he considered the incorporation of other messages as weakening the party's appeal, citing this as one of the reasons he left the party.

> I think AAP's messaging [since 2015] is quite lost. It is trying to communicate too many things, about education, health, all this … Before there was a clarity in the mind of AAP, we are here to fight corruption, change the system … change politics in India – L2

After winning the 2015 election, AAP has chosen not to base its entire narrative around honesty and anti-corruption. However, this ex-party leader feels that without consistent callbacks to anti-corruption and anti-establishment rhetoric, voters will find that AAP simply does not have enough of an exciting, systemic narrative to offer. This also points to a larger national vs. state communication divide evident in several of the interviews; AAP's policy messaging is successful at the level of Delhi, but, unlike the simplicity and strength of the anti-corruption narrative, may not provide a cohesive enough national message, especially to counter that of the BJP.

Discussion and conclusion

Our case study of AAP shows a divergence across dimensions of institutionalization. On one hand, we find party workers pushed towards personalistic, inconsistent, and often even conflicting messaging. This interferes with institutionalization across measures, impeding internal routinization processes through leadership turnover and centralization, as well as disrupting internal and external reification. Often, these disruptions are exacerbated by the affordances and composition of social media, which can reward contradictory and simplistic messaging, particularly in a party that gained initial prominence through a massively viral social movement. However, we also recognize the overwhelming mandate of AAP in the 2020 Delhi elections, which solidifies its institutionalized position on objective measures of adaptability – as it has weathered significant turnover, centralization, and a rapidly evolving national political environment – as well as on external measures of perceived lasting power, cementing the party as a key player in the state of Delhi. Thus, while these dimensions need not co-occur, and each has value in its own right, the differing outcomes leave open the question of AAP's future as an institutionalized electoral force in India.

There are notable limitations to our study. First, our interviewees were overwhelmingly concentrated in Delhi, and a richer picture of AAP's functioning would have involved more national diversity in data gathering. Second, in focusing on a qualitative and subjective exploration of the AAP's institutionalization through interviews and document analysis, we likely did not capture the full picture of AAP's institutionalization process. Third, AAP is still in its early stages – our analysis would benefit from a re-evaluation and recontextualization after more time has passed.

Despite these limitations, the current analysis serves to paint a fascinating and contradictory picture of AAP's initial institutionalization, rooted in the experiences of those who carried out and constructed it. First, we see that party strategists have heavily pushed personalistic and leader-centric messaging around the current leader, Arvind Kejriwal since 2015, a strategic communications choice that seems to be consistently moving AAP in the direction of personalization. However, at the same time, AAP workers across leadership levels also highlighted the narrative of an ideologically-driven, social movement-based party, whose main goal is and always would be the eradication of corruption in government – often standing in direct conflict with both the personalistic structure of the party, as well as the party's now nearly decade-long presence in Delhi politics.

Building atop this contradiction, a focus (at least from party leaders, if not canvassers) on a creating a diverse, non-traditional, and stable electoral coalition indicates a desire for external institutionalization. However, to be successful, this would require such a base to be stable, reliable, and long-lasting: a complicated proposal, given the range of opposing promises and narratives being constructed. Complicating the reification process, the party has also begun incorporating gentle nods to soft *Hindutva* (Hindu nationalist rhetoric), as recently seen in Kejriwal's nationalistic response to COVID-19 and to recent Chinese military action (Hindustan Times, 2020; Rahul Shrivastava, 2020). Since the 2019 general elections, the word 'secular' has not once appeared on the party's official site – aamaadmiparty.org, likely an attempt to broaden the 'ideal' voter coalition by appealing to BJP voters in Delhi. In fact, when the BJP overturned Article 370 to change the status of Kashmir, AAP supported the move, and when Dalit leaders joined the party prior to the 2019 state elections, the party referred to it as a Gharwapsi, a term specific to a Hindu 'return-to-fold' (AAP, 2019). This further calls into question the ideological core of the party and indicates that the search for a solid party identity, both internally and externally, is ongoing.

Thus, despite objective electoral successes, and a measure of external, institutional perception, internal routinization, as well as both internal and external reification, is not yet complete. Previously, we have often seen that movement parties eventually commit to a reified identity which is internally and externally cohesive, as they institutionalize. A party may become a personalistic vehicle, like Le Pen's Front National (Pappas, 2016), or commit to egalitarian, social movement, anti-establishment rhetoric, like the Communist Party of India (Hicken & Kuhonta, 2015), or be entrenched in the political establishment, creating a stable, fairly centrist voter base, like the Brazilian Worker's Party (Goirand, 2014). However, AAP has not yet settled on such an identity. Without discounting AAP's policies, it is clear that the pervasive presence of digital messaging has contributed to this ability to sustain these often conflicting identities, with a slew of differently targeted content cycling through the party's online presence: a post of Kejriwal's face next to a slogan about tech-forward governance, immediately preceded by an in-depth look at education reform and followed by a rousing call to oust the corrupt industrialists of Delhi. For the time being, this seems to be a winning strategy – at least in Delhi – contributing to objective measures of success. And yet, as in the case of M5S, we have seen the dangers of initial electoral successes belying narrative and organizational contradictions. While AAP has significantly more concrete policy successes than M5S, what remains to be seen is whether this combination of narrative tactics and strategies can work long-term outside of the particularities of an urban capital, or whether AAP will have to take a more traditional approach as it again attempts to expand nationally.

Disclosure statement

One of the authors volunteered with the initial AAP campaigns, and was an advisor to the Delhi Government.

Funding

This work was supported by Microsoft Research.

References

AAP. (2019). *CM Kejriwal welcomes Dalit activist Raj Kumar Anand back into party – Aam Aadmi Party*. https://aamaadmiparty.org/cm-kejriwal-welcomes-dalit-activist-raj-kumar-anand-back-into-party/

Arter, D., & Kestilä-Kekkonen, E. (2014). Measuring the extent of party institutionalisation: The case of a populist entrepreneur party. *West European Politics*, *37*(5), 932–956. https://doi.org/10.1080/01402382.2014.911486

Basedau, M., & Stroh, A. (2008). *Measuring party institutionalization in developing countries: A new research instrument applied to 28 African political parties*.

Bastos, M. T., Mercea, D., & Charpentier, A. (2015). Tents, tweets, and events: The interplay between ongoing protests and social media. *Journal of Communication*, *65*(2), 320–350. https://doi.org/10.1111/jcom.12145

Bennett, W. L. (2012). The personalization of politics: Political identity, social media, and changing patterns of participation. *The ANNALS of the American Academy of Political and Social Science*, *644*(1), 20–39. https://doi.org/10.1177/0002716212451428

Bennett, W. L., & Segerberg, A. (2012). The logic of connective action: Digital media and the personalization of contentious politics. *Information, Communication & Society*, *15*(5), 739–768. https://doi.org/10.1080/1369118X.2012.670661

Bickerton, D. (2018). *Language and species*. University of Chicago Press.

Bornstein, E., & Sharma, A. (2016). The righteous and the rightful: The technomoral politics of NGOs, social movements, and the state in India. *American Ethnologist*, *43*(1), 76–90. https://doi.org/10.1111/amet.12264

Chhibber, P., & Verma, R. (2019). The rise of the second dominant party system in India: BJP's new social coalition in 2019. *Studies in Indian Politics*, *7*(2), 131–148. https://doi.org/10.1177/2321023019874628

Corbetta, P., Colloca, P., Cavazza, N., & Roccato, M. (2018). Lega and five-star movement voters: Exploring the role of cultural, economic and political bewilderment. *Contemporary Italian Politics*, *10*(3), 279–293. https://doi.org/10.1080/23248823.2018.1524678

Coretti, L., & Pica, D. (2015). The rise and fall of collective identity in networked movements: Communication protocols, Facebook, and the anti-Berlusconi protest. *Information, Communication & Society*, *18*(8), 951–967. https://doi.org/10.1080/1369118X.2015.1043317

Deseriis, M. (2019). Digital movement parties: A comparative analysis of the technopolitical cultures and the participation platforms of the Movimento 5 Stelle and the Piratenpartei. *Information, Communication & Society*, *23*(12), 1770–1786. https://doi.org/10.1080/1369118X.2019.1631375

DeSouza, P. R. (2006). *India's political parties*. SAGE Publishing India.

Diwakar, R. (2016). Local contest, national impact: Understanding the success of India's Aam Aadmi Party in 2015 Delhi assembly election. *Representation*, *52*(1), 71–80. https://doi.org/10.1080/00344893.2016.1241296

Eipe, J. J., Varghese, T., & Veranani, S. M. (2012). India against corruption movement: An online version of a non-violent mass movement. *Quarterly Journal of the Gandhi Peace Foundation*, *34*(3), 343–353.

Gianolla, C. (2017). Party-movement's power dynamics in transcultural perspectives: The AAP and the M5S between participation and electoral politics. *Glocalism: Journal of Culture, Politics and Innovation*, *1*, 1–40. https://doi.org/10.12893/gjcpi.2017.1.8

Goirand, C. (2014). The worker's party, from contention to public action: A case of institutionalization. *Journal of Politics in Latin America*, *6*(3), 95–127. https://doi.org/10.1177/1866802X1400600305

Guest, G., MacQueen, K. M., & Namey, E. E. (2012). Introduction to applied thematic analysis. *Applied Thematic Analysis*, *3*, 50–65.

Harmel, R., Svasand, L., & Mjelde, H. (2016). *Party institutionalization and de-institutionalization: Concepts and indicators*. 44th ECPR Joint Sessions of Workshops, Pisa, Italy, April 2016.

Harmel, R., & Svåsand, L. (1993). Party leadership and party institutionalisation: Three phases of development. *West European Politics*, *16*(2), 67–88. https://doi.org/10.1080/01402389308424961

Hicken, A., & Kuhonta, E. M. (2015). *Party system institutionalization in Asia: Democracies, autocracies, and the shadows of the past*. Cambridge University Press.

Hindustan Times. (2020, June 22). 'Fighting 2 wars against China, will win them both': Arvind Kejriwal on Covid-19 fight. *Hindustan Times*. https://www.hindustantimes.com/india-news/our-soldiers-didn-t-back-down-we-too-won-t-retreat-kejriwal-on-covid-19-fight/story-66qqoZqwtUbmDatyCy6TaK.html

Horowitz, J. (2020, January 18). As Five Star Party risks implosion, Italy fears the fallout. *The New York Times*. https://www.nytimes.com/2020/01/18/world/europe/italy-five-star.html

Jaffrelot, C. (2015). The Modi-centric BJP 2014 election campaign: New techniques and old tactics. *Contemporary South Asia*, 23(2), 151–166. https://doi.org/10.1080/09584935.2015.1027662

Janda, K. (1980). *Political parties: A cross-national survey*. Free Press; Collier Macmillan.

Kelly Garrett, R. (2006). Protest in an information society: A review of literature on social movements and new ICTs. *Information, Communication & Society*, 9(02), 202–224. https://doi.org/10.1080/13691180600630773

Kitschelt, H. (2006). Movement parties. *Handbook of Party Politics*, 1, 278–290. https://doi.org/10.4135/9781848608047.n24

Kouki, H., & González, J. F. (2018). Syriza, podemos and mobilizations against austerity: Movements, parties or movement-parties?. In J. Roose, M. Sommer, & F. Scholl (Eds.), *Europas Zivilgesellschaft in der Wirtschafts-und Finanzkrise* (pp. 123–140). Springer.

Kuenzi, M., & Lambright, G. (2001). Party system institutionalization in 30 African countries. *Party Politics*, 7(4), 437–468. https://doi.org/10.1177/1354068801007004003

Kumar, A. (2019). A timeline of the Aam Aadmi Party's years in government. *The Citizen*. Accessed September 28, 2019, from https://www.thecitizen.in/index.php/en/NewsDetail/index/2/16488/A-Timeline-of-the-Aam-Aadmi-Partys-Years-in-Government

Leichty, G. B., D'Silva, M. U., & Johns, M. R. (2016). Twitter and Aam Aadmi Party: Collective representations of a social movement turned political party. *Intercultural Communication Studies*, 25(2).

Levitsky, S. (1998). Institutionalization and Peronism: The concept, the case and the case for unpacking the concept. *Party Politics*, 4(1), 77–92. https://doi.org/10.1177/1354068898004001004

Mainwaring, S., & Scully, T. (1995). *Building democratic institutions: Party systems in Latin America*. Stanford University Press.

Mainwaring, S., & Torcal, M. (2006). Party system institutionalization and party system theory after the third wave of democratization. *Handbook of Party Politics*, 11(6), 204–227. https://doi.org/10.4135/9781848608047.n19

Manucci, L., & Amsler, M. (2018). Where the wind blows: Five Star movement's populism, direct democracy and ideological flexibility. *Italian Political Science Review/Rivista Italiana Di Scienza Politica*, 48(1), 109–132. https://doi.org/10.1017/ipo.2017.23

Mercea, D. (2012). Digital prefigurative participation: The entwinement of online communication and offline participation in protest events. *New Media & Society*, 14(1), 153–169. https://doi.org/10.1177/1461444811429103

Micó, J.-L., & Casero-Ripollés, A. (2014). Political activism online: Organization and media relations in the case of 15M in Spain. *Information, Communication & Society*, 17(7), 858–871. https://doi.org/10.1080/1369118X.2013.830634

Mossige, D. D. (2009). *The personalistic movement-party and the dangers of duality*, 522.

Musella, F. (2015). Personal leaders and party change: Italy in comparative perspective. *Italian Political Science Review/Rivista Italiana Di Scienza Politica*, 45(3), 227–247. https://doi.org/10.1017/ipo.2015.19

NDTV. (2018). Minority, Dalit wings formed in Aam Aadmi Party. *NDTV.Com*. https://www.ndtv.com/delhi-news/delhi-minority-dalit-wings-formed-in-aam-aadmi-party-1936986

Pal, J. (2015). Banalities turned viral: Narendra Modi and the political tweet. *Television & New Media*, 16(4), 378–387. https://doi.org/10.1177/1527476415573956

Panebianco, A. (1988). *Political parties: Organization and power* (Vol. 6). Cambridge University Press.

Pappas, T. S. (2016). Are populist leaders "charismatic"? The evidence from Europe. *Constellations (oxford, England)*, 23(3), 378–390. https://doi.org/10.1111/1467-8675.12233

Pedahzur, A., & Brichta, A. (2002). The institutionalization of extreme right-wing charismatic parties: A paradox? *Party Politics, 8*(1), 31–49. https://doi.org/10.1177/1354068802008001002

Rahul Shrivastava. (2020, February 12). Populism mixed with soft-Hindutva makes Arvind Kejriwal a force to reckon with. *India Today*.

Rajesh Ramachandran. (2016). Why is there no adequate representation by common men & women in the AAP Cabinet in Delhi? *Economic Times*. https://economictimes.indiatimes.com/news/politics-and-nation/why-is-there-no-adequate-representation-by-common-men-women-in-the-aap-cabinet-in-delhi/articleshow/50977916.cms?from=mdr

Randall, V., & Svåsand, L. (2002). Party institutionalization in new democracies. *Party Politics, 8*(1), 5–29. https://doi.org/10.1177/1354068802008001001

Rohlinger, Deana A., & Bunnage, Leslie A. (2015). Connecting people to politics over time? Internet Communication Technology and retention in MoveOn.Org and the Florida Tea Party Movement. *Information, Communication and Society, 18*(5), 539–552.

Rose, R., & Mackie, T. T. (1988). Do parties persist or fail? The big trade-off facing organizations. *When Parties Fail: Emerging Alternative Organizations*, 533–558. https://doi.org/10.1515/9781400859498.533

Sengupta, M. (2012). Anna Hazare and the idea of Gandhi. *The Journal of Asian Studies, 71*(3), 593–601. https://doi.org/10.1017/S0021911812000617

Silverman, D. (2005). *Doing qualitative research: A practical*.

Sitapati, V. (2011). *What Anna Hazare's Movement and India's new middle classes say about each other. 30*, 6.

Sriram, J. (2015, April 21). AAP expels Yogendra Yadav, Prashant Bhushan. *The Hindu*. https://www.thehindu.com/news/cities/Delhi/aap-expels-four-rebel-leaders/article7123615.ece

Subrahmaniam, F. V. (2015). Reaching for the stars: The incredible rise of Arvind Kejriwal. *The Hindu Centre for Politics and Public Policy, 25*.

Tripathy, J. (2017). The broom, the muffler and the Wagon R: Aam Aadmi party and the politics of de-elitisation. *International Quarterly for Asian Studies, 48*(1–2), 77–95. https://doi.org/10.11588/iqas.2017.1-2.4074

Turner, E. (2013). The 5 Star movement and its discontents: A tale of blogging, comedy, electoral success and tensions. *Interface: A Journal for and About Social Movements, 5*(2), 178–212.

Udupa, S. (2014). Aam Aadmi: Decoding the media logics. 7, 3.

Vignati, R. (2015). The organization of the Movimento 5 Stelle: A contradictory party model. *Beppe Grillo's Five Star Movement: Organisation, Communication and Ideology*, 29–52.

Weissenbach, K., & Bukow, S. U. (2019). Travelling concepts of party institutionalization? A comparative perspective. *Zeitschrift Für Vergleichende Politikwissenschaft, 13*(2), 157–174. https://doi.org/10.1007/s12286-019-00426-4

Ziegfeld, A. (2012). Coalition government and party system change: Explaining the rise of regional political parties in India. *Comparative Politics, 45*(1), 69–87. https://doi.org/10.5129/001041512802822905

Reverting trajectories? UKIP's organisational and discursive change after the Brexit referendum

Ofra Klein [ID] and Andrea L. P. Pirro [ID]

ABSTRACT
The article focuses on the transformation of the UK Independence Party (UKIP) after the 2016 Brexit referendum. It describes how, after securing its chief political demand, UKIP opened up to grassroots far-right politics and assesses whether this strategy involved a concomitant shift towards a more radical discourse. Against a backdrop of organisational change, the findings refine the notion that a far-right turn within its ranks led to a significant shift in the (online) communication of the party towards issues like immigration, Islam, and gender. Indeed, these issues were mostly 'outsourced' to the cultural wing of the party, War Plan Purple. The article therefore critically links changes in UKIP's organisation with shifts in online communication, adding new insights into the unorthodox politics and forms of mobilisation of the far right.

Introduction

The 2016 British referendum on European Union (EU) membership clearly bore momentous consequences. It monopolised the political agenda thereafter, tipping the balance of contention in Brexiteers' favour; and ultimately brought about changes at different institutional levels (Pirro & Taggart, 2018). After Cameron's resignation as Prime Minister and Leader of the Conservatives (July 2016), it took the United Kingdom (UK) two snap elections and four governments to formally leave the EU in January 2020. The inability of Westminster to deliver Brexit after triggering Article 50 of the EU Treaty testified to a power reconfiguration across British politics, as well as within individual parties. This article specifically focuses on the organisational and discursive changes occurred within the UK Independence Party (UKIP), the main instigator of the Brexit referendum and driving force behind the 'Leave' camp.

UKIP took its first political steps as a cross-party pressure group named Anti-Federalist League and was eventually established as a party in 1993. It gradually evolved from a single-issue hard-Eurosceptic party to a populist radical right party under the leadership of Nigel Farage (e.g., Ford & Goodwin, 2014; Taggart, 1998; Usherwood, 2019). After securing its chief political demand, UKIP underwent significant organisational transformation. UKIP leader and Brexit kingmaker Farage initially announced his resignation from office in July 2016. He then quit the party altogether in December 2018, reportedly amid concerns over the new leadership's obsession with English Defence League (EDL) co-founder Tommy Robinson and fixation with the issue of Islam (Dallison, 2018; Davidson & Berezin, 2018, p. 486). Taking these considerations at face value, the trajectory undertaken by UKIP begs two interrelated questions: *How did UKIP turn to the far-right grassroots sector? Did the party shift its discourse in concomitance with these organisational changes?* Both organisationally and discursively, it is possible to reconcile UKIP's opening up to far-right movements and activists to the burgeoning literature on 'movement parties' (Kitschelt, 2006) and its discursive shifts to the notion of 'hybridisation' (Chadwick, 2007).

Movement parties are a relatively new species of political party addressing concerns such as the environment and immigration (Gunther & Diamond, 2003). Most recent examples of movement parties include the far-right Movement for a Better Hungary, the ideologically ambiguous 5 Star Movement in Italy, and the far-left *Podemos* in Spain (della Porta et al., 2017; Pirro, 2019). These collective actors are essentially 'coalitions of political activists who emanate from social movements and try to apply the organizational and strategic practices of social movements in the arena of party competition' (Kitschelt, 2006, p. 280). It is vital for them to pursue political goals 'outside or against the institutionalised channels of political communication and politicians inserted in them' (Kitschelt, 2006, p. 279). While UKIP has invested in the electoral and institutional arenas throughout its political lifecycle, notable changes took place after the Brexit referendum. Unlike other contributions that focused on UKIP's interaction with movements like Britain First (Davidson & Berezin, 2018), this article examines how *the party itself* has transformed since 2016. With its recent organisational shift towards the far-right grassroots sector, UKIP seemingly attempted a transition towards the movement-party form.

Organisational and discursive changes may be also driven by a process of hybridisation, according to which established parties would adapt to the digital repertoires of (far-right) movements. Social media are particularly suitable for hybridisation, as new technologies allow for fast 'repertoire switching' between protest and electoral politics (Chadwick, 2007, p. 284). Research on the communication and use of social media by far-right organisations is on the rise (Berntzen, 2020; Froio & Ganesh, 2019; Klein & Muis, 2019), although very few of these studies addressed how social media link with hybrid strategies (Davidson & Berezin, 2018). The study of party change may thus benefit from taking political communication into account: understanding how the far right uses social media adds new insights into its unorthodox politics and forms of mobilisation. With regard to the British case, if the outcome of the Brexit referendum accelerated a process of internal change within UKIP, any shift at the organisational level should in principle reveal change at the discursive level (e.g., Albertazzi et al., 2018; Stockemer & Barisione, 2017).

This article focuses on UKIP's transformation after Brexit and unpacks party strategy as a bundle made of, among other things, organisational and discursive choices. As a first attempt in this direction, the study accounts for developments that have taken place online and offline. Whereas the organisational changes occurring after the Brexit referendum – and especially under the leadership of Gerard Batten (2018–2019) – have perceptibly steered UKIP further towards the right, a concomitant emphasis on 'cultural issues' (i.e., immigration, Islam, and gender) can only be ascertained empirically. Hence, the aim of this article is to describe the reconfiguration of UKIP at the meso level, and analyse changes that occurred in its online political communication. While showing UKIP's projection into a new phase of its political lifecycle, the findings qualify the notion that the party has radicalised its (online) discourse as a result of (offline) organisational changes.

Unpacking UKIP's strategy after the Brexit referendum

Brexit directly affected the strategy of UKIP, robbing its main and most vocal advocate 'of its central policy issue and of its leader' (Usherwood, 2019, p. 1224). Since 2016, the party has been in constant search for a new identity and new leaders. This highlights the value of focusing on crises as exogenous shocks unfolding at the meso level and understand how they might affect individual organisations (e.g., Harmel & Janda, 1994; Panebianco, 1988). The article therefore focuses on the transformation of UKIP under subsequent post-Brexit party leaderships and addresses how the party has turned to the far-right grassroots sector and adapted its discourse in response to this shift.

The trajectory taken by UKIP after the Brexit referendum resonates in good part with the literature on movement parties, though in ways that have not been properly theorised and investigated. As the concept suggests, movement parties are hybrid collective actors whose status is inherently transitional (Kitschelt, 2006; Pirro & Castelli Gattinara, 2018). Yet, movement parties generally conform to a pattern of movement institutionalisation. Simply stated, movements may decide to take the electoral option while preserving their commitment to street politics. Power and electoral dilemmas would however confront the movement party with questions of survival, ultimately forcing it to opt for institutionalised forms of political action (Panebianco, 1988). Instances of far-right mobilisation across the protest and electoral arenas are not necessarily at odds with each other (Castelli Gattinara & Pirro, 2019; Pirro, 2019; Pirro & Castelli Gattinara, 2018), but are unlikely to be evenly sustained over time (Pirro et al., 2019).

The case of UKIP is noteworthy. UKIP stems from the Anti-Federalist League, a cross-party pressure group established in 1991 by British academic Alan Sked, which subsequently evolved into a self-standing political party in 1993. The party lingered at the margins of the British electoral arena until the 2000s, scoring a series of unimpressive results until the accomplishments in the European Parliament (EP) elections of 2004 and 2009 (Ford & Goodwin, 2014). UKIP's performance reached its peak under the leadership of Farage, gaining over 4.3 million votes (27.5% and 24 seats) in the 2014 EP elections and almost 3.9 million votes (12.6% and one seat) in the 2015 general elections. Its demise after the Brexit referendum has been, on the other hand, quite rapid: UKIP returned an overall 1.8% in the 2017 general elections and an all-time low 0.1% in the 2019 general elections.

After the Brexit referendum, and the departure of its leader Nigel Farage, the party joined the ranks of other 'weakly organised, poorly led, and divided' British far-right parties (Carter, 2005). Amid internal organisational struggles, and especially under the leadership of Batten (2018–2019), UKIP started flirting with the far-right subculture and opened up to the movement sector. Among other things, Batten's injection of far-right activists into the party was instrumental in establishing War Plan Purple (WPP) as the culturalist branch of UKIP in July 2018. Ultimately, UKIP's drift towards far-right territories prompted former leader Farage to leave the party in late 2018 and form the Brexit Party in early 2019. With the stated objective of delivering UK withdrawal from the EU, the Brexit Party gained the largest share of votes in the 2019 EP election (30.5%). UKIP gained only 3.2%.

UKIP's strategy to enlist far-right activists within its ranks and invest in parallel grassroots organisations is theoretically coherent with a shift towards the movement-party form and practically compatible with the rise of a more radical faction within the party. UKIP has a long-standing story of internal factionalism. Already by the late 2000s, when UKIP broadened its policies to immigration and multiculturalism, the party leadership faced the internal resistance of members solely concerned with UK withdrawal from the EU (Ford & Goodwin, 2014; Hanna & Busher, 2019; Usherwood, 2016).

UKIP's opening up to street politics and grassroots movement actors is however unprecedented, and its occurrence at such a late stage in its political lifecycle is fairly unique. Furthermore, reversing movement-party trajectories has not been covered by theories of movement-electoral interactions (McAdam & Tarrow, 2010; Pirro, 2019). To be sure, the far right might take movement-party features without necessarily stemming from the movement sector (Kitschelt, 2006). But if it moves along the movement-party continuum are to be interpreted as a one-way progression leading to transformation into political party, UKIP made investments to revert this monodirectional course. This primarily materialised through *organisational change*.

The contemporary far right has demonstrated high margins of adaptability. For each strategic turn involving organisational or leadership change, a shift in discourse has almost invariably followed. This applies indistinctly to movement parties and fully institutionalised parties (Albertazzi et al., 2018; Pirro, 2019; Stockemer & Barisione, 2017; Widfeldt, 2008). The analytical portion of this article is therefore concerned with *discursive change* and asks whether UKIP's discourse adapted to its organisational shift further to the right. It is worth noting that Farage left UKIP in 2018 claiming that its new leader, Gerard Batten, was increasingly obsessed with Islam and anti-Muslim policies (Walker, 2018a). The expectation would therefore be that UKIP under Batten has adjusted its discourse and started giving more prominence to far-right 'cultural issues' such as immigration, Islam, and gender over topics such as the EU and Brexit.

H1: Under Batten's leadership, UKIP's discourse emphasised cultural issues over 'Europe'.

UKIP under Batten seemed fascinated with Gramsci's notion of 'cultural hegemony', to be interpreted here as a means to challenge the intellectual and cultural dominance of the left and the liberal-democratic status quo (e.g., Griffin, 2000). In the online sphere, the establishment of WPP seemed to respond to similar purposes: between 2018 and 2019, WPP presented itself as a direct emanation of UKIP 'on the front lines of the culture war'.[1] While ascertaining organisational continuity between UKIP and WPP, it may as well be that, under the mounting pressure of internal factionalism, Batten tried to diversify UKIP's communication strategy to appease the more liberal faction of the party, or simply address different audiences: a mainstream audience made of traditional UKIP voters and a subcultural radical audience endorsing cultural issues. Hence, one could expect that, during Batten's leadership, cultural issues were primarily voiced by WPP, instead of UKIP.

H2: During Batten's leadership, WPP placed more emphasis on cultural issues than UKIP.

The organisational and discursive changes outlined so far can be reconciled with the hybridisation encouraged by the internet. On social media, actors can swiftly adapt forms, change identities, and switch action repertoires. These opportunities effectively propelled new, hybrid, forms of activism (Chadwick, 2007). The creation of a new 'wing' of UKIP under Batten, specifically organised by, and tailored for, tech-savvy alt-right and online activists, fits this idea and is consistent with UKIP's attempt to rebrand itself. This study tests these hypotheses through UKIP's and WPP's communication on Twitter.

Through social media platforms, far-right actors can spread their views without the filter of the traditional media. Social media platforms helped far-right movements like the EDL and PEGIDA gain support and organise rallies (Berntzen & Weisskircher, 2016). Social media are considered a successful tool for far-right parties in particular, as these platforms favour highly emotional, simplified, and dramatised content (Engesser et al., 2017, p. 1313). Their non-hierarchical nature and the opportunity to speak directly to the people without a media filter fit well the populist ideals of these actors (Bartlett, 2014, p. 106; Engesser et al., 2017, p. 1286).

Twitter represents a vehicle for unmediated communication and one of the most important political outreach tools for far-right parties and leaders (Jacobs & Spierings, 2016; Larsson & Moe, 2012; Van Kessel & Castelein, 2016). Research on online communication has often focused on Twitter, a platform that offers relatively easy access to scholars, but with a much smaller and more specific demographic than other social media platforms (Cihon & Yasseri, 2016). Twitter reaches, however, a broader audience than traditional media as the platform is an important source for journalists (Engesser et al., 2017; Stier et al., 2018). The platform has several features that make it suitable for political communication. The opportunity to search for keywords and hashtags as well as the availability of retweet buttons easily allows one to spread content across the network (Halupka, 2014, p. 162; Bossetta, 2018, p. 476). The option to share links underlines that Twitter is a suitable medium for communicating information to followers (Bossetta, 2018). It has thus been described as a platform primarily used for information consumption and distribution (Hermida, 2010). Social media, and Twitter in particular, offer an additional advantage: unlike political manifestos, which are issued in concomitance with elections (Budge et al., 1987), they deliver a regular stream of political views on multiple subjects and represent effective tools for self-promotion (Golbeck et al., 2010). As the timeframe of analysis rests on leadership changes, rather than elections, Twitter provides a very sensitive platform for studying the effects of these changes.

Research design, data, and methods

The article is concerned with UKIP's transformation after Brexit. It thus examines the changes that occurred in the organisation and online discursive practices across leadership periods. Tackling organisational change responds to a descriptive objective and is assessed qualitatively by reconstructing UKIP's network composition after Brexit. To analyse how organisational change influenced shifts in discourse, tweets were collected from the accounts of UKIP and War Plan Purple, covering the period between January 2015 and May 2019. Data were gathered through the Twitter API using the Python libraries Tweepy and Selenium (Roesslein, 2017). Besides the content of the tweet, the data reported the time-date stamp of the post, the number of likes, replies, and retweets that each tweet received. A total of 12,368 tweets were posted on the page of UKIP between January 2015 and May 2019. From its establishment in July 2018 until May 2019, 3,731 tweets were extracted from the page of WPP.

For the purpose of this study, retweets and replies were filtered out of the data. This proved necessary as the number of replies was especially high for WPP. More than 50% of the tweets collected from this page were retweets. Most of these replies seemed to reflect a trolling culture aimed at bashing users. Tweets solely consisting of a link and/or emoji were also filtered out as these could not be analysed automatically. The analysis therefore reflects only the textual content posted on the Twitter accounts of UKIP and WPP, namely a selection of 10,816 tweets for UKIP and 914 tweets for WPP (Table 1).

Table 1 provides an overview of UKIP and WPP pages, and the interaction of users on them. WPP interacted much more with their followers, as most of the tweets consisted of replies to other users. Conversely, UKIP was geared towards delivering information, as less than 2% of its tweets consisted of replies. UKIP on average enjoyed more interactions in terms of likes, replies, and retweets by users. However, looking at the higher number of UKIP followers, it is possible to conclude that WPP had a comparatively higher engagement. Interesting differences emerge comparing the tweets and engagement of users on the page of UKIP over the different leadership periods. Under Steve Crowther and Gerard Batten, UKIP interacted more with users than under other leaders: replies during these periods amount to about 7.5% and about 9% of tweets, respectively. UKIP under Nigel Farage, Diane James, and Paul Nuttal had very few replies (less than 1% of all tweets); even under Henry Bolton, this figure was less than 3%. The number of engagements that UKIP received under Batten is remarkable: likes, replies, and shares experienced a threefold increase compared to the previous leadership period. While more interactions could be due to the growing number of followers, they may also testify UKIP's greater investments in the online sphere during Batten's leadership.

Discursive change is assessed in terms of shifts in issue salience. To illustrate the results, the study reports quotes based on a qualitative reading of all tweets for any given topic. The topics included relate to European issues and cultural issues, i.e., immigration, Islam, and gender. This research strategy notably expands on previous studies that focused on the salience of the EU and immigration in UKIP's press releases and media coverage (Usherwood, 2019). Due to the brevity of many tweets, the quantitative analysis relied on a dictionary approach instead of a topic modelling approach (cf. Puschmann & Scheffler, 2016). Dictionaries were created ad hoc, based on the reading of UKIP electoral manifestos between 2009 and 2018, as well as tweets from UKIP and WPP pages (Table 2). These dictionaries were refined by comparing the outcomes of the dictionary classification with those by a human coder. Keywords were added to or removed from the dictionaries on the basis of potential inconsistencies. This process was repeated several times to improve the precision (i.e., how often a tweet that is identified by the dictionary is also about the topic of the dictionary) and recall (i.e., how often the dictionary fails to detect relevant tweets) of the dictionaries. Table 3 outlines the precision, recall, and F1 measures for the dictionaries used in this study. These measures are based on a manual coding of 300 randomly selected tweets (see also Sheafer et al., 2014).

Data were pre-processed using the Quanteda package in R to remove numbers, punctuation, links, stopwords, and set the characters to lower cases (Benoit et al., 2018). The

Table 1. Descriptive statistics of the Twitter pages of UKIP and WPP, per leader and total.

	UKIP Farage	UKIP James	UKIP Nuttal	UKIP Crowther	UKIP Bolton	UKIP Batten	UKIP total	WPP total
Followers (by end of leadership)	139,168	140,833	165,408	173,123	179,963	212,488	212,000	6,152
Data timeline	01/01/2015 to 16/09/2016 05/10/2016 to 28/11/2016	16/09/2016 to 04/10/2016	28/11/2016 to 09/06/2017	09/06/2017 to 28/09/2017	29/09/2017 to 17/02/2018	17/02/2018 to 02/06/2019	01/01/2015 to 10/05/2019	03/07/2018 to 10/05/2019
Tweets (incl. replies)	8332	222	1315	188	620	1691	12,368	3731
Tweets (excl. replies)	8315	222	1309	174	603	1537	12,160	1665
Percentage tweets (excl. replies)	99.80	100	99.54	92.55	97.26	90.89	98.33	44.63
Tweets (excl. URLs)	7525	188	1128	124	507	1344	10,816	914
Mean likes per tweet excl. replies (SD)	39.07 (49.04)	36.05 (44.70)	67.06 (87.21)	87.40 (119.76)	112.55 (132.41)	382.15 (562.16)	89.73 (237.05)	59.44 (165.46)
Mean replies per tweet (SD)	5.90 (8.33)	3.18 (5.11)	12.00 (25.10)	14.43 (16.29)	19.45 (40.60)	41.84 (81.24)	11.84 (34.31)	5.84 (14.87)
Mean retweets per tweet excl. replies (SD)	45.05 (61.46)	23.33 (32.47)	41.29 (54.98)	46.42 (55.93)	56.04 (64.55)	175.76 (262.42)	61.34 (117.42)	18.67 (62.86)

Table 2. Dictionaries.

Topic	Words
Europe	('eu*', 'brussel*', 'lisbon treaty', 'superstate', 'autocratic', 'bureaucrats', 'withdraw*', 'membership', 'sovereign*', 'brexit', 'negotiation*', 'european integration*', 'ecb', 'anti-eu', 'no2eu', 'greece', 'turkey')
Immigration	('immigra*', 'migra*', 'foreigner*', 'border', 'asylum', 'refugee*', 'illegal*', 'racist', 'diversity', 'multicultural*')
Islam	('islam*','burqa', 'niqab', 'mosque*', 'sharia', 'muslim*', 'imam*', 'preacher*', 'terror*', 'extrem*')
Gender	('women', 'emancipation', 'gay', 'lesbian', 'bisexual', 'transgender*', 'lgbt', 'transsexual*')

Table 3. Recall, precision, and F1 measures for the dictionaries.

	Recall	Precision	F1
Europe	0.85	0.85	0.85
Immigration	1.00	0.95	0.97
Islam	0.80	0.88	0.84
Gender	0.92	0.92	0.92
Total	0.88	0.88	0.88

package was used to count how often each dictionary occurred in the tweets, indicating whether at least one word in the dictionary was present in the tweet (1) or not (0). Independent *t*-tests with Bonferroni corrections were carried out to see whether the mean number of tweets discussing the different topics significantly changed on the page of UKIP before and during Batten's leadership (H1). Finally, *t*-tests were conducted to ascertain differences in issue salience between the Twitter pages of UKIP and WPP during Batten's leadership period (H2).

Organisational change

UKIP's electoral growth under the leadership of Farage largely put internal dissent to rest. His demise after the Brexit referendum, however, projected the party into a soul search punctuated by several personnel changes and defections. Diane James was UKIP's leader-elect between September and October 2016 but resigned before taking office. Farage continued serving as acting leader until the 2016 leadership election. Paul Nuttall was elected as new leader in November 2016 but resigned in June 2017 after failing to win a seat in the general elections. Henry Bolton was chosen over Anne Marie Waters in the 2017 leadership election. Waters is the founder and director of Sharia Watch UK; in 2016, she launched PEGIDA UK with Tommy Robinson and former UKIP candidate Paul Weston. She left UKIP after the leadership election and went on to form and lead the far-right party For Britain. Bolton held office until February 2018, when he was ousted following a controversy over racist comments. Gerard Batten was elected in April 2018 and remained in office until UKIP's disappointing performance at the 2019 EP election.

Across these leadership changes, UKIP also experienced a drain of members. From the 34,000 members reported by the Electoral Commission in December 2016, the party went down to 18,000 by February 2018. This trend was reverted upon Batten's election to chairman, when UKIP allegedly bounced back to about 30,000 members.[2] Such an increase is associated to Batten's investments to attract far-right activists within party ranks (Walker, 2018b; Walker & Halliday, 2019). In this regard, a notable development was Tommy Robinson's appointment to Batten's personal advisor in November 2018. A former British

National Party (BNP) member, Robinson (born Stephen Yaxley) is the founder and former leader of EDL – a far-right movement that gained significant exposure and following in the early 2010s for its vocal opposition to Islam (Busher, 2015). Robinson left EDL in 2013 but later set up the British chapter of PEGIDA. While not a formal member of UKIP, he stood as independent candidate at the 2019 EP elections, also earning the support of Anne Marie Waters (Halliday, 2019). Robinson's nomination took place in open defiance of UKIP's rulebook, which prevents members of far-right organisations like EDL to join the party (UKIP, 2018). Such a move seemed to testify a radicalisation of the party, anticipating the prominence of anti-Muslim discourses in UKIP's campaigning (Payne, 2018).

Another move substantiating UKIP's organisational change included allowing social media activists Paul Joseph Watson, Mark Meechan, Carl Benjamin, and Milo Yiannopoulos into the party in the summer of 2018 (Spence & Di Stefano, 2019; Walker, 2018c). The four far-right activists have large online followings and have expressed controversial views. Watson's YouTube channel, PrisonPlanetLive had 1.6 million subscribers as of June 2019. He uttered anti-Muslim and anti-immigrant opinions and is also senior editor at InfoWars, a US-based website that deals in conspiracy theories and promotes fake news. The website, founded by Alexander Jones, was launched in 1999 and has a monthly reach of 10 million visits. Meechan, also known as Count Dankula, is a Scottish YouTuber with over half a million subscribers. He was fined £800 in early 2018 for posting a video of a pug dog giving Nazi salutes. Meechan ran as candidate on the UKIP list in Scotland for the 2019 EP election. Benjamin is a conspiracy theorist and anti-feminist, who expressed views against Islam and political correctness. He is best known online as Sargon of Akkad. His YouTube channel lists almost one million subscribers at the time of writing. Benjamin also ran as UKIP candidate at the 2019 EP election. Finally, Yiannopoulos was the technology editor of the far-right Breitbart News Network and gained fame after he was suspended from Twitter over the abuse of actress Leslie Jones. Yiannopoulos was one of the key figures of the American alt-right and played a big role in the misogynist Gamergate movement online. He reportedly joined Benjamin on his campaign trail for the 2019 EP elections (Spence & Di Stefano, 2019).

The enrolment of these (online) activists is directly connected to the establishment of War Plan Purple as the cultural wing of UKIP in July 2018. WPP represented 'UKIP's new social media-savvy demographic of the nation' (Kipper Central, 2018), organising protests and speaking at rallies. WPP has both a Twitter and Facebook page[3], as well as a closed Facebook group.[4] The group first affiliated with the party by showing 'UKIP' in its logo. After Batten's tenure, however, WPP is no longer affiliated to the party and renamed itself from 'UKIP Liberalists' into 'UK Liberalists'.

Throughout this period, UKIP's Facebook and Twitter pages both followed and liked WPP on social media, and UKIP mentioned WPP in several of its tweets. WPP is linked to The Liberalists (or The Liberalist Society), a movement focused on activism – mostly in the form of events, protests, activities, and international campaigns – whose main goal is to 'uphold, promote, and spread classical Liberalism'.[5] In their own understanding, 'the term is a declaration of opposition to collectivist ideologies such as socialism, communism, feminism, Islamism and fascism'.[6] The Liberalists draw inspiration from Carl Benjamin's own articulation of the seven 'Liberalist Principles', i.e., individual rights, democracy, economic freedom, freedom of speech, self-reliance, blind justice, and secularism.[7] Therefore, between 2018 and 2019, there has been organisational continuity between The Liberalists,

Discursive change

How did UKIP's issue focus change over time? How did the Brexit referendum and subsequent leadership changes affect the discourse of the party? Figure 1 shows UKIP's issue focus on Twitter, over time. Figure 2 illustrates how issue salience was distributed on the page of UKIP and the affiliated War Plan Purple during Batten's leadership. The figures were generated with the R package Ggplot2 (Wickham, 2016).

Out of all changes ensuing after the Brexit referendum, the article hypothesised a shift in issue salience under Batten's leadership. In light of the recruitment of far-right activists within UKIP ranks, the first hypothesis anticipated cultural issues to override concerns over 'Europe' and Brexit. To test whether such changes took place under Batten, a t-test with Bonferroni corrections was carried out to compare the discourse of UKIP before Batten became leader (Table 4). Only the leaders after Farage were included in the analysis.

Compared to previous leadership periods, UKIP under Batten did not significantly differ in the salience of immigration, Islam, and gender (Table 4). During the leadership of Nuttal, for example, UKIP denied allegations of racism, but also denounced excessive political correctness, arguing that the party supporters shall 'stop being scared of being called names'.[8] Under Bolton, transgender people turned into a political target and gender

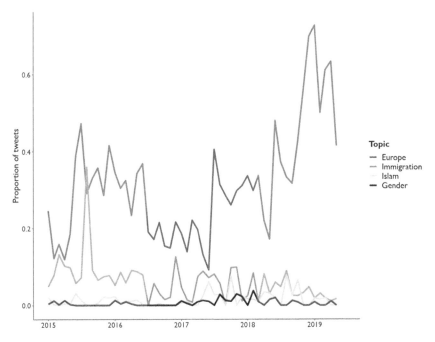

Figure 1. Proportion of tweets on Europe, immigration, Islam, and gender on the page of UKIP. Note: The figure distinguishes between three periods. The first period refers to the phase preceding the Brexit referendum (Farage leadership), the second period to the post-referendum leadership periods (except Batten), and the third period to Batten's leadership.

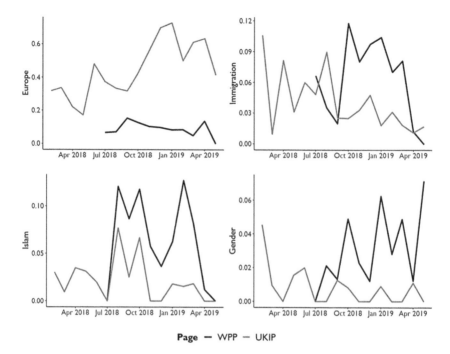

Figure 2. Proportion of tweets on Europe, immigration, Islam, and gender on the Twitter pages of UKIP and WPP during Batten's leadership.

was used to attack political elites. Politicians were blamed for 'transgenderism'[9], and the government was seen to 'push transgender books on primary schools'.[10] Debates on gender change were heated, as in a post arguing that 'declaring your sex as optional' was 'madness'.[11] A similar discourse on transgender issues continued under Batten. One tweet described gender-affirmation treatment of young children as 'child abuse of the highest order'.[12] The discourse even went as far as describing transgender people as a threat. This was the case for a news item about a woman sexually abused by a transgender inmate in an all-female prison. The tweet stated that UKIP has 'warned countless times' for the danger of such 'obsessive virtue signalling'.[13]

There was no statistically significant difference in the frequency with which Islam was discussed before and during Batten's mandate as a UKIP leader. The issue was already addressed on Twitter before his leadership. During Nuttal's tenure, for example, Sharia courts were a point of discussion, as was Islamic fundamentalism, which was described as a 'dangerous cancer in our society'.[14] Under the leadership of Bolton, then, the issue

Table 4. Percentage of tweets on Europe, immigration, Islam, and gender before and during Batten on the page of UKIP (only leaders after Farage included) (*$p < 0.017$, **$p < 0.003$, ***$p < 0.0003$).

	Before Batten		Batten		T (df = 3289)
	Mean	SD	Mean	SD	
Europe	0.209	(0.406)	0.457	(0.498)	−15.69***
Immigration	0.0539	(0.226)	0.0379	(0.191)	2.12
Islam	0.0149	(0.121)	0.0223	(0.148)	−1.58
Gender	0.00924	(0.0957)	0.00744	(0.0860)	0.55

Table 5. Percentage of tweets on Europe, immigration, Islam, and gender before and after the Brexit referendum (*$p < 0.017$, **$p < 0.003$, ***$p < 0.0003$).

	Before referendum		After referendum		T (df = 10814)
	Mean	SD	Mean	SD	
Europe	0.271	(0.444)	0.305	(0.460)	−3.74***
Immigration	0.0862	(0.281)	0.045	(0.208)	7.74***
Islam	0.00912	(0.095)	0.0165	(0.127)	−3.38**
Gender	0.00470	(0.0684)	0.008	(0.088)	−2.03

of Islam was framed as a cultural threat, stating how the "appeasement of Islam' threatens Christianity'.[15] These pleas reflected quite clearly in other tweets, whereby 'people are concerned about rising tide of Islam in communities'.[16] The discourse did not change substantively under Batten, as UKIP reiterated the fear of an Islamic takeover. Several tweets mentioned that 'Britons are being converted to literalist Islam – this is a major threat to our country. We cannot be silent any longer'.[17] Another post argued that veils were 'weaponised by Islamists' so as to 'impose [an] Islamic character on communities'.[18] In a more 'liberal' spell (see Berntzen, 2020), tweets voiced the danger that Islam posed to Western society, specifically to homosexuals and Jews.

The findings overall show a clear and significant increase in salience of European issues and Brexit under Batten ($t = -15.69$***). This evidence goes against the expectations formulated in H1, and against the notion that UKIP transformed into a far-right organisation 'fixated with Islam' under Batten's leadership. While proving that the delivery of Brexit remained a prime concern for UKIP, the analysis also corroborates that UKIP had emphasised anti-immigration stances long before Batten's tenure (e.g., Ford & Goodwin, 2014).

Delving deeper into these aspects, it is worth asking: How does this trend compare to the pre-referendum period? Was UKIP's communication under Farage, and before the Brexit referendum, substantively different? The *t*-test, evaluating the issue salience before and after the referendum, seems to reflect a similar focus on Europe (Table 5). Findings indicate that the issue of Islam became more common in tweets after the referendum ($t = -3.38$**). Yet, the mean number of tweets focusing on this issue is still very low, and much lower than the issues of immigration and Europe. Reference to European issues also strongly increased after the referendum ($t = -3.74$***). Against this backdrop, immigration was discussed more often before the referendum took place ($t = 7.74$***).

Despite the attention devoted to immigration before the Brexit referendum, UKIP's account referred to the 'non-racist & non-sectarian' nature of the party[19], stating that extremist comments on Islam – or any other religion – were 'totally unacceptable'.[20] This notwithstanding, UKIP under Farage argued that 'In almost every area, net migration, overall UK immigration, EU immigration, non-EU immigration, the government has failed catastrophically'.[21] This paired with concerns such as: 'Rapid implementation of common EU migration and asylum policy could lead to Islamic extremists coming to the UK'.[22]

There was no statistically significant difference in the frequency with which gender was discussed before and after the referendum. However, there seems to be a qualitative shift in the discussion on gender. Gender primarily referred to issues of gay and women's rights under Farage's leadership. UKIP once had its own LGBT section, and the discourse on homosexuality and women was neutral if not outright positive. The page included posts such as 'UKIP and homosexuality: a gay member's view' or stated that UKIP was not against gay adoption.[23] On the issue of women's right, UKIP engaged in posts such as 'we think women are smart enough to get by on merit. They do in UKIP' or 'A female UKIP Councillor makes the case for why the party isn't an old boys' club'.[24] These are notable qualitative differences between successive leaderships.

Since discursive change on cultural issues is not clearly discernible after the Brexit referendum, it is interesting to evaluate whether immigration, Islam, or gender were 'outsourced' to WPP, UKIP's cultural wing under Batten (H2). To test this second hypothesis, the analysis compared the tweets of UKIP and WPP exclusively under Batten's leadership period (2018–2019). Table 6 confirms that the pages overall focused on different issues. European issues are discussed much more often by UKIP ($t = 19.42^{***}$), while cultural issues are consistently discussed more often by WPP. This is the case for immigration ($t = -2.67^*$), Islam ($t = -6.49^{***}$), and gender ($t = -3.92^{***}$). Generally speaking, the idea of discursive diversification across multiple platforms is consistent with the findings: WPP's page discussed all cultural issues more often than UKIP (H2), which in turn placed significantly more emphasis on European issues. Even under Batten, UKIP seemed then concerned with discursive continuity, possibly not to estrange its traditional voter base or appease the more liberal faction of the party.

For example, WPP delivered a harsher stance on gender compared to UKIP. The page asked 'whether it is acceptable to encourage children to be gay'[25], and stating that 'most women are not retarded'[26] and that 'half of misogynistic tweets [are] sent by women'.[27] At times, the discourse took a conspiracist flair, with posts such as 'kids as young as three are being sent to an NHS transgender clinic accused of 'live experimenting' on them'.[28] At the same time, WPP used a protective frame towards women, stating that migrants had to be stopped otherwise they would rape women. Similarly, a tweet appeared on the WPP page about homosexuals being 'badly beaten in Paris by refugees for the crime of being gay'.[29] The link between paedophilia and Islam returns quite often, using terms such as 'Islamic grooming gangs' to describe how 'Pakistani Muslim rape gangs' targeted 'non-Muslim girls as young as 11 for sexual abuse'.[30] In addition to these issues, WPP adopted a 'political correctness' frame, blaming the elites for looking away and flinching from speaking up about the problematic aspects of Islam.

The evidence presented therefore corroborates that, even before Batten's rise to chairman, UKIP had done little to disprove allegations of far-right leanings at the discursive level, but actually attempted to normalise abusive rhetoric on gender and Islam. The subscription to radical views was then more apparent on the Twitter account of WPP, UKIP's cultural wing during Batten's leadership. During this period, WPP moved indistinct

Table 6. Percentage of tweets on Europe, immigration, Islam, and gender for Batten's UKIP and WPP ($^*p < 0.017$, $^{**}p < 0.003$, $^{***}p < 0.0003$).

	UKIP		WPP		T (df = 2256)
	Mean	SD	Mean	SD	
Europe	0.457	(0.498)	0.0996	(0.300)	19.42***
Immigration	0.0379	(0.191)	0.0624	(0.242)	−2.67*
Islam	0.0223	(0.148)	0.0799	(0.271)	−6.49***
Gender	0.007	(0.080)	0.0284	(0.166)	−3.92***

attacks against Muslims, feminists, and LGBTQ people, using a discourse that was, in all probability, deemed too extreme for a more mainstream audience of over 200,000 UKIP followers.

Discussion and conclusions

The Brexit referendum bore seismic consequences for UK politics. UKIP, as the most vocal and recognisable advocate of UK withdrawal from the EU, was swiftly projected into chaos after securing its main political goal. Farage's decision to step down from leadership in 2016 and leave the party in 2018 further contributed to internal instability. Since 2016, UKIP saw no less than eight leaders in office amid declining membership and consensus. During his stint as UKIP leader, Batten responded to these challenges trying to impose a change of strategy. Such a strategy first and foremost entailed opening up to far-right grassroots politics. Commentators widely anticipated a 'far-right turn' in UKIP's campaigning (Walker, 2018a). The article therefore reconstructed the organisational changes underlying this turn and assessed the discursive implications of far-right activists' recruitment. These aims resonate with the scholarship on movement parties and, even more so, with the hybridisation of action repertoires.

At the organisational level, enlisting far-right activists entailed opening up to the grassroots sector, both offline and online. The appointment of Tommy Robinson as Batten's personal advisor and the establishment of War Plan Purple as the cultural wing of UKIP were, in this sense, paradigmatic and substantiated a movement-party turn. This challenged standards and practices of movement-electoral interactions as UKIP provisionally reverted its institutional trajectory to venture down a social-movement route. Most interestingly, it did so at a rather late and consolidated stage of its political lifecycle.

At the discursive level, a significant far-right turn in UKIP's communication – as for prevalence of cultural over European issues – did not quite materialise. First, while European issues remained firmly at the heart of UKIP's discourse throughout the period analysed, it is also true that cultural issues were already salient before Batten stepped in as chairman. The analysis showed that pre-Batten's UKIP was more concerned with immigration than Batten himself, prompting to reconsider the magnitude of discursive change occurred under his leadership. A stronger emphasis on cultural issues was however visible on the page of WPP. Through the establishment of WPP, Batten and UKIP took on a more hybrid approach, diversifying their communication. By means of this strategy, WPP served as a platform to engage UKIP supporters attracted by extremist ideas, while keeping UKIP clear from (further) controversy. Batten was however unable to gain the upper hand over UKIP's more liberal faction and impose his vision as a long-term strategy. Internal infighting within UKIP ultimately forced Batten and his successor, Richard Braine, to resign from the party (Cockburn, 2019). With their departure, WPP also discontinued its affiliation to UKIP. This notwithstanding, UKIP has temporarily provided a platform for far-right activists and vloggers, whose extremist ideas propagated across mainstream political circles. Through this time period, UKIP and WPP filled a discursive gap after the BNP, Britain First, and EDL were censored from social media platforms (Hern, 2019).

The article unpacked party change as a bundle of organisational and discursive strategies, encouraging to factor in, and delve into, the activist component of far-right politics. This study also went the extra mile to review qualitative shifts in discourse, thus moving beyond assessments purely based on shifts in issue salience. For instance, while the analysis did not detect significant changes in salience for issues like gender and Islam, it highlighted a radical turn in the way these issues were discussed across subsequent leadership periods. The study generally rested on the assumption that communication on Twitter is a representative proxy for the ideological stances of individual organisations and those of their leaders. However, alternative approaches could also probe the personal profiles of leaders on Twitter and other social media, as well as the discursive practices of their followers.

Further research should finally consider whether movement-party hybridisation is part of a broader process within the far right. From the French *Front National* onwards, the history of the contemporary far right abounds with instances of mobilisations occurring in both the protest and electoral arenas (Pirro, 2019). More critically, reverting trajectories seems possible and, as the Flemish *Vlaams Belang* has shown, opening up to the movement sector decades after its foundation can also bear significant electoral fruits. The recruitment of Dries van Langehoven, the founder of the youth movement *Schild & Vrienden*, as well as a fine-tuned online communication strategy could in part explain their recent electoral comeback (Cerulus, 2019). However, the recent ousting of *Der Flügel* from the *Alternative für Deutschland* (Müller, 2020) shows that the establishment of a more radical wing is not always, nor necessarily, a successful endeavour.

The study of movement parties and hybridisation processes represents a new frontier in far-right research. Focusing on such aspects requires swift and timely effort, not least due to the often-transitory nature of cooperation among different far-right actors or the ever-more stringent criteria set by social media with regard to incitement of hatred. Notwithstanding these potential limitations, studies have shown that networks matter as do platform architectures for the discourse that is presented (e.g., Bossetta, 2018; Pirro et al., 2019). While this study concentrated on party change at a particular juncture, the boundaries between online and offline mobilisation have become porous – and this holds especially true for the far right and its reduced ability to access mainstream media.

Notes

1. https://twitter.com/warplanpurple.
2. Gerard Batten on BBC's Andrew Marr Show, 14 April 2019.
3. https://www.facebook.com/WarPlanPurple.
4. https://www.facebook.com/groups/UKIPLiberalists.
5. The quote was retrieved from http://theliberalists.net/about in June 2019. The Liberalists now only have one registered domain (http://liberalists.org), which does not include an 'About' section.
6. http://liberalists.org/faq/.
7. http://liberalists.org/principles/.
8. https://twitter.com/UKIP/status/872011917279219712.
9. https://twitter.com/UKIP/status/943169369709916160.
10. https://twitter.com/UKIP/status/940937131282792449.
11. https://twitter.com/UKIP/status/917391388668518400.
12. https://twitter.com/UKIP/status/1115746893064228864.
13. https://twitter.com/UKIP/status/1037991569872302082.
14. https://twitter.com/UKIP/status/862741940235841536.
15. https://twitter.com/UKIP/status/940880382546849799.

16. https://twitter.com/UKIP/status/937034996224806912.
17. https://twitter.com/UKIP/status/1027931141762899968.
18. https://twitter.com/UKIP/status/1028935059049459713.
19. https://twitter.com/UKIP/status/179533286350139393.
20. https://twitter.com/UKIP/status/190773608677781504.
21. https://twitter.com/UKIP/status/601322712431206400.
22. https://twitter.com/UKIP/status/593343864301301760.
23. https://twitter.com/UKIP/status/274171260966146048.
24. https://twitter.com/UKIP/status/402735603500208129; https://twitter.com/UKIP/status/367211481953075200.
25. https://twitter.com/WarPlanPurple/status/1030018958563389440.
26. https://twitter.com/WarPlanPurple/status/1093946696076271616.
27. https://twitter.com/WarPlanPurple/status/1125671030964535301.
28. https://twitter.com/WarPlanPurple/status/1115735893124558849.
29. https://twitter.com/WarPlanPurple/status/1052561253980430336.
30. https://twitter.com/WarPlanPurple/status/1054012954901991426.

Acknowledgements

An earlier draft of this article was presented at the 'Social Movements and Parties in a Fractured Media Landscape' symposium held at the Scuola Normale Superiore, Florence, 1–2 July 2019, and at the XXXIII Meeting of the Italian Political Science Association (SISP), Lecce, 12–14 September 2019. We would like to thank the participants of both events as well as Dan Mercea, Lorenzo Mosca, and the anonymous reviewers for their thorough and constructive comments on our work.

Disclosure statement

No potential conflict of interest was reported by the author(s).

ORCID

Ofra Klein http://orcid.org/0000-0002-6847-1015
Andrea L. P. Pirro http://orcid.org/0000-0002-0111-4865

References

Albertazzi, D., Giovannini, A., & Seddone, A. (2018). 'No regionalism please, we are Leghisti!' The transformation of the Italian Lega Nord under the leadership of Matteo Salvini. *Regional & Federal Studies*, *28*(5), 645–671. https://doi.org/10.1080/13597566.2018.1512977

Bartlett, J. (2014). Populism, social media and democratic strain. In C. Sandelind (Ed.), *European populism and winning the immigration debate* (pp. 99–114). Fores.

Benoit, K., Watanabe, K., Wang, H., Nulty, P., Obeng, A., Müller, S., & Matsuo, A. (2018). Quanteda: An R package for the quantitative analysis of textual data. *Journal of Open Source Software, 3*(30), 774. https://doi.org/10.21105/joss.00774

Berntzen, L. E. (2020). *Liberal roots of far right activism: The anti-Islamic movement in the 21st Century*. Routledge.

Berntzen, L. E., & Weisskircher, M. (2016). Anti-Islamic PEGIDA beyond Germany: Explaining differences in mobilisation. *Journal of Intercultural Studies, 37*(6), 556–573. https://doi.org/10.1080/07256868.2016.1235021

Bossetta, M. (2018). The digital architectures of social media: Comparing political campaigning on Facebook, Twitter, Instagram, and Snapchat in the 2016 US election. *Journalism & Mass Communication Quarterly, 95*(2), 471–496. https://doi.org/10.1177/1077699018763307

Budge, I., Robertson, D., & Hearl, D. (1987). *Ideology, strategy and party change: Spatial analyses of post-war election programmes in 19 democracies*. Cambridge University Press.

Busher, J. (2015). *The making of anti-Muslim protest: Grassroots activism in the English Defence League*. Routledge.

Carter, E. (2005). *The extreme right in Western Europe: Success or failure?* Manchester University Press.

Castelli Gattinara, P., & Pirro, A. L. P. (2019). The far right as social movement. *European Societies, 21*(4), 447–462. https://doi.org/10.1080/14616696.2018.1494301

Cerulus, L. (2019). Inside the far right's Flemish victory. *Politico*. https://www.politico.eu/article/inside-the-far-rights-flemish-victory/

Chadwick, A. (2007). Digital network repertoires and organizational hybridity. *Political Communication, 24*(3), 283–301. https://doi.org/10.1080/10584600701471666

Cihon, P., & Yasseri, T. (2016). A biased review of biases in Twitter studies on political collective action. *Frontiers in Physics, 4*(34), 1–8. https://doi.org/10.3389/fphy.2016.00034

Cockburn, H. (2019, October 30). Ukip loses eighth leader since Brexit referendum as Richard Braine resigns ahead of general election. Independent. https://www.independent.co.uk/news/uk/politics/richard-braine-ukip-leader-resign-brexit-general-election-latest-a9177516.html

Dallison, P. (2018, April 12). Nigel Farage quits UKIP. *Politico*. https://www.politico.eu/article/nigel-farage-quits-ukip/

Davidson, T., & Berezin, M. (2018). Britain first and the UK Independence Party: Social media and movement-party dynamics. *Mobilization: An International Quarterly, 23*(4), 485–510. https://doi.org/10.17813/1086-671X-23-4-485

della Porta, D., Kouki, H., Fernandez, J., & Mosca, L. (2017). *Movement parties against austerity*. Polity Press.

Engesser, S., Ernst, N., Esser, F., & Büchel, F. (2017). Populism and social media: How politicians spread a fragmented ideology. *Information, Communication & Society, 20*(8), 1109–1126. https://doi.org/10.1080/1369118X.2016.1207697

Ford, R., & Goodwin, M. J. (2014). *Revolt on the right: Explaining support for the radical right in Britain*. Routledge.

Froio, C., & Ganesh, B. (2019). The transnationalisation of far right discourse on Twitter. *European Societies, 21*(4), 513–539. https://doi.org/10.1080/14616696.2018.1494295

Golbeck, J., Grimes, J., & Rogers, A. (2010). Twitter use by the U.S. Congress. *Journal of the American Society for Information Science and Technology, 61*(8), 1612–1621. https://doi.org/10.1002/asi.21344

Griffin, R. (2000). Interregnum or endgame? The radical right in the 'post-fascist'. era. *Journal of Political Ideologies, 5*(2), 163–178. https://doi.org/10.1080/713682938

Gunther, R., & Diamond, L. (2003). Species of political parties: A new typology. *Party Politics, 9*(2), 167–199. https://doi.org/10.1177/13540688030092003

Halliday, J. (2019, April 25). Tommy Robinson announces plans to stand as MEP. *Guardian*. https://www.theguardian.com/uk-news/2019/apr/25/tommy-robinson-stand-mep-manchester-event-community-leaders-condemn-anti-islam-activist

Halupka, M. (2014). Clicktivism: A systematic heuristic. *Policy & Internet*, *6*(2), 115–132. https://doi.org/10.1002/1944-2866.POI355

Hanna, J., & Busher, J. (2019). UKIP and the UK's radical right: A tale of movement party success? In M. Caiani, & O. Císar (Eds.), *Radical right movement parties in Europe* (pp. 46–62). Routledge.

Harmel, R., & Janda, K. (1994). An integrated theory of party goals and party change. *Journal of Theoretical Politics*, *6*(3), 259–287. https://doi.org/10.1177/0951692894006003001

Hermida, A. (2010). From TV to Twitter: How ambient news became ambient journalism. *Media/Culture Journal*, *13*(2), 1–6. http://www.journal.media-culture.org.au/index.php/mcjournal/article/view/220

Hern, A. (2019, April 18). Facebook bans far-right groups including BNP, EDL and Britain First. *Guardian*. https://www.theguardian.com/technology/2019/apr/18/facebook-bans-far right-groups-including-bnp-edl-and-britain-first

Jacobs, K., & Spierings, N. (2016). *Social media, parties, and political inequalities*. Palgrave Macmillan.

Kipper Central. (2018, August 20). EXCLUSIVE: Who are war plan purple? https://kippercentral.com/2018/08/20/kipper-central-exclusive-who-are-war-plan-purple/

Kitschelt, H. (2006). Movement parties. In R. S. Katz & W. J. Crotty (Eds.), *Handbook of party politics* (pp. 278–290). Sage Publishing.

Klein, O., & Muis, J. (2019). Online discontent: Comparing Western European far-right groups on Facebook. *European Societies*, *21*(4), 540–562. https://doi.org/10.1080/14616696.2018.1494293

Larsson, A., & Moe, H. (2012). Studying political microblogging: Twitter users in the 2010 Swedish election campaign. *New Media & Society*, *14*(5), 729–747. https://doi.org/10.1177/1461444811422894

McAdam, D., & Tarrow, S. (2010). Ballots and barricades: On the reciprocal relationship between elections and social movements. *Perspectives on Politics*, *8*(2), 529–542. https://doi.org/10.1017/S1537592710001234

Müller, A. (2020, March 21). Der Flügel flattert weiter. *Der Spiegel*. https://www.spiegel.de/politik/deutschland/afd-der-fluegel-flattert-trotz-aufloesungsbeschluss-weiter-a-782f1b69-31a8-44e0-94a4-b78426c86a31

Panebianco, A. (1988). *Political parties: Organization and power*. Cambridge University Press.

Payne, S. (2018). Ukip's transformation into a far-right party is complete. *Financial Times*. Retrieved from: https://www.ft.com/content/c43857ca-ef16-11e8-89c8-d36339d835c0

Pirro, A. L. P. (2019). Ballots and barricades enhanced: Far-right 'movement parties' and movement-electoral interactions. *Nations and Nationalism*, *25*(3), 782–802. https://doi.org/10.1111/nana.12483

Pirro, A. L. P., & Castelli Gattinara, P. (2018). Movement parties of the far right: The organization and strategies of nativist collective actors. *Mobilization: An International Quarterly*, *23*(3), 367–383. https://doi.org/10.17813/1086-671X-23-3-367

Pirro, A. L. P., Pavan, E., Fagan, A., & Gazsi, D. (2019). Close ever, distant never? Integrating protest event and social network approaches into the transformation of the Hungarian far right. *Party Politics*, 1–13. https://doi.org/10.1177/1354068819863624

Pirro, A. L. P., & Taggart, P. (2018). The populist politics of Euroscepticism in times of crisis: A framework for analysis. *Politics*, *38*(3), 253–262. https://doi.org/10.1177/0263395718770579

Puschmann, C., & Scheffler, T. (2016). *Topic modeling for media and communication research: A short primer* (Report No. 2016-05). Das Alexander von Humboldt Institut für Internet und Gesellschaft.

Roesslein, J. (2017, November 10). *Tweepy Documentation, release 3.5.0*. https://buildmedia.readthedocs.org/media/pdf/tweepy/v3.5.0/tweepy.pdf

Sheafer, T., Shenhav, S. R., Takens, J., & Van Atteveldt, W. (2014). Relative political and value proximity in mediated public diplomacy: The effect of state-level homophily on international frame building. *Political Communication*, *31*(1), 149–167. https://doi.org/10.1080/10584609.2013.799107

Spence, A., & Di Stefano, M. (2019, May 8). Under siege for his comments about rape, UKIP's star candidate Carl Benjamin has recruited Milo Yiannopoulos to join his campaign. *BuzzFeed*. Retrieved from: https://www.buzzfeed.com/alexspence/ukips-european-election-campaign-has-a-new-recruit-milo

Stier, S., Bleier, A., Lietz, H., & Strohmaier, M. (2018). Election campaigning on social media: Politicians, audiences, and the mediation of political communication on Facebook and Twitter. *Political Communication*, *35*(1), 50–74. https://doi.org/10.1080/10584609.2017.1334728

Stockemer, D., & Barisione, M. (2017). The 'new' discourse of the Front National under Marine Le Pen: A slight change with a big impact. *European Journal of Communication*, *32*(2), 100–115. https://doi.org/10.1177/0267323116680132

Taggart, P. (1998). A touchstone of dissent: Euroscepticism in contemporary Western European party systems. *European Journal of Political Research*, *33*(3), 363–388. https://doi.org/10.1111/1475-6765.00387

UKIP. (2018). Rules of procedure. Retrieved from: https://www.ukip.org/uploads/party_rules.pdf

Usherwood, S. (2016). The UK Independence Party: The dimensions of mainstreaming. In T. Akkerman, S. L. de Lange, & M. Rooduijn (Eds.), *Radical right-wing populist parties in Western Europe* (pp. 247–267). Routledge.

Usherwood, S. (2019). Shooting the fox? UKIP's populism in the post-Brexit era. *West European Politics*, *42*(6), 1209–1229. https://doi.org/10.1080/01402382.2019.1596692

Van Kessel, S., & Castelein, R. (2016). Shifting the blame. Populist politicians' use of Twitter as a tool of opposition. *Journal of Contemporary European Research*, *12*(2), 594–614. https://www.jcer.net/index.php/jcer/article/view/709

Walker, P. (2018a, December 4). Nigel Farage quits Ukip over its anti-Muslim fixation. *Guardian*. https://www.theguardian.com/politics/2018/dec/04/nigel-farage-quits-ukip-over-fixation-anti-muslim-policies

Walker, P. (2018b, August 2). Ukip membership surges 15% in a month. *Guardian*. https://www.theguardian.com/politics/2018/aug/02/ukip-membership-surges-15-per-cent-in-a-month

Walker, P. (2018c, June 25). Ukip welcomes social media activists linked to 'alt-right' into party. *Guardian*. https://www.theguardian.com/politics/2018/jun/25/ukip-welcomes-social-media-activists-linked-to-alt-right-into-party

Walker, P., & Halliday, J. (2019, March 3). Revealed: Ukip membership surge shifts party to far right. *Guardian*. https://www.theguardian.com/world/2019/mar/03/new-ukip-members-shifting-party-far-right

Wickham, H. (2016). *Ggplot2: Elegant graphics for data analysis*. Springer-Verlag.

Widfeldt, A. (2008). Party change as a necessity: The case of the Sweden democrats. *Representation*, *44*(3), 265–276. https://doi.org/10.1080/00344890802237031

Social networks and digital organisation: far right parties at the 2019 Australian federal election

Jordan McSwiney

ABSTRACT
This paper analyses the social media networks and content of four Australian parties, assessing their relationship to the far right at the time of the 2019 Australian federal election. Using social network analysis, I map their relationship to a broader network of far-right actors in Australia on Facebook and Twitter, identifying pathways of communication, mobilisation and recruitment. The structure of the parties' networks points to highly centralised, leader-centric organisations, placing them in a vulnerable position in terms of sustainability. This is combined with qualitative content analysis, which finds little evidence of party organisation or campaign mobilisation on either platform, despite the context of a first-order election. Instead, these parties use social media primarily for the construction of collective identities and the development and dissemination of interpretive frames, practices typically associated with social movements rather than political parties.

Introduction

The digital is no longer disruptive (Cramer, 2015). Internet technologies are intertwined with the organisational life of parties and movements, reshaping how they campaign and organise. Digitalisation promotes a culture of organisational experimentation, facilitating the adoption of hybrid organising practices (Chadwick, 2007; Chadwick & Stromer-Galley, 2016). This interplay between party and movement dynamics – so-called 'movement parties' (Kitschelt, 2006) – includes the use of both parliamentary and extra-parliamentary mobilisation, the formation of lose supporter networks rather than formalised membership structures, and limited investment in party structures. How these dynamics are reflected in their social media activity is vital to understanding the organisation of far right parties[1] in a climate where academic access is often limited. Digital networks are therefore an invaluable proxy (Caiani & Parenti, 2013a), reflecting the overall organisational preferences of a party (Bennett et al., 2018). In Australia, where the study of political parties is characterised by a 'general culture of secrecy surrounding the[ir] internal organization' (Gauja & McSwiney, 2019, p. 48), analysis of digital trace data is especially useful. The aims of this paper are twofold. Firstly, to map the manner in which far-right

---

Supplemental data for this article can be accessed at https://doi.org/10.1080/1369118X.2020.1757132

parties relate to the broader Australian far right, assessing potential pathways of recruitment, mobilisation and communication. Secondly, to assess how these platforms are used to facilitate party organisation. As the analysis centres on a first-order election, the use of social media is expected to focus on engaging with existing supporters and members (as well as recruiting new ones), organising and promoting party activities such as campaign mobilisations, and disseminating the parties' messages.

To answer these questions, I conduct a social network analysis of four parties, exploring their relationship to the Australian far right through Facebook and Twitter, the two most popular social networking platforms in Australia. This is combined with a qualitative content analysis of the content posted to these platforms during the federal election. This article focuses on three far-right parties: Pauline Hanson's One Nation (PHON), Australia's oldest and most successful far-right party; Fraser Anning's Conservative National Party (FACNP), the newest and most explicitly racist; and the Yellow Vest Alliance (YVA), with its extensive connections to the international counter-jihad movement. In addition, the article also examines the ideologically dubious United Australia Party (UAP), a party which has demonstrated a willingness to engage in and reproduce far-right memes, testing whether (and how) the party relates the far right. Though these parties differ significantly in terms of resources, political ambitions and histories, and with limited electoral impact, they are nevertheless important cases for understanding how far-right parties organise and relate to a broader movement. Lacking the organisational infrastructure and resources of larger parties such as the Australian Labor Party (ALP) or the Liberal-National Coalition (henceforth Coalition) – those most likely to form government in Australia – these parties turn to the internet, and in particular social media, as a way to better operationalise their comparatively limited resources.

Findings indicate that PHON, FACNP and the YVA are closely connected to far-right actors present on the platforms, as expected. The UAP on the other hand is poorly connected despite its efforts to penetrate the milieu. The networks on both platforms are not especially centralised, suggesting a heterogeneous ecosystem not amenable to vertical coordination by one of the parties. Nevertheless, Pauline Hanson and PHON fulfil a structuring role, with various other organisations coalescing around them. In terms of organisation, there is little evidence of developed intra-party networks, with minimal investment in horizontal party infrastructure such as local or regional branches. Instead, their party networks indicate highly centralised and hierarchical organisations built around the national office and party leaders, confirming anecdotal accounts. Despite expectations that the digital activity would centre on party organisation, especially in the context of a first-order election contest, this was not the case. Instead, it is primarily used in the construction of collective identities, along with the production and dissemination of 'interpretive frames' (Benford & Snow, 2000) for particular topics, namely Islam and the ALP – mobilising practices associated more with movement organisational repertoires (Pirro, 2019).

The internet, the far right and political party organisation

The internet has long served as an important space for the far right, allowing a characteristically fragmented, decentralised and often sectarian political family to connect and coalesce in both cooperative and competitive interactions (Caiani et al., 2012). Active on popular social media like Facebook and Twitter, these platforms enable the far right to connect with a larger audience than ever before. Crucially, they allow for direct communications between party elites (namely the party leader) and supporters without distortion from potentially hostile media or various layers of the party bureaucracy (Pedersen & Saglie, 2005). Content shared via these networks is typically aimed at creating a collective identity among supporters (Burris et al., 2000) and includes the construction of interpretive frames which help to define the issues around which to mobilise (Caiani et al., 2012). For example, Islamophobia is one of the most important frames for mobilising the far right today (Froio & Ganesh, 2018; Minkenberg, 2018b).

As well as helping facilitate the control of information, the architecture of these platforms can aid in mobilisation and recruitment (Caiani & Parenti, 2013b), connecting parties with supporters without the need for on-the-ground organising (Ward & Gibson, 2010). Individuals can affiliate themselves and materially support a party – for example by sharing or retweeting their posts – without necessarily investing significant amounts of time in its internal life, lowering the barriers to membership and participation (Gibson et al., 2017; Lusoli & Ward, 2004). Digitalisation serves to replace physical branch structures, while still providing a means to engage members and supporters. As well as extending a party's reach into society, these processes respond to efficiency considerations given the high cost of maintaining physical party infrastructure (Gerbaudo, 2019). These trends have tended to reinforce existing power relations (Gibson, 2015), although this may be masked behind moderator practices or the platform's architecture (Gerbaudo, 2019; Lovink, 2016).

Reliance on the internet also fosters a culture of organisational experimentation, as elements of political party and social movement blend together through the selective transplantation of organisational repertoires (Chadwick, 2007; Chadwick & Stromer-Galley, 2016). This movement-like experimentation or 'movement party' model of organisation (Kitschelt, 2006) is characterised by limited investment in party structure, with no formalised membership roles and a lack of extensive communicative and organisational infrastructure. It helps these organisations to cope with the potential lack of a coherent ideology among members and elites, intra-party competition, or the lack of a formalised branch structure (Chadwick & Stromer-Galley, 2016), and highlights the complex interdependence between the parliamentary and extra-parliamentary far right (Kitschelt, 2006; Minkenberg, 2018a). While far right movement parties do not usually originate from social movements, their application of movement organisational and strategic practices, as well as a 'permanent politics of contention' (Minkenberg, 2018a, p. 481), suggest they often behave more like movements than parties.

In Australia, the enthusiasm for social media among the far right has not been lost on scholars. Various attempts have been made to map the ideological landscape of the Australian far right using digital trace data (Dean et al., 2016; Hutchinson, 2019). Others have used it to explore their discourses. For example, Peucker et al. (2019) point to divergent narratives to illustrate the Australian far right's heterogeneity, while Davis (2019) looks to the broadening of these narratives beyond race. In a similar vein, Miller (2017) analysed anti-Islam discourses for Australian anti-Islam groups such as PHON on Facebook, identifying security (terrorism) and political threats as key to their framing. There has also been close analysis of individual actors, particularly Hanson and PHON (Grant et al.,

2019; Sengul, 2019), and militant street movements like the True Blue Crew (Nilan, 2019). While this emerging body of scholarship offers exciting (and overdue) analyses of various elements of the Australian far right, it lacks organisational perspectives. Hence, very little is known about how these groups operate, outside of some anecdotal accounts (e.g. Broinowski, 2017). This article builds on this existing scholarship, exploring how the four parties relate to a broader far right, and providing a first account of their organising dynamics.

Data and methods

Social network analysis is especially suited to addressing the question of the organisation of these parties, shedding light on 'activity and social exchange' between different actors (Caiani & Parenti, 2013a, p. 55). While digital ties are 'cheaper' and do not necessarily represent formal relations, they nevertheless point to pathways of communication, collective action and recruitment, as well as ideological affinities (Burris et al., 2000). Exploring the pattern of relations among and between actors therefore helps to understand their organisational dynamics, highlighting practices of 'coalition building, overlapping membership, processes of collective action and counter mobilisation' (Caiani, 2014, p. 373). In terms of their internal life, analysis of their digital networks serves as a suitable proxy for understanding party organisation. The network structure provides an indication of the complexity of organisation, in so far as their concentration or dispersion over various territorial units such as national, regional and local branches. This also provides an indication of the extent of party centralisation and distribution of power across different levels of leadership and party units.

To do so, this paper uses electronic trace data from social media, operationalising the 'likes' between Facebook fan-pages and interactions ('mentions', 'replies' and 'retweets') between Twitter users. Without an exhaustive directory of social media accounts, it is impossible to determine the 'real' dimensions of a network, preventing the development of a representative sample (Caiani, 2014). Instead, a sample of key organisations is purposively selected as a starting point for exploratory searches (Appendix A), with new accounts added through snowballing (Scott, 2017). This starting sample includes (where possible) two official accounts on each platform for PHON, FACNP, YVA and the UAP. It also includes the main pages and handles for five other far right parties registered for the 2019 federal election and an additional 12 Australian far-right organisations including alternative media, social movements and subcultural milieus. These additional actors are drawn from the literature (e.g. Campion, 2019; Dean et al., 2016; Fleming & Mondon, 2018; Miller, 2017) and are purposively selected to provide a cross-section of the differing organisational forms, tactics, and ideologies which comprise the far right in Australia. These additional organisations are important in helping to understand what, if any, relationship the four parties may have to the far right. Including them in the starting searches helps capture potential connections to the far right that do not originate with the four parties and therefore provides a better indication of their interrelationship. Of these only 14 were present on both platforms. A further six were present on only one, and five were not present on either Facebook or Twitter at the time. Those without a presence on the platforms are therefore unable to be included in the sample. This creates a problem of network incompleteness into the analysis (O'Callaghan et al., 2013). This likely introduces biases into the findings, with a network potentially smaller and less connected than it is in reality. It may also produce a more 'moderate' network in terms of its ideological character, as those absent from the platforms tend to be groups more prone to violence, as well as those with more extreme ideologies. Nevertheless, despite the limitations created by network incompleteness, given the generally secretive nature of the far right – and Australian parties more generally – the method has genuine empirical and scholarly value as it is the best available means of assessing their organisation and interaction.

Network data was collected from May 22-24, 2019, using the NodeXL Pro (Smith et al., 2010) data importation features for Facebook and Twitter. This collects only publicly available data via the application programming interface, ensuring legal requirements regarding data-scraping and its use by third parties is met. In acknowledgement of ethical restrictions regarding the publication of personal data collected from social media, the analysis focuses only on public pages with only the names of public figures (i.e. election candidates and party leaders) included in publication (Klein & Muis, 2019). Due to the variation in platform rate limiting and the type of network data being collected, there is also a variation in the depth of the search conducted. Facebook fan-pages were searched to a depth of two (i.e. two 'steps' from the starting node) and includes interactions among and between these adjacent nodes. This provides a picture of the broader network structure and the location of the parties within it. Twitter interactions were search to a depth of one, and do not include the interactions among and between adjacent nodes. This gives a more limited picture of the network structure, but provides a better basis for exploring the relations between the parties in question and the broader network since it captures potentially multiple interactions over time, rather than a single interaction as per Facebook fan-page likes. Visualisations were produced using Gephi (Bastian et al., 2009).

This is supplemented with qualitative content analysis (Krippendorff, 2018), a combination of methods common in the study of the far right (e.g. Froio & Ganesh, 2018). Data for the content analysis was collected manually from the principle Facebook and Twitter accounts of the four parties for the duration of the election campaign, as well as the two days following the election (11 April–20 May). Content was coded thematically with an original codebook (Appendix B), which was developed inductively. Individual posts were treated as distinct coding units and coded for their manifest content, including post content (e.g. text, image), topic, and purpose. Post topic coded for the subject(s) discussed in the post, for example Islam or party organisation. Post purpose coded for the intent of the post, such as providing commentary on an issue, recruiting party members, or mobilising followers for campaign activities via a call to action. Such posts might include links to membership forms or encouragements to 'join today' (coded: 'Recruitment') or requests to participate in activities like attending polling booths on election day (coded: 'Call to Action – Campaigning'). Post purpose also captured posts aimed at the construction and maintenance of social boundaries through the development of in- and out-group identities. That is, posts which construct an 'inside' expressed in positive or favourable terms, and an oppositional 'outside' expressed in negative or adverse terms. These identities range from individuals and specific organisations, to broad sections of the community and manufactured constituencies like 'the people' constructed in populist terms (Mudde, 2007).

Case outline

The 2019 Australian federal election took place on Saturday, May 18th, with all 151 seats in the House of Representatives up for election, along with 40 of the 76 Senate seats. The Australian electoral system uses two different systems of voting for each house. The House of Representatives uses a 'distinct alternative' method which aggregates the majority of voter's preferences into legislative seats, making it harder for smaller parties to achieve plurality. In contrast, the Senate uses a proportional electoral system, distributing seats in proportion to the percentage of vote a party receives in each state or territory, providing greater electoral opportunities to smaller parties. In addition, Australia's system of compulsory voting creates an additional institutional barrier to minor parties, reducing their capacity to increase their vote share simply by having a more mobilised base, while ensuring large numbers of electors who are not especially politically engaged vote, typically for the major parties (Mackerras & McAllister, 1999).

Perhaps unsurprisingly then, the election results for the four parties were underwhelming. One Nation secured another Queensland senator, but lost one in Western Australia, despite a near 3% growth in its national first preference vote to just over 8%. While FACNP managed to stand 70 candidates across both the House and Senate – an enormous effort for a party registered just nine days before the election – it failed to achieve even 1% of the first preference vote, with its founder and leader Fraser Anning losing his seat. Similarly, and despite a record campaign expenditure of AUD$60 m, the UAP failed to elect any of its candidates, with its only sitting member Brian Burston also failing to be re-elected. Worse still, the YVA, which stood just four Senate candidates, achieved less than 0.1% of the vote. Despite their lacklustre electoral performance, the four parties remain useful cases for analysing how parties use social media, and what if any relationship these parties have to the non-party sector of the far right, while shifting the focus away from the 'usual suspects' of far-right party studies (Mudde, 2016).

One Nation is the most significant in this regard. Founded in 1997, the party has been a lightning rod for issues of immigration, multiculturalism and Aboriginal reconciliation (Mondon, 2013). It returned to prominence at the 2016 federal election, achieving a record 4.29% of the first preference Senate vote resulting in the election of four PHON senators including Hanson. This was followed with success at subsequent state elections in Western Australia and Queensland (2017), and later New South Wales (2019). Despite boasting of an active and growing party membership, no verifiable numbers are available. The party has expanded, establishing a South Australian branch while rejuvenating existing state branches, but the extent to which these structures exist outside of a handful of state MPs and party elites is unclear. The party has also been beset by poor discipline, resulting in a number of defections and high-profile scandals involving senior party officials.

One of these defectors was Queensland senator Fraser Anning, who later founded the eponymous Fraser Anning's Conservative National Party. The FACNP represents the most extreme elements of the Australian far right, with Anning attending a number of rallies linked to white supremacists, and allegedly employing white supremacist activists on his parliamentary staff. The Yellow Vest Alliance is the political party project of the highly secretive Q Society of Australia, which describes itself as 'Australia's leading Islam-critical organisation' (Q Society of Australia, n.d.). Formerly the Australian Liberty Alliance, the party changed its name in an effort to capture the success of the French *gilets jaunes* (yellow vest) movement. Despite a negligible electoral impact the party is significant due to its extensive contacts with the international far right, including Geert Wilders (Party for Freedom), and is considered a 'key player' in the global counter-jihad movement (Hope Not Hate, 2018). Little is known about either the FACNP or YVA's organisational strength. Given the federated nature of the Australian polity, the efforts of both parties to stand candidates across multiple states suggests at least the intention of establishing state-level party organisations, but the extent to which these parties exist beyond a handful of organisational elites is unclear.

Lastly, the UAP is the party of Australian mining magnate Clive Palmer. Its first iteration as the Palmer United Party enjoyed significant initial success (Kefford & McDonnell, 2016), but was deregistered in 2017. Following the defection of a second PHON senator, Brian Burston, the party was relaunched as the UAP, with Burston as its only sitting representative and Palmer returning as leader. The party's ideology is difficult to pin down owing to a policy outline of only 177 words at the time of the election (UAP, 2019b). Nevertheless, the party has repeatedly produced materials employing the symbolism of the 'Alt-Right' (McSwiney, 2018). It claims to have established a number of state and even sub-state, regional offices (i.e. Northern Queensland), drawing on disaffected former PHON candidates and staffers to do so. The party also explicitly stated an aim to capture PHON's support base, and therefore serves as an interesting test case in terms of how parties emerging from outside the far right may nevertheless relate to the milieu.

Findings

Facebook and Twitter networks

Figure 1 illustrates the complex network of relations between the four parties and those elements of the Australian far right present on Facebook. The resulting directed network contains 3,074 nodes and 10,491 ties. It is comprised of one large central cluster, with a number of smaller peripheral clusters. Though seemingly well integrated, connectivity is extremely low, with 0.1% of all potential ties active. The Twitter network (Figure 2), is comprised of 2,435 nodes and 3,630 ties. It is slightly more compartmentalised than the Facebook network, with a clearer differentiation between clusters and is also poorly connected. Across both networks, a number of key nodes play a structuring role, with various other nodes coalescing around them. Different colours signify these communities, which generally reflect organisational affiliations, such as green for PHON and nodes in its community in Figure 1.

There are no major cleavages in either network, however the UAP as well as more extreme actors like the neo-fascist Australia First Party are persistently marginalised. There is no direct connection between any of the four parties on Facebook, indicating a competitive rather than collaborative relationship. There is some connection between the four on Twitter, however the number of interactions is negligible, apart from the activity between Anning's handle *(Fraser_Anning)* and accounts affiliated with the YVA. Interestingly, though the Facebook network contains a larger number of nodes, the Twitter network is more diverse, including handles linked to the ALP, Coalition and Australian Greens, as well as numerous Australian news media. This is likely the result of differences in platform architecture and search parameters, where the Twitter data

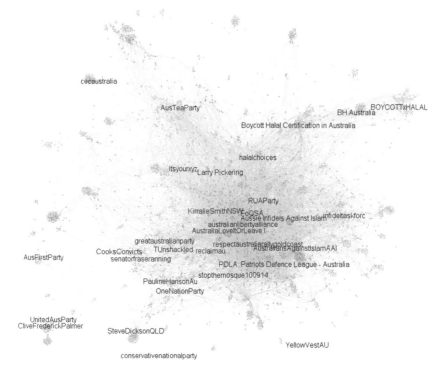

Figure 1. Facebook fan-page network, April 2019.

captured interactions (like sharing an article from a newspaper) while the Facebook data captured only static 'likes' between pages. There is also an increased prominence of the international far right on Twitter, most notably Geert Wilders, US President Donald Trump and the Canadian white supremacist Lauren Southern, suggesting the Twitter network is better internationalised.

Accounts affiliated with PHON are among the best connected on both Facebook and Twitter, with some of the highest number of inbound connections (in-degree) on either platform. This places PHON and in particular Hanson 'in the thick of things' (Scott, 2017, p. 96), reflecting a position of prestige and leadership within the milieu despite the arrival of competitors like the FACNP and the YVA. The prominence of Hanson's personal accounts over other PHON pages and handles, including the national party, illustrates her centrality and structural significance, with the network of PHON accounts coalescing around her. On Facebook in particular, Hanson's personal page (*PaulineHansonAu*) occupies an important brokerage position based on betweenness centrality measures, meaning the node sits on the shortest path between pages which otherwise would not be connected. In this sense, Hanson serves as a unifying figure, mediating connections between various actors in the network. Most notable among these on Facebook are Islamophobic organisations representing anti-mosque and anti-halal certification campaigns such as *halalchoices, BH.Australia*, and *stopthemosque100914*. These are better placed than many of the parties on Facebook, but their presence is much smaller on Twitter. Nevertheless, these movements clearly represent important pathways of recruitment and mobilisation for parties such as PHON. They also serve as important links in chains

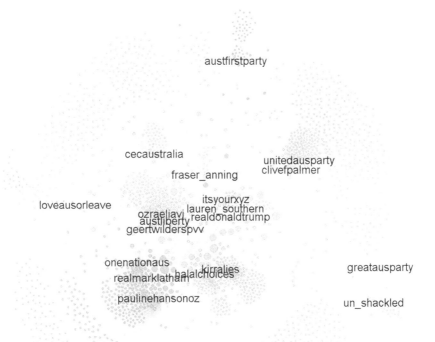

Figure 2. Twitter interaction network, April 2019.

of communicative diffusion, helping to disseminate and amplify a party's message (Gonzalez-Bailón, 2014).

In contrast, FACNP, YVA, and the UAP are markedly less connected to the networks, albeit to varying degrees and for different reasons. Like PHON and Hanson, Anning has many connections from anti-mosque campaigns, especially on Facebook, with a greater concentration of campaigns based in Queensland. Despite this, Anning and the FACNP are not especially well connected. The FACNP page (*ConservativeNationals*) has an in-degree of zero, and only Anning himself is present on Twitter. The limited connectivity is likely due to the newness of the party. It may also be a consequence of network incompleteness, with various extreme-right figures and organisations Anning has collaborated with not present or otherwise removed from the platforms for breaching community standards. For the YVA, the timing and decision to rebrand from the Australian Liberty Alliance appears the key reason for their lack of connection, with the Alliance's Facebook and Twitter extremely well integrated. So, where the YVA nodes are completely isolated, those still under the Alliance banner enjoy similar connectivity to PHON, with a notable relationship to various anti-mosque campaigns. The Alliance also connects to the Patriots Defence League of Australia and the Australian branch of the Australian Soldiers of Odin, two violent street organisations imported from Europe. Conversely, the UAP lacks any significant connection to far-right actors on either platform. What little relationship the party has is brokered almost entirely through former PHON senator Burston. This marginalisation at the periphery of the networks attests to a lack of integration into the far right, despite disseminating 'Alt-Right' memes and hiring former PHON personnel.

Though the parties differ in regard to their relationship with members of the far-right on Facebook and Twitter, they are quite comparable in terms of their intra-party networks. All four are highly centralised, their networks dominated by party elites with minimal representation of state or local party organisations. One Nation, FACNP and the UAP are all structured around their respective leaders. The YVA's network on the other hand coalesces around the pages and accounts under party's former moniker, as well as the activist and former candidate Avi Yemini (*ozraeliavi*). The FACNP and YVA nodes contain no evidence of local or state party organisations. This might be expected for a party like the FACNP, which registered just days before the election, but the YVA has been registered since 2015. Even as PHON and the UAP have a number of state-based party accounts in their networks, particularly on Twitter, the rate of engagement is markedly lower compared to interactions with federal party elites. This is especially so with the UAP. Many of the Twitter handles created for candidates at the 2019 election having only one or two interactions with the central party *(unitedausparty)* or the party leader *(clivepalmer)*. Instead, much of the party's Twitter activity is directed towards two key elites, Palmer and Senator Burston. This suggests a quantity-over-quality approach, with the party applying its broader saturation advertising campaign to the development its digital presence.

Use of Facebook and Twitter

Expectations that the principal use of social media, particularly during an intense election campaign, would be for party organisation and election mobilisation purposes were not borne out in the data. Instead, the largest share of the 298 posts analysed related to the development of collective identities through the construction of in- and out-group dynamics. Each of the parties constructed themselves as champions of an embattled Australian people, facing a dual threat both internal (corrupt elites represented by their political opposition) and external (China, Islam, and immigration). The following examples are characteristic of such posts:

> [Rural and regional Australia] need a break from the tired old parties … There is no stopping One Nation, we never give up on Australians (One Nation Australia, 2019)

> We must stop Muslim immigration to protect our nation for our kids & grandkids! (Senator Fraser Anning, 2019a)

> Mr Palmer is using his own funds to promote Australian interests, while Labor conspires with Communists, to recruit ALP members and approve the takeover of strategic assets [by the Chinese government]. (United Australia, 2019a)

There is limited evidence of the use of the platforms for mobilisation. Few posts contained a call to action for electoral campaigning, such as candidate announcement events or for supporters to hand out materials on election day. Similarly, there is little evidence of online engagement, such as requests to share a post or comment, or attempts to solicit donations.

Recruitment was similarly underrepresented, with little in the way of manifest efforts to recruit members, consistent with the organisational practices of movement parties (Kitschelt, 2006).

Topically, the content more closely resembled what might be expected during an election period. Posts regarding candidates for election and those identifying allies and opponents comprise the largest share. Posts discussing electoral politics more generally, as well as those outlining party policies were similarly common. The identification of allies and opponents generally corresponded with in- and out-group construction, with negative posts targeting political opponents while trying to align a sector of the electorate onside. It should be noted however that almost half of the candidate content (and a significant share of the dataset overall [12%]) is comprised of a UAP content dump, where the party handle tweeted campaign flyers for each of its 173 House and Senate candidates over two days, all with the caption '@UnitedAusParty #auspol' Figure 3.

Islamophobia emerged as a central frame to much of the PHON, FACNP and YVA content, forming a core pillar of their broader nativist ideology. Typically, these frames corresponded with topics of immigration and national security. For example, the YVA (2019) warns of a dual threat posed by 'Immigration and Islamisation' in a post on their Facebook, and Hanson emphasises her 'harsh stance' of no return for the children of Australians who fought with the Islamic State (Pauline Hanson's Please Explain, 2019a). The FACNP is especially vehement: 'Islam is an evil barbaric cult & is not comparable with a Judeo Christian Society' (Senator Fraser Anning, 2019a); 'hypocrisy from

Figure 3. Examples of Islamophobic framing on Facebook and Twitter.

our traitorous politicians since this attack has unfolded, shows they are more interested in bowing down to Islam and destroying Christian Europeans then ensuring public safety' (Fraser Anning Official, 2019). All three framed Muslims and Islam as a clear and present threat to Australia and the Australian 'way of life', consistent with previous research on Australian anti-Islam groups (Miller, 2017). While the UAP did not rely on Islamophobia, the party regularly employed an anti-Chinese framing, with particular concern over the Chinese ownership of Australian agricultural and transport infrastructure. For example: 'This is a disgrace that the Chinese Government is allowed in such an underhanded manner to become involved in our election like this. The @UnitedAusParty is campaigning to protect our strategic assets such as ports, airports and gas infrastructure from foreign govt ownership' (United Australia, 2019b) Figure 4.

Alongside the anticipated anti-Islam framing, anti-elite messaging emerged as vitally important to all four parties. Curiously, though one might expect anti-elite framing to be leveraged against the government of the day (the Coalition), in this case it was overwhelming centred on the centre-left opposition, the Australian Labor Party. This focused particularly on Opposition leader Bill Shorten, framing him (and the ALP at large) as out-of-touch elites who will 'sell out' Australia. Moreover, such framing was heavily reliant the Coalition's own re-election platform. In this sense, it served to reproduce a radicalised version of Coalition campaign, with particular emphasis on tax reform (the 'death tax' and

Figure 4. Examples of Anti-ALP framing on Facebook and Twitter.

franking credits) and the border security. PHON and the UAP were the most frequent to integrate the Coalition's tax reform talking points into their anti-ALP framing:

> The United Australia Party has major concerns over the proposed death tax, franking credits ... and the leadership of Bill Shorten (UAP, 2019b).

> If Bill Shorten will lie about his family history, what else will he lie about? Is he lying about death taxes? Carbon taxes? Immigration? Foreign aid? Bill Shorten will say anything to get elected (PHON, 2019).

One Nation, FACNP and YVA also regularly reproduced a radicalised version of Coalition talking points on immigration and border security. The following tweet from PHON is characteristic of such posts: 'spread this warning far and wide and help One Nation stop Labor and the Greens from opening the floodgates for illegals boat arrivals, squeezing millions of more migrants into our overcrowded cities and opening Australia into ruin' (Pauline Hanson's Please Explain, 2019b).

Discussion and conclusion

Lacking the size and electoral potential of its European and American counterparts, the Australian far right has tended to be overlooked in the literature. However, its steady domestic rise and growing international prominence make it a valuable case for the analysis of far right party organisation and their use of social media. Each of the parties analysed have sought to create active networks of followers through their digital activities, utilising the connective architecture of platforms like Facebook and Twitter to develop interactive communities of engagement that do not distinguish between dues-paying members and supporters. The lack of a clearly structured network suggests a heterogeneous assortment of far-right actors on the platforms, poorly suited to vertical coordination, even if Hanson and PHON are of greater structural significance. Anti-mosque campaigns serve as important entry points and spaces of recruitment and mobilisation for PHON, FACNP and YVA, with all three recruiting election candidates from these groups, underlining the importance of social movement actors to these political parties (Minkenberg, 2018a). In addition, the FACNP and YVA are connected to the more militant street-level far right organisations on the platforms, such as the Australian Soldiers of Odin. This, along with the relationship between FACNP and YVA suggests their constituency is drawn from more militant segments of the Australian far right associated with social movements, as well as sharing a more explicitly racialized and Islamophobic outlook. Without minimising the nativist and Islamophobic content of PHON, its network location suggests it is a more 'generalist' far-right party, capable of appealing to a broader cross section of the milieu (and beyond). However, the overall lack of extreme-right actors on either platform due to network incompleteness limits the scope of the findings in this regard, reducing the potential ties captured for a party like FACNP, while favouring PHON with a more 'moderate' network. Furthermore, the UAP is markedly isolated, its lack of integration indicating that the party's reproduction of far-right symbols and active recruitment of former PHON officials and candidates is the product of opportunism rather than ideology. This is consistent with research on the party's previous iteration, the Palmer United Party, described as having 'no fixed ideological abode', instead attempting to present 'crowd-pleasing policy proposals without much concern for coherence' (Kefford & McDonnell, 2016, p. 184).

There is minimal representation of regional or local party units in the networks. There is none for FACNP or the YVA, and only limited representation for state-based organisation for PHON and the UAP. Those present are marginalised within their own party's networks pointing to a limited organisational role. Given the importance of local organising in the electoral viability the far right (Art, 2011), its absence does not bode well for the electability of these parties. The lack of organisational complexity evidenced by the absence of a distributed party organisation will hinder mobilisation efforts and limit the available pool of skilled activists and candidates. However, this may be a response to efficiency considerations, with 'the party on the Web' replacing 'the party on the ground' (Gerbaudo, 2019, p. 97). Organisational power is highly concentrated in the national party, and for PHON, FACNP and the UAP, in the party leader. Combined with the predominance of select party elites on both platforms this suggests a reproduction of extant party hierarchies reinforcing the parties' vertical organisation as per Bennett et al. (2018). The leader-centric structure places these three parties in a precarious position in terms of electoral sustainability, especially in terms of leadership renewal. Even as social media use has created new spaces for members and supporters to engage with the parties, this opening up at the bottom has not resulted in a diffusion of power. Participation remains largely limited to the 'like' and 'share' features of the platform with little evidence of the parties soliciting member or supporter involvement in party life more broadly. These findings, though anticipated, provide empirical confirmation of anecdotal accounts of the internal life of these parties. This congruence suggests one can have confidence in their utility in assessing the organisational strength of these parties despite methodological limitations.

Given the surprising lack of organisational content present in each of the parties' social media content, the Australian case challenges to some extent the expected impact of internet technologies as an organising and mobilising tool for the far right. Only a small number of posts included a call to action, such as participating in campaign activities, and fewer still were aimed at recruitment. The parties instead use the platforms primarily for the construction of collective identities and the production and dissemination of frames, especially regarding Islam and the ALP. The centrality of Islamophobic framing for PHON, FACNP and YVA is consistent with the findings of Miller (2017) and provides a complimentary account to Campion's (2019) work on the narratives of Australian right-wing extremists. The importance of elite distrust, which Miller (2017) identifies as a secondary consideration is here refined into a specific frame targeting the ALP and is consistent across all four parties. The decision to emphasise on the party of opposition, rather than the current government, seems a contradictory logic in their anti-elite messaging.

Another unexpected finding was the extent to which the parties reproduced the Coalition's talking points. This suggests that rather than original policy or ideological positions, much of the parties' content is simply a radicalisation of existing centre-right positions (Mudde, 2010). Even as the parties have not actively utilised the platforms for party organisation or electoral mobilisation, they still play a vital role in the dissemination of the parties' messages, especially when the network is decentralised (Gonzalez-Bailón, 2014) as is the case here. Moreover, they represent a rich ecosystem of potential collaboration, useful for post-election reorganising. However, these findings are tempered by the fact that Facebook fan-pages and Twitter interactions are only one facet of their respective platforms – which also include closed groups and private messaging (among other features) – and are themselves part of a larger fractured media landscape in which the far right operates (Ellinas, 2010). As such, while these public-facing components are most feasible for scholars, further research should look to the role of closed or semi-closed spaces such as Facebook groups as organisational spaces, though this introduces a litany of new challenges in terms of accessibility and research ethics.

Lastly, all four parties appear to be attempting to straddle the conceptual space between parties and movements. Although they have contested elections in order to gain representation their emphasis on mobilising support around specific interpretive frames resembles 'in more than one way the *modus operandi* of social movements' (Pirro, 2019, p. 785). Though none began as social movements PHON and the YVA are tied a wave of far-right protests in 2015-16 (Fleming & Mondon, 2018), while the FACNP has worked closely with more militant street-level organisations. Though lacking connection to social movements, the UAP shares with the other parties an evident lack of investment in party infrastructure and limited emphasis on formal membership vis-à-vis recruitment. However, whether this is the result of deliberate organisational considerations, or simply consequence of limited party size and resources remains unclear. In the case of the YVA and PHON there seems to be some indication the movement-party parallels are deliberate, with both parties actively portraying themselves as movement-like: PHON's homepage exclaims 'JOIN THE MOVEMENT' and the YVA positions itself as an antipodean *gilets jaunes*. Further analysis of the extent of movement party hybridisation– and the role of the internet in it – in Australia and elsewhere therefore seems a fruitful avenue for future research.

Note

1. This paper follows Mudde's (2007, 2019) interpretation of the far right: a heterogeneous family of political actors distinguished by a shared ideological core of nativism combined with authoritarianism.

Acknowledgements

The author would like to thank Anika Gauja and Ofra Klein for their helpful comments on previous versions of this paper.

Disclosure statement

No potential conflict of interest was reported by the author(s).

Funding

This work was supported by the Australian National University's Herbert and Valmae Frielich Project early career research small grants scheme.

References

Art, D. (2011). *Inside the radical right: The development of anti-immigrant parties in Western Europe*. Cambridge University Press.

Bastian, M., Heymann, S., & Jacomy, M. (2009). Gephi: An open source software for exploring and manipulating networks. *Icwsm*, *8*, 361–362.

Benford, R., & Snow, D. (2000). Framing processes and social movements: An overview and assessment. *Annual Review of Sociology*, *26*(1), 611–639. https://doi.org/10.1146/annurev.soc.26.1.611

Bennett, L. W., Segerberg, A., & Knüpfer, C. B. (2018). The democratic interface: Technology, political organization, and diverging patterns of electoral representation. *Information, Communication & Society*, *21*(11), 1655–1680. https://doi.org/10.1080/1369118X.2017.1348533

Broinowski, A. (2017). *Please explain: The rise, fall and rise again of Pauline Hanson*. Random House Australia.

Burris, V., Smith, E., & Strahm, A. (2000). White supremacist networks on the internet. *Sociological Focus*, *33*(2), 215–235. https://doi.org/10.1080/00380237.2000.10571166

Caiani, M. (2014). Social network analysis. In D. Della Porta (Ed.), *Methodological practices in social movement research* (pp. 368–396). Oxford University Press.

Caiani, M., della Porta, D., & Wagemann, C. (2012). *Mobilizing on the extreme right: Germany, Italy, and the United States*. Oxford University Press.

Caiani, M., & Parenti, L. (2013a). *European and American extreme right groups and the Internet*. Routledge.

Caiani, M., & Parenti, L. (2013b). Extreme right organizations and online politics: A comparative analysis of five Western democracies. In P. Nixon, R. Rawal, & D. Mercea (Eds.), *Politics and the Internet in Comparative Context: Views from the Cloud* (pp. 135–153). Routledge.

Campion, K. (2019). Australian right wing extremist ideology: exploring narratives of nostalgia and nemesis. *Journal of Policing, Intelligence and Counter Terrorism*, *14*(3), 208–226. https://doi.org/10.1080/18335330.2019.1667013

Chadwick, A. (2007). Digital network repertoires and organizational hybridity. *Political Communication*, *24*(3), 283–301. https://doi.org/10.1080/10584600701471666

Chadwick, A., & Stromer-Galley, J. (2016). Digital media, power, and democracy in parties and election campaigns: Party decline or party renewal? *The International Journal of Press/Politics*, *21*(3), 283–293. https://doi.org/10.1177/1940161216646731

Cramer, F. (2015). What is 'post-digital'? In D. Berry & M. Dieter (Eds.), *Postdigital aesthetics* (pp. 12–26). Springer.

Davis, M. (2019). Transnationalising the anti-public sphere: Australian anti-publics and reactionary online media. In M. Peucker & D. Smith (Eds.), *The far-right in contemporary Australia* (pp. 127–150). Palgrave MacMillan.

Dean, G., Bell, P., & Vakhitova, Z. (2016). Right-wing extremism in Australia: the rise of the new radical right. *Journal of Policing, Intelligence and Counter Terrorism*, *11*(2), 121–142. https://doi.org/10.1080/18335330.2016.1231414.

Ellinas, A. (2010). *The media and the far right in Western Europe: Playing the nationalist card*. Cambridge University Press.

Fleming, A., & Mondon, A. (2018). The radical right in Australia. In J. Rydgren (Ed.), *The Oxford handbook of the radical right* (pp. 651–666). Oxford University Press.

Fraser Anning Official (Fraser_anning). (2019, April 22). [Tweet]. https://twitter.com/fraser_anning/status/1120324990153281536.

Froio, C., & Ganesh, B. (2018). The transnationalisation of far right discourse on Twitter. *European Societies*, *21*(4), 513–539. https://doi.org/10.1080/14616696.2018.1494295

Gauja, A., & McSwiney, J. (2019). Do Australian parties represent? In K. Heidar & B. Wauters (Eds.), *Do parties still represent?* (pp. 47–65). Routledge.

Gerbaudo, P. *The digital party: Political organisation and online democracy*. London.

Gibson, R. (2015). Party change, social media and the rise of 'citizen-initiated' campaigning. *Party Politics*, *21*(2), 183–197. https://doi.org/10.1177/1354068812472575

Gibson, R., Greffet, F., & Cantijoch, M. (2017). Friend or foe? Digital technologies and the changing nature of party membership. *Political Communication*, *34*(1), 89–111. https://doi.org/10.1080/10584609.2016.1221011

Gonzalez-Bailón, S. (2014). Online social networks and bottom-up politics. In M. Graham & W. Dutton (Eds.), *Society and the internet: How networks of information and communication are changing our lives* (pp. 209–222). Oxford University Press.

Grant, B., Moore, T., & Lynch, T. (2019). *The rise of right-populism: Pauline Hanson's One Nation and Australian politics*. Springer.

Hope Not Hate. (2018). Key players: The international Islamophobia scene. https://www.hopenothate.org.uk/research/islamophobia-hub/profiles/key-players/.

Hutchinson, J. (2019). The new far-right movement in Australia. *Terrorism and Political Violence*, *1* (23), 1–23. https://doi.org/10.1080/09546553.2019.1629909.

Kefford, G., & McDonnell, D. (2016). Ballots and billions: Clive Palmer's personal party. *Australian Journal of Political Science*, *51*(2), 183–197. https://doi.org/10.1080/10361146.2015.1133800

Kitschelt, H. (2006). Movement parties. In R. Katz & W. Crott (Eds.), *Handbook of party politics* (pp. 278–290). Sage.

Klein, O., & Muis, J. (2019). Online discontent: comparing Western European far-right groups on Facebook. *European societies*, *21*(4), 540–562. https://doi.org/10.1080/14616696.2018.1494293

Krippendorff, K. H. (2018). *Content analysis: An introduction to its methodology* (3rd edn). Sage Publications.

Lovink, G. (2016). *Social media abyss: Critical internet cultures and the force of negation*. Polity.

Lusoli, W., & Ward, S. (2004). Digital rank-and-file: Party activists' perceptions and use of the Internet. *British Journal of Politics & International Relations*, *6*(4), 453–470. https://doi.org/10.1111/j.1467-856X.2004.00150.x

Mackerras, M., & McAllister, I. (1999). Compulsory voting, party stability and electoral advantage in Australia. *Electoral Studies*, *18*(2), 217–233. https://doi.org/10.1016/S0261-3794(98)00047-X

McSwiney, J. (2018). Alt-Right memes and Clive Palmer's return to politics. https://poppoliticsaus.wordpress.com/2018/09/27/alt-right-memes-and-clive-palmers-return-to-politics/.

Miller, C. (2017). Australia's anti-Islam right in their own words: Text as data analysis of social media content. *Australian Journal of Political Science*, *52*(3), 383–401. https://doi.org/10.1080/10361146.2017.1324561

Minkenberg, M. (2018a). Between party and movement: Conceptual and empirical considerations of the radical right's organizational boundaries and mobilization processes. *European Societies*, *21*(4), 463–486. https://doi.org/10.1080/14616696.2018.1494296

Minkenberg, M. (2018b). Religion and the radical right. In J. Rydgren (Ed.), *The Oxford handbook of the radical right* (pp. 2–14). Oxford University Press.

Mondon, A. (2013). *The mainstreaming of the extreme right in France and Australia: A populist hegemony?* Ashgate Publishing Ltd.

Mudde, C. (2007). *Populist radical right parties in Europe*. Cambridge University Press.

Mudde, C. (2010). The populist radical right: A pathological normalcy. *West European Politics*, *33* (6), 1167–1186. https://doi.org/10.1080/01402382.2010.508901

Mudde, C. (2016). The study of populist radical right parties: Towards a fourth wave. *C-REX Working Paper Series*, *1*(1).

Mudde, C. (2019). *The far right today*. John Wiley and Sons.

Nilan, P. (2019). Far-right contestation in Australia: Soldiers of Odin and True Blue Crew. In M. Peucker & D. Smith (Eds.), *The far-right in contemporary Australia* (pp. 101–126). Palgrave MacMillan.

O'Callaghan, D., Greene, D., Conway, M., Carthy, J., & Cunningham, P. (2013). *Uncovering the wider structure of extreme right communities spanning popular online networks*. Proceedings of the 5th Annual ACM Web Science Conference. May 2-4. (pp. 276–285).

One Nation Australia (OneNationAus). (2019a, May 15). [Tweet].

Pauline Hanson's One Nation Party (OneNationParty). (2019, 9 May). [Facebook post]. https://www.facebook.com/OneNationParty/posts/2153627041381533.

Pauline Hanson's Please Explain (PaulineHansonAu). (2019a, April 16). [Facebook post]. https://www.facebook.com/PaulineHansonAu/posts/978452415692404.

Pauline Hanson's Please Explain (PaulineHansonAu). (2019b, May 1). [Facebook post]. https://www.facebook.com/PaulineHansonAu/posts/987836294754016.

Pedersen, K., & Saglie, J. (2005). New technology in ageing parties: Internet use in Danish and Norwegian parties. *Party Politics*, *11*(3), 359–377. https://doi.org/10.1177/1354068805051782

Peucker, M., Smith, D., & Iqbal, M. (2019). Not a monolithic movement: The diverse and shifting messaging of Australia's far-right. In M. Peucker & D. Smith (Eds.), *The far-right in contemporary Australia* (pp. 73–100). Palgrave MacMillan.

Pirro, A. L. P. (2019). Ballots and barricades enhanced: far-right 'movement parties' and movement-electoral interactions. *Nations and Nationalism*, *25*(3), 782–802. https://doi.org/10.1111/nana.12483

Q Society of Australia. (n.d.). Q Society of Australia. http://www.qsociety.org.au/.

Scott, J. (2017). *Social network analysis*. Sage Publications Ltd.

Senator Fraser Anning (senatorfraseranning). (2019a, April 29). [Facebook post]. https://www.facebook.com/senatorfraseranning/posts/699672723781758.

Sengul, K. (2019). Critical discourse analysis in political communication research: a case study of right-wing populist discourse in Australia. *Communication Research and Practice*, *5*(4), 376–392. https://doi.org/10.1080/22041451.2019.1695082

Smith, M., Ceni, A., Milic-Frayling, N., Shneiderman, B., Mendes Ridrugyes, E., Leskovec, J., & Dunne, C. (2010). NodeXL: A free and open network overview, discovery and exploration add-in for Excel 2007/2010/2013/2016. Social Media Research Foundation.

United Australia Party. (2019a). United Australia Party national policy. https://www.unitedaustraliaparty.org.au/national_policy/.

United Australia Party (UnitedAustraliaParty). (2019b, April 29). [Facebook post]. https://www.facebook.com/UnitedAusParty/posts/2039984419464193.

United Australia (UnitedAusParty). (2019a, May 6). [Tweet]. https://twitter.com/UnitedAusParty/status/1125263828340563969.

United Australia (UnitedAusParty). (2019b, May 6). [Tweet]. https://twitter.com/UnitedAusParty/status/1125264324782460930.

Ward, S., & Gibson, R. (2010). European political organizations and the internet: Mobilization, participation, and change. In A. Chadwick & P. Howard (Eds.), *Routledge handbook of internet politics* (pp. 25–40). Routledge.

Yellow Vest Australia (YellowVestAu). (2019, May 17). [Facebook post]. https://www.facebook.com/YellowVestAU/videos/1239134249568219/.

Decentralizing electoral campaigns? New-old parties, grassroots and digital activism

Josep Lobera and Martín Portos

ABSTRACT
Recent studies suggest that new parties display new patterns of digital mobilization. We shed light on this debate: do new party supporters engage in online political activities to a greater extent during electoral campaigns? Do they share political images or quotes on social media, participate in political forums, or exchange political messages with their friends more often than supporters of traditional parties? No. Drawing on a post-electoral survey dataset in Spain, we find that offline extra-institutional political activities are key predictors of the level of online political engagement. Even in the context of a polarized electoral campaign and the emergence of new electoral forces such as Podemos, extra-institutional political participation drives digital activism to the detriment of institutional variables, such as turnout or partisan preferences. Thus, all parties depend on extra-institutional activists to boost their online campaigns. Since grassroots activists increasingly influence the communicative strategy of all political parties, we interpret this process within a long-term digital-based post-material transformation of the political culture, with major implications for partisan organization, mobilization, and polarization in many democracies. We contend that the overrepresentation of grassroots activists in producing and disseminating political content in social media may have favored an increase of the visibility and public support of political outsiders in several countries.

Introduction

The increasing use of digital media worldwide has generated a more fragmented and diverse media environment in the last decade, resulting in a flow of information that is more fluid and harder to control. A broad range of political actors can bypass the mainstream media using digital platforms, reducing the influence of the traditional gatekeepers (Schulz, 2014), as they are able to produce and disseminate political content (Castells, 2015). These changes in the digital public sphere become particularly significant during electoral campaign periods, where political exchanges intensify.

Following the 2008 financial and economic crisis, protests spread worldwide to voice political discontent and strong opposition to rising inequality and welfare retrenchment. Activists' use of digital media played an instrumental role in the recruitment and rapid diffusion of mobilizations (Micó & Casero-Ripollés, 2014) – e.g., Facebook pages were used to mobilize, gain feedback from members (Kavada, 2015), and moderate the influence of repression on the diffusion of the movement (Suh et al., 2017). Also, tech and media activists set up alternative media publications, established autonomous technological infrastructures, and ran 24-hour livestreams (Costanza-Chock, 2014).

In contrast to the costly and complex organizational infrastructures that institutional organizations offer, Internet contributed to the decrease of such costs while increasing the power of entrepreneurial activists (della Porta & Mosca, 2005). In a way, it favored 'organizing without organizations' (Klandermans et al., 2014; Shirky, 2008). Some scholars argue that these transformations challenge established views of what it means to be a 'member' (Chadwick, 2013), leading to a new type of 'connective action' characterized by the lack of clear leadership, weak organizational structure, predominantly personal action frames, and the centrality of network technologies (Bennett & Segerberg, 2012).

To what extent do these changes affect partisan activism? Several authors have pointed out that the new parties display new patterns of digital mobilization, since many of them rely on innovative forms of digital participation (e.g., Casero-Ripollés et al., 2016; della Porta et al., 2017). According to this perspective, supporters of these parties would have a higher level of digital activism (e.g., sharing partisan content on social media more often) compared to traditional parties.

On the other hand, one could argue that all parties would be affected by an increase in autonomous activist participation, regardless of the macro strategy of the political party. Following this approach, partisan digital activism would have similar conditions in all parties, reflecting profound changes in the organization and mobilization of the parties. Certain cultural changes and the extension of the political use of digital tools would favor an increase in autonomous logic in partisan participation, similar to what has occurred in recent decades in the organization of social movements.

The first general election in which Podemos ran in December 2015 presents a phenomenal setting to explore the association between electoral activism in practice and the evolution of political culture on the Net. In the context of new political competitors, what is the association between electoral behavior and digital political activism? To what extent is there an association between institutional participation (i.e., voting preferences) and digital political activism during an electoral campaign? Would digital activism be higher among new movement-related political parties? Does the emergence of a post-material political culture have an impact on digital political activism during an electoral campaign?

Digital media might mobilize citizens far from traditional channels of political representation (Mosca & Quaranta, 2017). Several scholars have noted that new information and communication technologies are important resources for new parties – and more generally for organisations that lack access to mainstream media (Ward & Gibson, 2009). Indeed, empirical evidence shows that people with more expertise and who are more active on Internet and on social networks are more likely to vote for new parties such as Podemos (e.g., Casero-Ripollés et al., 2016; Mosca & Quaranta, 2017).

We contend that this line of reasoning cannot be inverted: our results suggest that it is not whether they vote for one party or another that determines citizens' degree of political engagement in the digital sphere. Even in the context of a polarized electoral campaign and the emergence of new electoral forces, it is participation in offline extra-institutional political activities which ultimately determines the level of online political engagement. Our findings are in line with contributions that stress post-material political cultures, where political participation would gradually move away from the control of party elites (Bang & Sørensen, 1999; Beck, 1997; Bennett, 1998; Chadwick & Stromer-Galley, 2016), and have important implications for understanding the relationship of social media with the changing structure of political opportunities and political polarization. Digital activism of extra-institutional activists would be often outside the control of political elites, giving rise to new intermediation processes in the digital sphere and more opportunities for political challengers.

Our empirical analyses draw on original survey data collected right after the December 2015 election. In the next sections we survey relevant contributions to address our research questions, and place our contribution in relation to extant literature. We then introduce the Spanish case and its importance for the broader readership. After that, we present our data, lay out the empirical design, and discuss our results. Finally, in the concluding section we elaborate on the implications of our findings and signal some avenues for further inquiry.

Electoral turnout and digital activism

When it comes to the nexus offline-online political involvement, we can distinguish three main approaches in the literature on digital participation. Early contributions underscored the possibilities Internet could offer in terms of enhancing citizens' offline relationships and political involvement (Wellman et al., 2001). Internet would help restore community by overcoming limitations of space and time (Sproull & Kiesler, 1991), creating room for democratic deliberation, identity building, and organizational involvement (Wellman et al., 2001).

Indeed, Internet eases the dissemination of political content, facilitating the connection with like-minded users and the coordination of the different interest groups (Hoffmann & Lutz, 2017). Importantly, most relationships formed in cyberspace have a continuity in physical space (Rheingold, 2000). The opposite approach, often referred to as thesis of replacement, would posit that development of new technologies weakens offline engagement as people spend more time in front of the screens (Putnam, 1995), embracing 'clicktivism' activism and other forms of low intensity activism such as online petitioning and participation in social media and Internet fora. Moreover, Internet may cause depression, alienating people from face-to-face interaction (Kraut et al., 1998).

After subjecting the two preceding approaches to close empirical scrutiny, a third 'normalization' perspective developed, suggesting Internet does not substantially change the patterns of political involvement but reinforces pre-existing structures and inequalities (Bimber, 2000; Dahlgren, 2005). This way, Internet is incorporated into routine practices of everyday life, and thus

> a largely null finding of participation effects (…), [which] emerges from attempts to discover a stimulus effect from new technology on political engagement or learning at the individual level. It does not appear (…) that new technology leads to higher aggregate levels of political engagement. (Bimber, 2002, pp. 4–5)

While we know a great deal about the determinants of offline political engagement (including the non-effect of Internet), we know comparatively less about the determinants of online political participation (Feezell, 2016). Evidence on the importance of resource mobilization to understand changing levels and/or forms of digital political participation abounds (Anduiza et al., 2010; Best & Krueger, 2005; Gibson et al., 2005); in contrast, the association between offline and online political behavior is often assumed but seldom tested (see, e.g., Anduiza et al., 2009; Feezell, 2016; Hoffmann & Lutz, 2015). In countries like Spain where opportunities for participation are manifold, costs and restrictions on the circulation of information are relatively low, people who are keen to get involved in politics would have been able to do so through traditional channels in the first place (Bimber, 2000, 2002). Hence, in line with the normalization approach,

H.1 (Hypothesis 1): we would expect electoral turnout to be positively associated with higher levels of digital political activism.

New movements parties and digital activism

In May 2011 thousands of *indignados* ('outraged') activists demonstrated and occupied squares to protest against austerity policies and demand real democracy in Spain (Lobera, 2019; Portos, 2019). These protest events are part of a broader cycle of contention, which contributed to the birth of Podemos, a new party launched from scratch some months before the European Parliament election of 2014, when it gathered one million votes and got five MEPs on the basis of some indignados movement's core claims (Portos, 2019). With regards to organizational settings, research emphasized the continuities between square movements and Podemos, oftentimes referring to the latter as a 'movement party' (della Porta et al., 2017).

Kitschelt (2006, p. 280) defined movement parties as 'coalitions of political activists who emanate from social movements and try or apply the organizational and strategic practices of social movements in the arena of party competition.' Relative to traditional parties, Podemos is less institutionalized in terms of formal party structures and internal decision-making processes, relying to a greater extent on grassroots mobilization – at least, that was the case in its first general election campaign in 2015.

The rapid growth of Podemos flowed from thousands of volunteer groups, the so-called *círculos* ('circles'), which debated party positions and took direct action. Borrowed from the *indignados* movement, this organizational feature was conceived to promote grassroots participation within Podemos (Rodríguez-Teruel et al., 2016). The *círculos*' use of social networking services led to organizational hybridity, as parties adopted and adapted digital network repertoires typical of social movements (Casero-Ripollés et al., 2016; Lisi, 2018). By privileging communication as the central feature in its political action (Kioupkiolis, 2019), the party combined presence on broadcast television through the use of intense digital media to boost citizens' engagement and self-mediation, promoting connective action (Bennett & Segerberg, 2012; Casero-Ripollés et al., 2016).

In this vein, Paolo Gerbaudo (2018) finds that new political formations such as Podemos use social media to gain momentum and online participatory platforms to mobilize the rank-and-file. Specifically, the party followed a 'multi-layered techno-political strategy', where both 'the front end' (elites) and 'the back end' (grassroots) played an important role (Toret, 2015; Lobera & Parejo, 2019).

A number of contributions have stressed the populist character of left-wing formation Podemos (e.g., Font et al., 2019; Lobera, 2020). Broader scholarship on populism has stressed the central role that social media play in maintaining voters' support for populist candidates (see Kriesi, 2014). In this vein, Groshek and Koc-Michalska (2017, p. 1402) found that US voters more active in social media (creating and sharing political content) show higher levels of 'support for populist candidates than those that are more passive receivers of political online content' during the 2016 US election campaign.

Overall, there is solid evidence that people who are younger, more educated, more politically sophisticated, and with Internet skills tend to be more supportive of Podemos (Fernández-Albertos, 2015; Mosca & Quaranta, 2017; Ramiro & Gomez, 2017). Specifically, the frequent use of Internet and digital social media increase the probabilities of voting for Podemos (Fernández-Albertos, 2015; Mosca & Quaranta, 2017). This argument has important endogenous implications. Not only that being a more active and sophisticated Internet user makes you keener to vote for Podemos, but also,

H.2 (Hypothesis 2): we would expect Podemos's constituency to be more politically active in the Web during an electoral campaign than voters of other parties.

Extra-institutional political behavior and digital activism

Although sometimes forgotten in the literature, social movement actors are linked to routine political actors in electoral campaigns (McAdam & Tarrow, 2010). Movements often engage in proactive and reactive electoral mobilization and may 'introduce new forms of collective action that influence election campaigns' (McAdam & Tarrow, 2010, p. 533). Moreover, digital tools offer growing opportunities for social movements and entrepreneurial activists to exert influence on the electoral field.

On the other hand, researchers have noted a 'growing disconnection between formal bureaucratic modes of organizational maintenance and looser, more flexible, and less "dutiful" engagement repertoires' (Chadwick & Stromer-Galley, 2016, p. 4; Tormey, 2015; Wells, 2015). This happens in a broad context of decreasing levels of membership and trust, declining partisan identification and support among the wider electorate, which put under question the parties' ability to sustain themselves (Gibson & Ward, 2000; Mair & Van Biezen, 2001; Norris, 2011).

While some observers seem to have discarded all expectations that political parties can be 'resuscitated' (Wilson, 2006), others have issued calls for reform and renewal. Following political parties' cartelization over the last few decades (Katz & Mair, 2009) and the exceptional use of experts and professionals for creating campaigns, strategies, and marketing to strengthen its electoral appeal (Panebianco, 1988), political parties seem to be experiencing a long-term period of adjustment toward post-material political culture and attitudes toward political engagement (Chadwick & Stromer-Galley, 2016). These shifts in political values and participation would affect all constituencies and imply a move away from traditional forms of loyalty-based party engagement and toward issue-oriented campaigns, including participation through alternative forms of action, such as protesting, political consumerism, community involvement, and so on (Dalton, 2007; Tormey, 2015; Wells, 2015).

There is an ongoing, vivid debate in the literature about how alternative digital media may be fostering self-organization and open participation (Atton, 2004; Couldry &

Curran, 2003), challenging traditional membership (Chadwick, 2013), and favoring the surge of political outsiders (Jungherr et al., 2019). Similar to the changes observed in the social movements by Bennett and Segerberg (2012), we would also expect a weakening of the organizational structure of political parties, predominantly personal action frames, and a declining of party elite control, with a greater importance of network technologies. Digital tools promote cultures of organizational experimentation and a party-as-movement mentality that cause many to reject norms of hierarchical discipline and usual partisan adherence. Moreover, the effect of Internet use on institutional forms of political involvement, such as electoral turnout and contacting politicians, would be more moderate than on alternative forms of participation such as social movement activism (Dahlgren, 2011; Hoffmann & Lutz, 2015).

Earl and Kimport (2011) argue that Internet offers two key affordances relevant to activism: e-activists do not need to be physically present to act together, and the web sharply reduces costs for organizing and engaging in coordinated action. These authors find a positive effect between affordances' leverage and the transformative changes of organization and participation in contentious activities (*Ibid.*). More generally, the elective affinity between digital tools and post-material engagement is observed with different intensities in what Ulrich Beck called *sub-politics* (1997), Lance Bennett's *lifestyle politics* (1998), Henrik Bang and Eva Sørensen's *everyday makers* (1999), and Russell Dalton's *engaged citizenship* (2007). Accordingly,

> H.3 (Hypothesis 3): we would expect extra-institutional forms of participation to increase digital political activism, concealing the effect of electoral preferences on digital participation.

Digital political participation in Spain: the context

The wide use of digital tools in US presidential campaigns has dominated scholarly literature on digital political campaigning since 2000 (Hara, 2008). Developing empirically informed research that incorporates other cases can advance our knowledge and the undertheorized association between political engagement and digital activism (Postill, 2012). The Spanish case provides an analytically useful case to shed light on the interplay between these two factors for a number of reasons.

First, a deep transformation in the political landscape goes together with increasing relevance of the digital public sphere. Exchanges of information and political organization through Internet and social media were key to understand the level of anti-austerity mobilization in the country since 2011 and the subsequent transformation of the traditional bipartisan system (Micó & Casero-Ripollés, 2014).

Second, political practices in the digital environment developed early and in an intense way. Traditionally, Spain has been among the Western countries with lower levels of political and citizen participation (Morales, 2005). After a period of intense citizen mobilization around the Transition to democracy, Spaniards' political mobilization decreased during the following decades (Torcal, 1995). 'Tactical demobilization' has been identified as one of the necessary keys enabling the elites to negotiate and establish 'consensus politics' (Gunther, 2010, p. 24). Since the 1980s formal political participation decreased –e.g., party and union membership-, protracting a public sphere with no criticism towards the so-called 'Transition Culture' (Martínez, 2012).

In this context, the appearance of the Net led to the development of a digital public sphere in Spain with a marked 'dissident' nature and new social intermediations in the electoral information flows. Although traditional political actors still play an important role as a source of electoral information, they are increasingly sharing space with new social actors (Lobera & Sampedro, 2018). The general election held on 20th December, 2015 took place in a climate of increasing polarization, with an expectation to restructure the bipartisan system in the face of the emergence of new electoral competitors with greater mobilization capacity such as left-wing Podemos and center-right liberal Ciudadanos (Rodríguez-Teruel et al., 2016). The preceding campaign and ensuing election were marked by different issues, including corruption, citizens' distrust towards traditional parties and the consequences of the economic recession and austerity policies.

The vote resulted in the most fragmented parliament in the country's recent democratic history. While the conservative PP remained as the main force, total electoral support for the party went from 45% in the 2011 election to 28.7% in 2015 (which represents a loss of 64 seats). The main opposition party, social-democratic PSOE, got its worst electoral result to date since the Transition to democracy (22% support, 90 seats). Newcomer Podemos closely followed, winning some 20% of the vote share (69 seats). Centre-right challenger, Ciudadanos, ranked fourth (with 13.9% of electoral support and 40 seats).

All in all, this context lets us closely examine the determinants of the levels of digital political participation, providing evidence of whether new parties display different patterns of digital mobilization. More generally, the results allow us to better understand the current dynamics in party support and public opinion – in Spain and beyond.

Data and methods

To test our hypotheses about the determinants of digital political activism, we use information collected from 1,556 post-electoral structured interviews with Internet users (Lobera & Sampedro, 2018). The survey was fielded between December 21st and December 30th 2015, following the Spanish general election held on December 20th. The sample was built by a specialized polling agency (Netquest), implementing balanced quotas based on respondents' demographic information.[1] Specifically, online panellists were stratified by gender, age, region and size of town. The sampling has been done by randomly selecting, in each stratum, four records for each theoretical sample unit. The deviations of the sample distributions from the population characteristics have been corrected by weighting. The source used for weighting is the '2011 Survey on Equipment and Use of Information and Communication Technology in Households' from the National Statistics Institute (INE). Quality assurance and supervision systems were applied during the process (see Netquest, 2019).

The survey questionnaire focuses on Internet uses and online political participation, but it also includes a number of questions covering biographical features, participation during the electoral campaign, and broader information on socio-political behavior and attitudes. In our empirical analyses, we understand online political participation as a ladder made up of several rungs of intensity (see Bazurli & Portos, 2019; Pirro & Portos, 2020). Precisely, in order to build the dependent variable we rely on a battery of nine items that measure the frequency in which the following activities are carried out over the last three months (all of them are measured through an ordinal scale, 1–6, which ranges from 'never or almost never' to 'several times a day'): (1) 'upload political images or videos on social media such as Facebook, Twitter, etc.', (2) 'share political phrases, texts, or quotes via social media', (3) 'participate in forums, blogs, or chats about the elections or politics in general', (4) 'search information about the candidates' position on topics that interest me', (5) 'sign petitions, manifestos, or incriminations of a political nature', (6) 'visit a candidate's or party's website', (7) 'visit a civic, social or alternative information group's or organization's website', (8) 'send emails to political parties or candidates', (9) 'exchange emails with relatives or friends with comments on the campaign or forwarding political jokes'.

Since the level of intercorrelation between the items is moderate-to-high (0.32 < Pearson's r < 0.76), we carried out a Principal Component Analysis, which allowed us to construct a weighted additive scale that we used to measure the level of digital political activism.[2] The scale is reliable, and the Principal Component Analysis (PCA) offered a solution with one single component's Eigenvalue above the 1.00 threshold (Eigenvalue = 4.94; Cronbach's α = 0.89), which accounts for 54.84% of the total variation.

We perform a number of OLS regressions with robust standard errors.[3] The survey questionnaire includes information on past voting spells and electoral turnout in the preceding December 2015 national election, as well as participation in a number of extra-institutional political activities during the last four months such as protesting, membership of pressure groups and boycotting/buycotting. The last three items report a low-to-moderate level of correlation (Pearson's r < 0.30). In order to weigh our arguments against alternative explanations, we include a number of controls. The control variables measure grievances (whether the respondent is unemployed, household income), biographical availability (sex, age, education, municipality size), as well as political attitudes and values (ideology, trust, attention during the electoral campaign). Importantly, we also control for the effect the individual's expertise as an Internet user can have on the level of digital activism – in Table 1, we report the summary statistics; for the exact wording of the questionnaire, see Appendix II.

Table 1. Descriptive statistics.

	N	Mean	S.D.	Min.	Max.
Digital activism scale	1379	5.49	2.78	4	24
Sex	1502	0.50	0.50	0	1
Age groups	1502	2.17	0.77	1	3
Household Income	1418	1.84	0.80	1	3
Education	1502	2.51	0.61	1	3
Municipality size	1502	2.36	0.71	1	3
Employed	1502	0.75	0.43	0	1
Internet User	1502	2.85	0.42	1	3
Ideology	1502	2.32	1.30	1	5
Institutional trust	1502	2.79	2.29	0	10
Campaign attention	1502	2.21	0.85	1	4
Protest participation	1502	0.16	0.37	0	1
Member pressure group	1502	0.08	0.27	0	1
Boycotting/Buycotting	1502	0.45	0.50	0	1
Electoral turnout	1499	0.89	0.31	0	1
Party voted (ref. Podemos & allies)					
_PP	1291	0.14	0.35	0	1
_PSOE	1291	0.13	0.34	0	1
_Ciudadanos	1291	0.16	0.37	0	1
_Izquierda Unida	1291	0.08	0.26	0	1
_Other minority	1291	0.12	0.33	0	1

Results

We study the determinants of the level of digital activism in election campaigns. In the first specifications we include only the predictors related to institutional participation and the sociodemographic controls (Models 1–2, Table 2). While in Model 1 we incorporate a dummy on electoral turnout, we include a multinomial variable in Model 2, taking electoral support for Podemos (and its confluences in Catalonia, Galicia and Comunitat Valenciana) as the baseline category. Turning out to vote seems to have a positive impact on the level of online activism (Model 1, Table 2). Relative to voting for Podemos (and its allies), we observe a negative association between opting for traditional forces (PP, PSOE) and Ciudadanos (Model 3, Table 2).[4] Coefficients for voting IU or other minor parties relative to Podemos and allies are not significant.

When controlling for political attitudes and values, the effects of electoral turnout vanish (Model 3, Table 2). Self-declaring as a right-wing individual decreases online activism. Greater confidence in political institutions, and especially paying attention to the electoral campaign, and more frequent use of Internet are positively associated with the level of online political participation (Models 2–5, Table 2). Likewise, the effects of extra-institutional political behavior (i.e., attending to protests and rallies, belonging to a pressure group, and engaging in boycotts/buycotts) are strong and robust (Models 4–5, Table 2).

On the one hand, the regression analyses show a robust, statistically significant, and positive association between non-electoral offline participation and the degree of political involvement in the digital public sphere. Specifically, the value on the scale for a person who has not participated in demonstrations or protests is 5.22, keeping the rest of the constant predictors adjusted to their means. Conversely, if the respondent has participated in a demonstration or protest, the prediction on the digital activism frequency scale is 6.83 (Figure 1).

In a similar way, the predicted value of the digital political activism scale fluctuates between 5.28 and 7.69, depending on whether the person belongs to a political pressure group, *ceteris paribus* (Figure 1). The value on the digital activism frequency scale changed from 5.19 to 5.84 if they have bought or have stopped buying products for ethical or political reasons. On the other hand, the predicted value of the digital activism scale remains constant regardless of whether or not the respondent turned out to vote and regardless of his or her electoral preferences (Figures 1 and 2).[5]

Discussion

We compared the extent to which levels of digital political participation could be predicted by people's offline participation. The results were clear: *online* political participation functions as a complement not dissociable from *offline* participation, and electoral mobilization as an extension as the individual's extra-institutional participation. Although our results are not counter-intuitive nor do they contradict this line of thought, they do allow us to qualify previous findings, as not every form of offline political participation works as a determinant of online activism. Amid high levels of polarization and electoral mobilization, especially following the electoral emergence of new left-wing and movement-related parties such as Podemos that increased fragmentation, one could expect that electoral turnout in general (and voting for Podemos and allies in particular) would be associated with increased levels of online activism.

Table 2. OLS regressions with robust standard errors, DV: Digital Activism Scale.

	Model 1		Model 2		Model 3		Model 4		Model 5	
	Coef.	S.E.	Coef.	S.E.	Coef.	S.E.	Coef.	S.E.	Coef.	S.E.
Sex	−0.30	0.16	0.02	0.15	0.09	0.16	−0.03	0.13	0.02	0.15
Age groups	−0.12	0.10	−0.09	0.09	−0.01	0.10	−0.13	0.08	−0.08	0.09
Household Income	0.02	0.11	−0.11	0.10	−0.16	0.10	−0.15	0.09	−0.21	0.09
Education	0.14	0.13	−0.00	0.12	−0.07	0.13	−0.06	0.10	−0.09	0.12
Municipality size	0.15	0.11	−0.01	0.10	−0.04	0.11	−0.05	0.09	−0.08	0.10
Employed	−0.30	0.20	−0.10	0.18	−0.05	0.20	−0.06	0.16	−0.02	0.18
Internet User	0.62***	0.16	0.39*	0.15	0.59*	0.15	0.41*	0.14	0.63*	0.14
Ideology			−0.22***	0.06			0.00	0.05		
Institutional trust			0.09*	0.04	0.11*	0.04	0.07*	0.03	0.09*	0.04
Campaign attention			1.33***	0.09	1.33***	0.11	1.08***	0.08	1.05***	0.09
Protest participation							1.61***	0.26	1.53***	0.26
Member pressure group							2.41***	0.37	2.44***	0.39
Boycotting/Buycotting							0.64***	0.13	0.63***	0.14
Electoral turnout	1.02***	0.23	0.07	0.21			−0.07	0.19		
Party voted (ref. Podemos & allies)										
_PP					−0.84**	0.26			−0.14	0.24
_PSOE					−0.60*	0.28			−0.12	0.24
_Ciudadanos					−0.93***	0.19			−0.25	0.18
_Izquierda Unida					0.16	0.31			0.13	0.26
_Other minority					−0.03	0.31			−0.08	0.29
Constant	1.02***	0.23	8.01***	0.74	7.44***	0.72	6.71***	0.66	6.08***	0.66
N	1233		1233		1060		1233		1060	
Adj. R^2	0.0351		0.2133		0.2039		0.3668		0.3596	

*$p < 0.05$; **$p < 0.01$; ***$p < 0.001$.

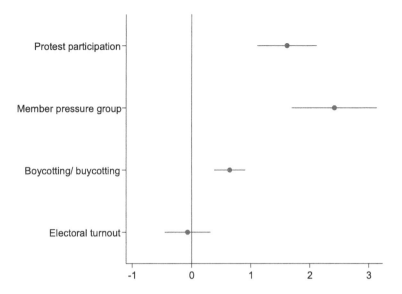

95% C.I.

Figure 1. Marginal effects of offline political participation (protest participation, member of pressure group, boycotting/ boycotting, and electoral turnout) on digital political activism scale (Model 4, Table 2).

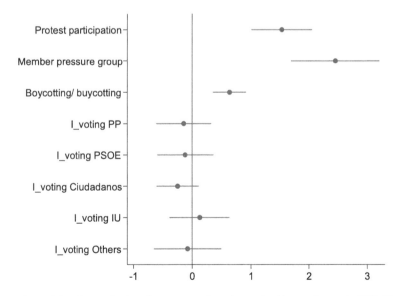

Multinomial voting spells: baseline category is Podemos (and its confluences). 95% C.I.

Figure 2. Marginal effects of offline political participation (protest participation, member of pressure group, boycotting/ boycotting, and voting spells) on digital political activism scale (Model 5, Table 2).

Contending with this approach, our results show that only the least formal and least conventional forms of offline political participation account for the frequency of digital political activism. Neither electoral turnout nor partisan preferences are relevant predictors of the general level of online activism, as their effect is concealed by extra-institutional political engagement such as protesting, pressure group membership and having boycotted/buycotted. In fact, these three explanatory variables are, along with political interest, the most relevant predictors in the models, strengthening the hypothesis that online political participation is connected to offline participation and can be interpreted as an extension of it.

Our results support Hypothesis 3 (to the detriment of H.1/H.2). Participation in offline extra-institutional political activities determines level of online political engagement more strongly than party preferences, in line with the observations of Dahlgren (2011) and Hoffmann and Lutz (2015). The individual's digital learning processes accumulated over the months and years (as a form of cultural capital) are transferred to his/her partisan activism during the electoral campaign. It is true that activists are increasingly aware and conscious of the mediation opportunity structure, being able to adapt to, appropriate, and develop media and communication practices (Cammaerts, 2012). Moreover, the changes produced in the field of social movements in the last decade seem to be transferring in new patterns in the digital participation during the electoral campaigns.

Notwithstanding limitations emerging from single-case studies, our results lead to important implications for other scenarios. Extra-institutional activists may be contributing to the surge of political challengers (Jungherr et al., 2019) and populist candidates (Groshek & Koc-Michalska, 2017), as empirical evidence from several countries testifies. Specifically, extra-institutional activists' over-representation in the generation and diffusion of political content within their parties may be increasing the visibility of more polarized messages in social media than those designed by the party elites, leading to a more polarized debate discussion among the party members themselves. This, in turn, may have contributed to the success of political challengers in several countries, including the United States, Germany, and China (see Jungherr et al., 2019).

The results add to the current state of the reflection on how digital technology can act as a driver of political change. As Jungherr et al. (2019) point out, while some have described digital media as an instrument that deterministically disrupts existing structures of political power (Gerbaudo, 2018; Margetts et al., 2015), others have referred to the role of technology in enlarging control by incumbents in the form of political elites (Gohdes, 2020; Howard, 2005; Robles & Córdoba-Hernández, 2019). As Tucker et al. (2017) suggest, this division may emerge as a sort of historical stage model of technology that starts by serving outsiders to defy the political elites, followed by a time in which the status quo readjusts and the same technologies are used to avert this defiance.

Our argument emphasizes the importance of extra-institutional grassroots activists both in the emergence of challengers as well as in the efforts of political elites to counter these challenges. In the latter case, the status quo will tend to develop co-optation (e.g., Gunitsky, 2015) or surveillance/repression mechanisms (e.g., Gohdes, 2020), due to the key importance of these actors in the political debate in the digital sphere. In the first stage, outsider candidates will try to persuade grassroots activists to support them, as a central strategy for their digital campaigns. This is the case of the UK Labour Party leader, Jeremy Corbyn (Dennis, 2019), and the three outsider candidates who challenged their parties in pursuit of the US Presidential nomination in the last years, Barack Obama (Katz et al., 2013), Bernie Sanders (Penney, 2017) and Donald Trump (Gervais & Morris, 2018).

In this vein, the remarkable higher digital political activity of extra-institutional activists *in all* parties observed in our results may help to explain observations in other contexts. These activists may be favoring messages of more radical candidates, polarizing the discourse of their own parties, away from the traditional discourse of the party elites. Groshek and Koc-Michalska (2017) noted that voters more active in social media showed higher levels of support for populist candidates in the 2016 US election campaign, but they found no support that ideologically constrained flows of information (*filter bubbles*) were related to increasing the likelihood of higher support for populist candidates; conversely, they found that greater heterogeneity actually increased the probability of endorsing specific (populist) candidates, both in the Republican and the Democratic side.

How could social media favor polarization in an environment of greater heterogeneity of political opinions? A grassroots-driven increasing polarization *within* each party may induce reactive polarization *outside* them. Experimental evidence shows that exposure to opposite messages on social networks increases the political polarization of individuals, particularly among conservatives (Bail et al., 2018), adding to the effects of the selective exposure and the principle of homophily in social media. Therefore, an increase of political polarization within a party due to the action of extra-institutional grassroots activists would induce an increase of political polarization in rival parties, particularly on those voters exposed to a higher level of information heterogeneity in social media. Given the increasing polarization that emerge for most political parties across countries, the role of digital activism as a determinant of political polarization will be an important avenue of inquiry.

Finally, our cross-sectional correlational study cannot demonstrate causality. It will require some other type of approaches and empirical evidence (e.g., experimental). Even though the endogeneity hypothesis cannot be fully ruled out, it does not preclude the fact that our rationale holds – and the findings in our article are robust and relevant.[6] Incorporating controls in multivariate designs also helps us to weigh our argument against alternative explanations.

Conclusions

The current study is useful in sharpening our understanding of digital political activism during electoral processes. Participation in extra-institutional forms of political involvement (e.g., protest participation, boycotting/ boycotting, and being a member of a pressure group) increases digital political activism, concealing the effect of electoral preferences on digital participation. Our results connect with the theory of normalization and the emergence of a post-material culture in political parties.

Digital technologies do not substantially change the patterns of political involvement but reinforce pre-existing structures and inequalities (Bimber, 2000; Dahlgren, 2005), blurring the separation between offline and online participation. The expansion of social media has weakened the power of political elites. However, this shift in the opportunity structure has not been seized equally by all individuals but mainly by those with greater participation in extra-institutional forms of political engagement. Importantly, this pattern is observed irrespective of electoral turnout and within *all* political parties.

Our findings might help understand the surge of populist candidates (Groshek & Koc-Michalska, 2017) and political outsiders (Jungherr et al., 2019). In short, rather than being determined by homophily, political polarization in social media might be determined by grassroots driven-polarization within each party. This mechanism can help explain the increase in polarization in contexts where social media induces an environment of greater heterogeneity of political opinions (Bail et al., 2018). Our results confirm that extra-institutional grassroots activists have become central actors of new political intermediations in the digital public sphere (Howard, 2005; Lobera & Sampedro, 2018), affecting all parties during the electoral campaigns. Decentralized activist participation and their influence through new information and communication technologies could under certain conditions 'hack' the official campaign, potentially forcing the campaign leaders to hybridize or adapt their initiatives to the activists' proposals.

Are political parties therefore being forced into a process of uncartelization? Not necessarily. The decentralization processes of electoral communication that we observe in our analysis is currently compensated for by the political parties through several re-centralizing strategies. These aim to recover the central influence of the political party on the new logic of decentralized digital activism. The changes in the digital sphere lead to an increasing tension between the centripetal tools of the political parties and the decentralizing dynamics of digital activists.

This tension is particularly salient during election campaigns. In societies with acute political conflict, the activity of extra-institutional activists will be greater (both in relative and absolute terms), and the effect of the preference falsification—suggested by Mutz (2006) as a fundamental intermediating factor between levels of online polarization and readiness to engage in political action—will diminish.

Notes

1. This established polling agency counts 'with more than 1,300,000 panelists in over 23 countries around the world' (see Netquest, 2019). Specifically, for Spain they have a large enough sample of 157,916 panelists, with an average response rate of 50-55% (Netquest, 2019). Panel members are recruited from a host of different sources, including standard advertising, strategic partnerships with websites, and so on. When a new panel member is recruited, Netquest records a host of socio-demographic information. For nationally representative samples, it draws a sub-sample of the panel that is representative in terms of a number of socio-demographic features, inviting this sub-sample to complete the survey.
2. We have built three alternative indices. First, instead of a cumulative index, we calculate a weighted average of the nine indicators. Second, we have created a simple additive scale based on the individual 1–6 scales (potential range: 6-54). Third, depending on the degree of online activist participation, we have distinguished between three groups within the simple additive scale (low, medium and high, which correspond to 39.5%, 35.5% and 25% of the observations, respectively). We have reproduced our statistical models with these three alternative dependent variables, and the overall findings are robust.
3. The histogram in the Appendix I shows the dependent variable is not normally distributed (Figure A1). The data are strongly skewed to the right. Further evidence confirms overdispersion. The latter happens provided the conditional variance exceeds the conditional mean. We run a test of the overdispersion parameter alpha. As alpha is significantly different from zero, we conclude that the Poisson distribution is not the most suitable modeling strategy. Although our measures are not discrete, the structure of our dependent variable is similar

to event counts, hence we replicate all models with negative binomial specifications in the Appendix I (Table A1).
4. We have excluded the ideological self-identification variable in Models 3 and 5 due to multi-collinearity concerns.
5. If using negative binomial regressions instead of OLS specifications with robust standard errors, these results remain unchanged (see Appendix I, Table A1; Figures A1 and A2).
6. In addition to the analyses reported here, we ran preliminary statistical analyses inverting the relationship of dependency between the key variables. While digital activism seems to be positively associated with electoral turnout, it vanishes when controlling for institutional trust and campaign attention. Similarly, while the effect of activism seems to be positively associated with voting for Podemos and allies— relative to voting for any other party—, it vanishes when controlling for extra-institutional participation. Consistent with the normalization approach, the effects from online political activism on offline political participation are far from robust, thus going against the reverse causality hypothesis.

Acknowledgements

An earlier draft of this article was presented at the 'Social Movements and Parties in a Fractured Media Landscape' symposium, at the Scuola Normale Superiore in Florence on 1–2 July 2019. We would like to thank all the participants, Dan Mercea, Lorenzo Mosca and Lorenzo Zamponi for their feedback, help, and support throughout the process. We would also like to offer special thanks to Víctor Sampedro, who has inspired this research and has secured funding for the fieldwork on which this work is based. We are also grateful to the anonymous reviewers and the editors of the journal for their constructive comments on our work.

Disclosure statement

No potential conflict of interest was reported by the author(s).

Funding

This work was supported by Secretaría de Estado de Investigacion, Desarrollo e Innovacion [grant number CSO2013-48612-C2-1-P].

ORCID

Josep Lobera ⓘ http://orcid.org/0000-0002-0620-6312
Martín Portos ⓘ http://orcid.org/0000-0003-1714-6383

References

Anduiza, E., Cantijoch, M., & Gallego, A. (2009). Political participation and the Internet: A field essay. *Information, Communication & Society*, *12*(6), 860–878. https://doi.org/10.1080/13691180802282720

Anduiza, E., Gallego, A., & Cantijoch, M. (2010). Online political participation in Spain: The impact of traditional and Internet resources. *Journal of Information Technology & Politics*, *7*(4), 356–368. https://doi.org/10.1080/19331681003791891

Atton, C. (2004). *An alternative Internet*. Edinburgh University Press.

Bail, C. A., Argyle, L. P., Brown, T. W., Bumpus, J. P., Chen, H., Fallin Hunzaker, M. B., Lee, J., Mann, M., Merhout, F., & Volfovsky, A. (2018). Exposure to opposing views on social media can increase political polarization. *Proceedings of the National Academy of Sciences*, *115*(37), 9216–9221. https://doi.org/10.1073/pnas.1804840115

Bang, H. P., & Sørensen, E. (1999). The everyday Maker: A New challenge to democratic Governance. *Administrative Theory & Praxis*, *21*(3), 325–341. https://doi.org/10.1080/10841806.1999.11643381

Bazurli, R., & Portos, M. (2019). Crook! The impact of perceived corruption on non-electoral forms of political behavior. *International Political Science Review*, https://doi.org/10.1177/0192512119881710

Beck, U. (1997). Subpolitics: Ecology and the disintegration of institutional power. *Organization & Environment*, *10*(1), 52–65. https://doi.org/10.1177/0921810697101008

Bennett, W. L. (1998). The uncivic culture: Communication, identity, and the rise of lifestylepolitcs. *PS: Political Science & Politics*, *31*(4), 741–761. https://doi.org/10.1017/S1049096500053270

Bennett, W. L., & Segerberg, A. (2012). The logic of connective action. *Information, Communication & Society*, *15*(5), 739–768. https://doi.org/10.1080/1369118X.2012.670661

Best, S. J., & Krueger, B. S. (2005). Analyzing the representativeness of internet political participation. *Political Behavior*, *27*(2), 183–216. https://doi.org/10.1007/s11109-005-3242-y

Bimber, B. (2000). The study of information technology and civic engagement. *Political Communication*, *17*(4), 329–333. https://doi.org/10.1080/10584600050178924

Bimber, B. (2002). *Information and American democracy: Technology in the evolution of political power*. Cambridge University Press.

Cammaerts, B. (2012). Protest logics and the mediation opportunity structure. *European Journal of Communication*, *27*(2), 117–134. https://doi.org/10.1177/0267323112441007

Casero-Ripollés, A., Feenstra, R. A., & Tormey, S. (2016). Old and new media logics in an electoral .campaign: The case of Podemos and the two-way street mediatization of politics. *The International Journal of Press/Politics*, *21*(3), 378–397. https://doi.org/10.1177/1940161216645340

Castells, M. (2015). *Networks of outrage and hope: Social movements in the Internet age* (2nd ed). Polity Press.

Chadwick, A. (2013). *The hybrid media system: Politics and power*. Oxford University Press.

Chadwick, A., & Stromer-Galley, J. (2016). Digital media, power, and democracy in parties and election campaigns: Party decline or party renewal? *The International Journal of Press/Politics*, *21*(3), 283–293. https://doi.org/10.1177/1940161216646731

Costanza-Chock, S. (2014). *Out of the shadows, into the streets! Transmedia organizing and the immigrant rights movement*. The MIT Press.

Couldry, N., & Curran, J. (2003). The paradox of media power. In N. Couldry, & J. Curran (Eds.), *Contesting media power: Alternative media in a networked world* (pp. 3–15). Rowman & Littlefield.

Dahlgren, P. (2005). The Internet, public spheres, and political communication: Dispersion and deliberation. *Political Communication*, *22*(2), 147–162. https://doi.org/10.1080/10584600590933160

Dahlgren, P. (2011). Young citizens and political participation online media and civic cultures. *Taiwan Journal of Democracy*, 7(2), 11–25. http://www.tfd.org.tw/export/sites/tfd/files/publication/journal/dj0702/002.pdf

Dalton, R. J. (2007). *The good citizen. How a younger generation is reshaping American politics*. CQ Press.

della Porta, D., Fernández, J., Kouki, H., & Mosca, L. (2017). *Movement parties against austerity*. Polity Press.

della Porta, D., & Mosca, L. (2005). Global-net for global movements? A network of networks for a movement of movements. *Journal of Public Policy*, 25(1), 165–190. https://doi.org/10.1017/S0143814X05000255

Dennis, J. (2019). A party within a party posing as a movement? Momentum as a movement faction. *Journal of Information Technology & Politics*, 1–17. https://doi.org/10.1080/19331681.2019.1702608

Earl, J., & Kimport, K. (2011). *Digitally enabled social change: Activism in the internet age*. MIT Press.

Feezell, J. T. (2016). Predicting online political participation: The importance of Selection Bias and selective exposure in the online setting. *Political Research Quarterly*, 69(3), 495–509. https://doi.org/10.1177/1065912916652503

Fernández-Albertos, J. (2015). *Los votantes de Podemos: Del partido de los indignados al partido de los excluidos*. Catarata.

Font, N., Graziano, P., & Tsakatika, M. (2019). Varieties of inclusionary populism? SYRIZA, Podemos and the five Star movement. *Government and Opposition*, 1–21. https://doi.org/10.1017/gov.2019.17

Gerbaudo, P. (2018). *The digital party. Political organisation and online democracy*. Pluto Press.

Gervais, B. T., & Morris, I. L. (2018). *Reactionary republicanism: How the tea party in the house paved the way for Trump's Victory*. Oxford University Press.

Gibson, R., Lusoli, W., & Ward, S. (2005). Online participation in the UK: Testing a 'contextualised' model of Internet effects. *British Journal of Politics and International Relations*, 7(2), 561–583. https://doi.org/10.1111/j.1467-856x.2005.00209.x

Gibson, R., & Ward, S. (2000). *Reinvigorating democracy? British politics and the Internet*. Ashgate.

Gohdes, A. R. (2020). Repression technology: Internet accessibility and state violence. *American Journal of Political Science*, https://doi.org/10.1111/ajps.12509

Groshek, J., & Koc-Michalska, K. (2017). Helping populism win? Social media use, filter bubbles, and support for populist presidential candidates in the 2016 US election campaign. *Information, Communication & Society*, 20(9), 1389–1407. https://doi.org/10.1080/1369118X.2017.1329334

Gunitsky, S. (2015). Corrupting the cyber-commons: Social media as a tool of autocratic stability. *Perspectives on Politics*, 13(1), 42–54. https://doi.org/10.1017/S1537592714003120

Gunther, R. (2010). The Spanish Model Revisited. In D. Muro, & G. Alonso (Eds.), *The politics and memory of democratic transition: The Spanish model* (pp. 17–40). Routledge.

Hara, N. (2008). Internet use for political mobilization: Voices of participants. *First Monday*, 13(7), https://doi.org/10.5210/fm.v13i7.2123

Hoffmann, C.P., & Lutz, C. (2017, July 28–30). *Spiral of Silence 2.0: Political self-Censorship among Young Facebook users*. Proceedings of the 8th International Conference on social media & society, ACM, p. 10.

Hoffmann, C. P., & Lutz, C. (2015). The impact of online media on stakeholder engagement and the governance of corporations. *Journal of Public Affairs*, 15(2), 163–174. https://doi.org/10.1002/pa.1535

Howard, P. N. (2005). Deep democracy, thin citizenship: The impact of digital media in political campaign strategy. *The ANNALS of the American Academy of Political and Social Science*, 597(1), 153–170. https://doi.org/10.1177/0002716204270139

Jungherr, A., Schroeder, R., & Stier, S. (2019). Digital media and the surge of political outsiders: Explaining the success of political challengers in the United States, Germany, and China. *Social Media+ Society*, 5(3), https://doi.org/10.1177/2056305119875439

Katz, J., Barris, M., & Jain, A. (2013). *The social media president: Barack Obama and the politics of digital engagement*. Palgrave Macmillan.

Katz, R. S., & Mair, P. (2009). The cartel party thesis: A restatement. *Perspectives on Politics, 7*(4), 753–766. https://doi.org/10.1017/S1537592709991782

Kavada, A. (2015). Creating the collective: Social media, the occupy movement and its constitution as a collective actor. *Information, Communication & Society, 18*(8), 872–886. https://doi.org/10.1080/1369118X.2015.1043318

Kioupkiolis, A. (2019). Late modern adventures of leftist populism in Spain. In G. Katsambekis, & A. Kioupkiolis (Eds.), *The populist radical left in Europe* (pp. 47–72). Routledge.

Kitschelt, H. (2006). Movement parties. In R. S. Katz, & W. J. Crotty (Eds.), *Handbook of party politics* (pp. 278–290). Sage.

Klandermans, B., van Stekelenburg, J., Damen, M. L., van Troost, D., & van Leeuwen, A. (2014). Mobilization without organization: The case of unaffiliated demonstrators. *European Sociological Review, 30*(6), 702–716. https://doi.org/10.1093/esr/jcu068

Kraut, R., Lundmark, V., Patterson, M., Kiesler, S., Mukopadhyay, T., & Scherlis, W. (1998). Internet paradox: A social technology that reduces social involvement and psychological well-being? *American Psychologist, 53*(9), 1017–1031. https://doi.org/10.1037/0003-066X.53.9.1017

Kriesi, H. (2014). The populist challenge. *West European Politics, 37*(2), 361–378. https://doi.org/10.1080/01402382.2014.887879

Lisi, M. (2018). Party innovation, hybridization and the crisis: The case of Podemos. *Italian Political Science Review, 49*(3), 245–262. https://doi.org/10.1017/ipo.2018.20

Lobera, J. (2019). Anti-austerity movements in Europe. In C. F. Fominaya, & R. Feenstra (Eds.), *Routledge handbook European social movements. Protest in turbulent times* (pp. 267–283). Routledge.

Lobera, J. (2020). Migrants and 'patria'. The imagined community of the radical left in Spain. *Teknokultura, 17*(1), 59–68. https://doi.org/10.5209/tekn.66912

Lobera, J., & Parejo, D. (2019). Streets and institutions? The electoral extension of social movements and its tensions. In R. Kinna, & U. Gordon (Eds.), *Routledge handbook of radical politics* (pp. 314–325). Routledge.

Lobera, J., & Sampedro, V. (2018). New intermediations of the electoral information flows: Changes in the digital public sphere in election campaigns in Spain (2008–15). *Social Science Information, 57*(4), 553–572. https://doi.org/10.1177/0539018418820239

Mair, P., & Van Biezen, I. (2001). Party membership in twenty European democracies, 1980–2000. *Party Politics, 7*(1), 5–21. https://doi.org/10.1177/1354068801007001001

Margetts, H., John, P., Hale, S., & Yasseri, T. (2015). *Political turbulence: How social media shape collective action*. Princeton University Press.

Martínez, G. (2012). *CT o la Cultura de la Transición: crítica a 35 años de cultura española*. Debolsillo.

McAdam, D., & Tarrow, S. G. (2010). Ballots and barricades: On the reciprocal relationship between elections and social movements. *Perspectives on Politics, 8*(2), 529–542. https://doi.org/10.1017/S1537592710001234

Micó, J. L., & Casero-Ripollés, A. (2014). Political activism online: Organization and media relations in the case of 15-M in Spain. *Information, Communication & Society, 17*(7), 858–871. https://doi.org/10.1080/1369118X.2013.830634

Morales, L. (2005). ¿Existe una crisis participativa? La evolución de la participación política y el asociacionismo en España. *Revista Española de Ciencia Política, 13*, 51–87. https://recyt.fecyt.es/index.php/recp/article/view/37411/20928

Mosca, L., & Quaranta, M. (2017). Voting for movement parties in Southern Europe: The role of protest and digital information. *South European Society and Politics, 22*(4), 427–446. https://doi.org/10.1080/13608746.2017.1411980

Mutz, D. C. (2006). *Hearing the other side: Deliberative Versus participatory democracy*. Cambridge University Press.

Netquest. (2019). *Netquest Panel Book*, https://www.netquest.com/panel/sample-calculator#panel-book

Norris, P. (2011). *Democratic Deficit: Critical citizens Revisited*. Cambridge University Press.
Panebianco, A. (1988). *Political parties: Organization and power*. Cambridge University Press.
Penney, J. (2017). Social media and citizen participation in "official" and "unofficial" electoral promotion: A structural analysis of the 2016 Bernie Sanders digital campaign. *Journal of Communication*, *67*(3), 402–423. https://doi.org/10.1111/jcom.12300
Pirro, A. L. P., & Portos, M. (2020). Populism between voting and non-electoral participation. *West European Politics*, 1–27. https://doi.org/10.1080/01402382.2020.1739451
Portos, M. (2019). Keeping dissent alive under the great recession: No-radicalisation and protest in Spain after the eventful 15M/*indignados* campaign. *Acta Politica*, *54*(1), 45–74. https://doi.org/10.1057/s41269-017-0074-9
Postill, J. (2012). Digital politics and political engagement. In H. Horst, & D. Miller (Eds.), *Digital anthropology* (pp. 165–184). Berg.
Putnam, R. D. (1995). *Bowling Alone: The Collapse and Revival of American community*. Simon & Schuster.
Ramiro, L., & Gomez, R. (2017). Radical-left populism during the great recession: Podemos and Its competition with the established radical left. *Political Studies*, *65*(1_suppl), 108–126. https://doi.org/10.1177/0032321716647400
Rheingold, H. (2000). *The virtual community: Homesteading on the electronic frontier* (2nd ed). MIT Press.
Robles, J. M., & Córdoba-Hernández, A. M. (2019). *Digital political participation, social networks and Big data: Disintermediation in the Era of Web 2.0*. Palgrave Macmillan.
Rodríguez-Teruel, J., Barrio, A., & Barberà, O. (2016). Fast and furious: Podemos' quest for power in multi-level Spain. *South European Society and Politics*, *21*(4), 561–585. https://doi.org/10.1080/13608746.2016.1250397
Schulz, W. (2014). Mediatization and New media. In F. Esser, & J. Strömbäck (Eds.), *Mediatization of politics: Understanding the transformation of Western democracies* (pp. 57–73). Palgrave Macmillan.
Shirky, C. (2008). *Here comes everybody: The power of organizing without organizations*. Penguin.
Sproull, L. S., & Kiesler, S. B. (1991). *Connections: New ways of working in the networked organization*. MIT Press.
Suh, C. S., Vasi, I. B., & Chang, P. Y. (2017). How social media matter: Repression and the diffusion of the Occupy Wall Street movement. *Social Science Research*, *65*, 282–293. https://doi.org/10.1016/j.ssresearch.2017.01.004
Torcal, M. (1995). *Actitudes políticas y participación política en España. Pautas de cambio y continuidad* [Doctoral dissertation]. Universidad Autónoma de Madrid. https://repositorio.uam.es/handle/10486/130981
Toret, J. (2015). Una mirada tecnopolítica al primer año de Podemos. Seis hipótesis. *Revista Teknokultura*, *12*(1), 121–135. https://doi.org/10.5209/rev_TK.2015.v12.n1.48889
Tormey, S. (2015). *The End of Representative politics*. Polity Press.
Tucker, J. A., Theocharis, Y., Roberts, M. E., & Barberá, P. (2017). From liberation to Turmoil: Social media and democracy. *Journal of Democracy*, *28*(4), 46–59. https://doi.org/10.1353/jod.2017.0064
Ward, S., & Gibson, R. (2009). European political organizations and the internet. In A. Chadwick, & P. N. Howard (Eds.), *Routledge handbook of Internet politics* (pp. 25–39). Routledge.
Wellman, B., Quan Haase, A., Witte, J., & Hampton, K. (2001). Does the Internet increase, decrease, or supplement social capital? Social networks, participation, and community commitment. *American Behavioral Scientist*, *45*(3), 436–455. https://doi.org/10.1177/00027640121957286
Wells, C. (2015). *The civic organization and the digital citizen: Communicating engagement in a networked age*. Oxford University Press.
Wilson, R. (ed.). (2006). *Post party politics: Can participation reconnect citizen and government*. Involve.

Appendices

Appendix I

Table A1. Negative binomial regressions, DV: Digital Activism Scale

	Model 1		Model 2		Model 3		Model 4		Model 5	
	Coef.	S.E.	Coef.	S.E.	Coef.	S.E.	Coef.	S.E.	Coef.	S.E.
Sex	−0.06*	0.03	0.00	0.03	0.01	0.03	−0.01	0.03	−0.01	0.03
Age groups	−0.02	0.02	−0.01	0.02	0.01	0.02	−0.02	0.02	−0.01	0.02
Household Income	0.00	0.02	−0.02	0.02	−0.03	0.02	−0.03	0.02	−0.04	0.02
Education	0.03	0.02	−0.00	0.02	−0.01	0.02	−0.01	0.02	−0.02	0.02
Municipality size	0.03	0.02	−0.00	0.02	−0.01	0.02	−0.01	0.02	−0.01	0.02
Employed	−0.05	0.03	−0.01	0.03	−0.01	0.03	−0.01	0.03	−0.00	0.03
Internet User	0.12**	0.04	0.08*	0.03	0.12**	0.04	0.08*	0.03	0.12**	0.04
Ideology			−0.04***	0.01			−0.00	0.01		
Institutional trust			0.02**	0.01	0.02**	0.01	0.01*	0.01	0.02**	0.01
Campaign attention			0.25***	0.02	0.24***	0.02	0.20***	0.02	0.19***	0.02
Protest participation							.24***	.03	.23***	.03
Member pressure group							.31***	.04	.31***	.04
Boycotting/Buycotting							.12***	.03	.12***	.03
Electoral turnout	0.21***	0.05	0.03	0.05			0.00	0.04		
Party voted (ref. Podemos & allies)										
_PP					−0.15**	0.04			−0.03	0.04
_PSOE					−0.10*	0.04			−0.02	0.04
_Ciudadanos					−0.17***	0.04			−0.05	0.04
_Izquierda Unida					0.03	0.05			0.03	0.05
_Other minority					−0.00	0.05			−0.00	0.04
Constant	1.13***	0.15	2.10***	0.14	1.99***	0.15	1.87***	0.14	1.77***	0.15
N	1233		1233		1060		1233		1060	
Adj. R^2	0.0090		0.0572		0.0539		0.0948		0.0919	

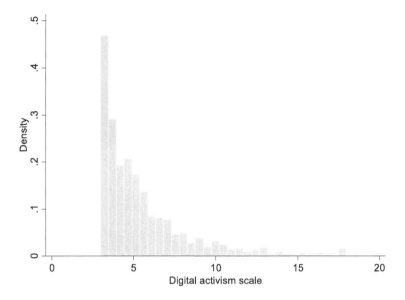

Figure A1. Histogram dependent variable (Digital Activism Scale).

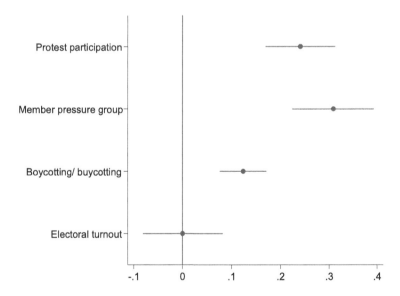

95% C.I.

Figure A2. Marginal effects of offline political participation (protest participation, member of pressure group, boycotting/ boycotting, and electoral turnout) on digital political activism scale (Model 4, Table A1).

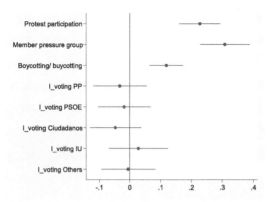

Multinomial voting spells: baseline category is Podemos (and its confluences). 95% C.I.

Figure A3. Marginal effects of offline political participation (protest participation, member of pressure group, boycotting/ buycotting, and voting spells) on digital political activism scale (Model 5, Table A1).

Appendix II: questionnaire and operationalization.

- Age groups: 1 = 30 years-old or less; 2 = 30-45 years-old; 3 = +45 years-old
- Household income: 1 = 1,200€ per month or less; 2 = 1,201-2,400€ per month; 3 = +2,400€ per month
- Education: 1 = primary; 2 = secondary; 3 = tertiary
- Municipality size: 1 = 10,000 inhabitants or less; 2 = 10,001-100,000 inhabitants; 3 = +100,000 inhabitants
- Internet user: 1 = 'sometimes every month' or less; 2 = 'several times a week'; 3 = 'daily'
- Ideology: 0 = extreme 'left', 5 = extreme 'right'
- Institutional trust: 0 = 'fully mistrust'; 10 = 0 = 'fully trust'
- Campaign attention: 1 = 'none'; 2 = 'little'; 3 = 'quite'; 4 = 'a lot'

Are digital platforms potential drivers of the populist vote? A comparative analysis of France, Germany and Italy

Lorenzo Mosca and Mario Quaranta

ABSTRACT

Populist parties are often argued to be very skilled in using digital media to attract supporters and strengthen linkages with their followers. However, only rarely has research shown this linkage empirically. This study explores whether arguments about the relation between digital platforms and populist voting can be substantiated using comparative survey data in France, Germany and Italy. Digital media include a variety of online platforms that can affect populist vote in different ways. This article addresses the relation between the *political use* of digital platforms and the populist vote. First, it looks at how the use of Social Networking Sites (SNS) and Mobile Instant Messaging Services (MIMS) is related to voting for populist parties. Second, it assesses whether the role of digital platforms is different for supporting digital 'immigrant' and digital 'native' populist parties. Third, it explores country differences in the relation between SNS and MIMS' use and the populist vote. Using original online surveys, the article shows that political activities on SNS and MIMS platforms (sending messages or posting, discussing or convincing others to vote for a candidate) increase the probability of voting for populist parties. However, it also finds that the political use of digital media is associated with the populist vote under certain (and limited) circumstances, that is only for a subset of populist parties. Finally, it identifies important differences in how SNS and MIMS are linked to the populist vote in countries presenting diverse institutional features, web regulations and constellations of media systems.

Introduction

Digital media have been said to greatly contribute to the emergence and success of the populist parties shaking the European party systems (Kriesi, 2014). Online platforms have often been considered natural allies of outsider parties challenging traditional parties and the mainstream media, which they accuse of being spokespersons for the establishment (Bennett & Pfetsch, 2018; Jungherr et al., 2019). Indeed, most populist parties appear very skilled at using digital media to attract supporters and strengthen linkages with their followers.

Despite the enduring relevance of the legacy media, in the hybrid media system an important slice of citizens' knowledge of political affairs comes from digital media. Online opportunities for populist actors are, however, not a property of the web as a whole, but they change according to contextual characteristics (Jungherr et al., 2019) as well as the diffusion, use and affordances of different online platforms. Therefore, we posit that diverse online media outlets provide different opportunities for political actors to spread their messages, affecting citizens' likelihood of voting for populist parties, and we analyse this link in France, Germany and Italy. In this article, we distinguish between Social Networking Sites (SNS) and Mobile Instant Messaging Services (MIMS). While the relation between the former and populist actors has become an important topic of discussion in the scientific debate, the role of MIMS in political communication has seldom been addressed (Valeriani & Vaccari, 2018). Furthermore, a systematic comparison of the association between the political use of SNS and MIMS and the vote for populist parties with varying characteristics in different countries is lacking.

We believe this gap in the literature should be addressed for several reasons. First, the increasing strength of populist parties can be related to recent changes affecting media systems. Digital media allow these actors to establish a direct link with people who often feel marginalized by traditional media (Gerbaudo, 2018). However, only rarely has research shown this linkage empirically. Therefore, this study explores whether often-made statements about the link between digital media – in our case, the political use of SNS and MIMS – and populist voting can be substantiated using comparative survey data. We follow the literature which argues that digital media favour populist parties and their support to demonstrate whether its claims hold. Second, existing research has focused on the internet and SNS without seriously envisioning different affordances of diverse platforms. MIMS tend to work as hybrids between mass and interpersonal communication channels, allowing users greater intimacy, like-mindedness and expression of emotions than SNS. Therefore, it might be possible that the two means work differently in relation to the populist vote. Third, in generically linking the populist vote and digital platforms, differences between parties we label 'digital natives' vs 'digital immigrants' have not been considered. Indeed, the former might be more attentive to digital media than the latter in their use of them for political campaigning. Fourth, such differences have not been systematically assessed in a comparative perspective but generally using single case-studies. In contrast, our study aims to explore these relationships in three European countries – France, Germany and Italy – which present different institutional features, web regulations and constellations of media systems, by means of original post-electoral online surveys.

Our findings show that the political use of digital platforms is associated with the populist vote. There are, however, some important nuances to take into consideration. First, the political use of SNS and MIMS seems to affect the populist vote differently, a finding that is supported by somewhat counterintuitive evidence. Second, 'newer' populist parties that have originated in the last decade effectively benefit from digital platforms while 'older' ones do not, and this might suggest that the 'digital' nature of such parties could be a crucial feature for their attractiveness of voters who use more the internet for political information and participation. Third, the strength of this relation varies across countries, with Italy displaying a greater association, Germany a lesser one and France resulting between these two countries. Therefore, the arguments about the affinity between digital media and populist support seems to hold empirically only for specific cases, at least according to our data.

Theoretical framework

The literature has shown that activity on SNS and MIMS can stimulate offline political participation (Boulianne, 2015). These platforms are argued to ease the collection of political information from several sources – from family or friends to mainstream or alternative media sources – which might in turn be used for political mobilization (Gil de Zúñiga et al., 2012). In particular, the political use of the internet is argued to have a positive effect on participation because it represents an interactive way of communicating, which in turn produces a feeling of accessibility to politics (Kruikemeier et al., 2014).

Digital platforms and the populist vote

The concept of populism, although contested, revolves around the contrast between the 'pure' people, who should hold sovereignty, and the 'corrupt' elite, which do not act in the interest of the former group (Mudde, 2004). Another conceptualization of populism sees it more as a 'communication style' (Jagers & Walgrave, 2007) which leaders use to connect with the people without intermediaries and spread their messages (Gerbaudo, 2018). Therefore, it is worth exploring whether digital platforms, such as SNS and MIMS, provide opportunities for populist parties' communication and attract voters.

We argue that populist parties have an advantage in the online environment vis-à-vis traditional political parties. Digital media allow populist actors to avoid traditional gatekeepers (i.e., journalists), establish direct connections with the people and keep an antagonistic stance with the mainstream parties and media (Engesser et al., 2017; Kriesi, 2014). Moreover, the interactive features of the web generate new chances for users to be involved in decision-making, as it is an environment echoing the direct democracy claims which are often at the core of populist discourse (Mudde, 2004). Eventually, digital platforms vehiculate anti-elitist content that is often unverified or false which tends to favour populist leaders (Guess et al., 2018).

In sum, according to Gerbaudo (2018) there is an 'elective affinity' between online platforms and populism. In fact, they are seen to give representation to the voiceless who are marginalized by mainstream media. Moreover, they allow the creation of groups of like-minded disaffected individuals that can be mobilized against the 'enemies of the people.' Both these features are particularly resounding with populist actors, who tend to deplore the mainstream media as the voice of the establishment and far from the concerns of common people. Specularly, it should be underlined that the features of digital media tend not to advantage the mainstream parties, as they prefer to establish good relationship with mainstream media, do not contest them, and tend to rely on 'facts' in their communication, avoiding spreading information on social media which may hinder their reputation (Schaub & Morisi, 2019).

With the rise of the internet, research has devoted much attention on the relationship between the use of digital tools and political behaviour and attitudes (Zhuravskaya et al., 2020), and also populism, although to a much lesser extent (Heiss & Matthes, 2017). Most of the available literature linking social media use and populist voting applies a 'supply-side' approach to explaining why the former could affect the latter. The general argument is that the internet and/or social media platforms facilitate the spreading of the messages of populist parties and leaders and that using them or being active on them exposes individuals to such messages (Zhuravskaya et al., 2020), which might, in turn, increase the likelihood of voting for these actors. A study by Groshek and Koc-Michalska (2017) argues that social media use – in particular active use (as posting, sharing, campaigning, forwarding content) in contrast to passive use (as receiving information) – may be linked to an increasing support for populist candidates. The study demonstrates that using Facebook and Twitter was related to an increased likelihood of supporting populist presidential candidates in the 2016 American primary elections. Focusing on the 2016 Trump campaign, Baldwin-Philippi (2019) proves the ability of populists to centre 'the people' through various digital platforms and strategies. Cremonesi and colleagues (2019) show that social media use is positively associated with populist attitudes in Italy.

Only few studies have instead looked into the 'demand-side,' that concerns the reasons why voters use platforms and how such use might be driven by partisanship. Regarding the first aspect, studies have shown that individuals with populist attitudes tend to use more frequently information coming from the internet (Newman et al., 2019; Schulz, 2019), trust less quality media and more commercial or tabloid media (Pew Research, 2018) and also selectively avoid the websites of legacy press media when surfing the internet (Stier et al., 2020). Despite a clear gap in the literature, the linkage between populist attitudes and trust in different media outlets (Fawzi, 2019) provides important indications concerning the relationship between the former and social media platforms. Since platforms are privately owned and driven by profit-seeking goals, they share important characteristics with commercial media. Accordingly, citizens with a populist worldview may be more prone to use them compared with non-populist citizens as they perceive these platforms as weapons in the hands of 'the good people' against 'the corrupt elite.'

In-between the two approaches, Hameleers (2018) claimed that what he calls 'populist mass-self communication' manifests itself at the intersections of the supply-side and the demand-side, since on social media platforms 'all actors can simultaneously and interchangeably take on the role of a sender and receiver of populist ideas' (p. 2178). This makes particularly complicate to clarify the causal order of the relationship between digital information and voting choices. However, recent research has tackled the issue of the direction of such an association, providing robust evidence that digital media use affects populist attitudes or voting, and not the other way around. Schumann and colleagues (2019) show that more frequent use of social media increases the likelihood of voting for populist radical right parties in Germany, showing that there is no evidence of reverse causation. Dealing with a similar problem, Schaub and Morisi (2019) address the issue of causality in the relationship between internet use and populist voting in Italy and Germany, and provide compelling evidence that the former affect the latter, and not the opposite.

Different platforms and the populist vote

Previous research on the opportunities provided by digital media for populist communication does not usually distinguish between different platforms. The extant research generally looks at internet or social media use in general, without considering other digital platforms when studying populist voting. In contrast, we consider the affordances respectively provided by SNS and MIMS in populist communication. Because of the impossibility of summarizing a lengthy and ongoing debate, we rely on the following definition of *affordance*: 'what various platforms are actually capable of doing and perceptions of what they enable, along with the actual practices that emerge as people interact with platforms' (Kreiss et al., 2018, p. 19).

As already mentioned, SNS have been found to be ideal platforms for personalized communication connecting leaders with followers, and there is growing evidence on their link with populist attitudes or support. However, while SNS have rapidly become one of the interests of media studies, consideration of MIMS and their potential contribution to political communication has been limited, at least in western European countries. MIMS are in fact one of the main tools for political propaganda in the Global South (i.e., Africa, Latin America, South-East Asia), where mobile phones can be the only available devices to access the internet (Balbi & Magaudda, 2018). Nonetheless, as we will discuss below, some interesting aspects of MIMS may help explain their political use in Western countries too, especially that by populist actors.

When comparing SNS and MIMS, it should be noticed that while the latter have been developed for, and are mostly used on, mobile devices (but desktop versions are also available), the former tend to be accessed from different types of hardware. Building on Bossetta's taxonomy (2018), we compare SNS and MIMS in Table 1. *Searchability* refers to the opportunities afforded by a platform to single out new accounts and access their contents. Unlike SNS, where politicians can easily create public pages that can be liked or followed by users, this feature can only be found on some MIMS (i.e., Messenger and Telegram) but not on WhatsApp, where new contacts cannot be searched for and added within the platform. *Filtering* governs how content is displayed to users and how the latter interact with the platform's features. While contents sorted on SNS tend to be filtered, MIMS just displays content chronologically. *Reach* describes the visibility of a post across the stream of contents on SNS. Whilst non-paid Facebook posts only reach a tiny minority of users, MIMS messages are always directly delivered to the addressee. Whereas *targeting* allows focusing on audiences that can be persuaded or mobilized, *analytics* permits monitoring and extracting data, which are used to modify campaigning in real time. Encryption seriously limits datafication in the case of WhatsApp, while secure communication is not set by default in Telegram and Messenger but can be enabled by the user. Consequently, SNS and MIMS can be located at the two extremes of a continuum since most of the above-mentioned characteristics are

Table 1. Main differences between SNS and MIMS.

Platform	Searchability	Filtering	Reach	Sophistication of targeting/analytics
SNS	High–medium	High	Low	High–medium
MIMS	Medium–low	Low	High	Low

Source: Own adaptation from Bossetta (2018).

particularly advanced on the former while they may only be present in a rudimentary way on the latter.

Undoubtedly, the features of SNS make them formidable tools for political campaigning. Apparently, the basic qualities of MIMS make them more suitable for interpersonal communication. However, some specific qualities of MIMS may make them interesting platforms for political communication, too. Comparing four different platforms, Waterloo and colleagues find that expressions of positive and negative emotions are more likely on WhatsApp compared to more public platforms, concluding that 'more private spaces in which one can communicate with a specific close friend allow for looser norms of emotion expression' (2018, p. 1827). Moreover, Dodds (2019) notices that this platform facilitates intimacy and trust between journalists and sources and also comradery and mutuality between different journalists. MIMS allow the creation of small homogeneous groups that, unlike SNS, tend to be characterized by stronger ties. For example, WhatsApp requires personal phone numbers to establish a connection. Consistently, it is perceived as a more personal/intimate medium and used to cultivate homophile relations among people sharing similar political views (Valeriani & Vaccari, 2018). While Telegram allows the creation of 'supergroups' with thousands of members, groups on WhatsApp and Messenger can only include up to 250 members. However, they can be scaled up and go viral. The possibility of forwarding messages circulating in groups to personal contacts and other groups potentially expands their audience exponentially.

In sum, messages circulating via MIMS are generally sent from trusted and known contacts and they directly reach users' devices. Compared to SNS, messages circulated through MIMS may have a greater impact as they are distributed from reliable and known sources. Because of these characteristics, MIMS can be conceived as 'a unique combination of mass and interpersonal communication channels' (Malka et al., 2015, p. 329). This original mix may facilitate more effective communication as it is based on the exchange of sensitive messages that would be less likely to surface on SNS. Furthermore, as populist communication is heavily based on emotions (Engesser et al., 2017), MIMS appear particularly suited to spreading and amplifying passionate messages among intimate and trustworthy networks. In this light, being active users of SNS or MIMS could be differently related to political choices, such as voting for populist parties. This is because the logic of such platforms assumes activity rather than passivity, which in turn may favour forms of offline participation, as voting for populist candidates or parties which are not well depicted by mainstream media (see Groshek & Koc-Michalska, 2017). Based on the above-mentioned literature, we formulate the following research questions:

(RQ1a) Does the political use of SNS and MIMS increase the chances of voting for a populist party compared to mainstream parties?
(RQ1b) Do the greater intimacy, like-mindedness and emotionality afforded by MIMS increase the chances of voting for a populist party more than SNS do?

'Digital native' vs 'digital immigrant' parties

We cannot classify populist parties in the countries included in the analysis along the left-right continuum because some of them – such as the Five Star Movement (in Italy) – present an eclectic ideology 'combining contradictory or elusive visions on policy issues crosscutting traditional cleavages' (Mosca & Tronconi, 2019, p. 1277). In addition, what unites left and right populist parties is that they share an ideology positing that society is divided in two groups – the 'corrupt elites' and the 'pure people' – and that the general will should be pursued in politics (Mudde, 2004, p. 543). In Europe, populism is often associated with the 'right' and with what comes with it – xenophobic politics, nationalism or opposition to multiculturalism – while populist traits can be found in a variety of actors, including on the 'left' (van Kessel, 2015, p. 2). Furthermore, what also unites left and right populist parties is the dimension of political communication. It has been argued that a different way of identifying populist parties is to apply a conception of populism as a 'strategy' or a 'style' which these actors employ to create a bond with voters (Jagers & Walgrave, 2007). Populist parties, on both sides, make use of communication emphasizing a link between the leader and the people (Gerbaudo, 2018), and in this regard Reinemann and colleagues argue that 'populist political communication should be restricted neither to the left nor to the right of the political spectrum' (2017, p. 14).

An alternative way to distinguish populist parties is to consider their date of foundation. The economic crisis of 2008 can be understood as a turning point in European politics for two distinct reasons: first, increased economic inequalities generated 'a notable but uneven surge [of populist parties] during crisis' (Pappas & Kriesi, 2015, p. 322); and second, because the spread of SNS and MIMS reached its peak in Europe at the end of that decade, i.e., 2010s (Chadwick, 2013). Therefore, we assume that parties founded during the Great Recession can be considered 'digital natives,' which naturally embed digital platforms in their everyday organization. On the contrary, populist parties that emerged before the economic crisis and the spread of digital media may be labelled 'digital immigrants,' adapting to digital technologies with much more caution, lagging behind in the process of adapting to new means of communication. We are aware that this generational juxtaposition is one of the myths surrounding digital media (Livingstone, 2017) and could be misleading. Nonetheless, similar arguments have been proposed, among others, by Karpf (2012) who notices that 'there are important generational differences between the ways that netroots and legacy organizations use information technology' (p. 18). A path-dependency of organizational cultures (Pettigrew, 1979) could in fact explain different patterns of digital media adoption by diversely-aged parties. According to Gerbaudo (2019), traditional parties are very careful about using digital platforms and consider mainstream media their main campaigning ground, while new-founded ones fully employ digital media both for external communication and for internal decision-making. Accordingly, we formulate the following research question:

(RQ2) Does the political use of SNS and MIMS increase the probability of voting for 'new' rather than 'old' populist parties compared to mainstream parties?

Digital platforms in context

Regarding differences in the countries selected that may affect the use and the role of digital platforms in supporting the populist vote, we can briefly refer to institutional features, the characteristics of party systems, the configuration of media systems and the regulation of internet contents. Compared to the other two countries, the German party system is characterized by greater stability combined with much more stringent web regulation (see Caiani & Parenti, 2013 and also the recent law on hate speech), a lower spread of SNS and a public sphere where newspapers still play an important role compared to digital media. In fact, 78% of Germans watch TV while 50% read the press and 32% use SNS.[1] Germans are very trustful of traditional media and distrustful of digital ones (70% for TV, 70% for newspapers and 17% for SNS, respectively). All these features may act as barriers to the effectiveness of populist communication on digital media. From this point of view, Italy is in an opposite situation as it displays a very unstable party system (Chiaramonte & Emanuele, 2017), limited regulation of internet contents (Caiani & Parenti, 2013) and a TV-centred public sphere associated with widespread use of digital media. TV is watched daily by 90% of Italians, while newspapers are read by 26%, and SNS are used by 37%. Comparatively, Italians tend to display less trust in all kinds of media (56% for TV, 60% for newspapers and 19% for SNS, respectively). France occupies an intermediate position between polarized pluralist countries (e.g., Italy) and democratic-corporatist countries (e.g., Germany) (Hallin & Mancini, 2004). France also presents important institutional differences such as semi-presidentialism, which could potentially act as a very powerful driver of personalization and the political use of digital platforms. This effect might, however, be balanced by the fact that our data refer to the 2017 legislative election and not a presidential one. Regarding media use, TV is watched by 77%, newspapers are read by 26% and SNS used by 40%. These media are trusted by 63%, 71% and 27%, respectively.[2] Compared to the EU average, Germany displays higher trust in traditional media and lower trust in digital ones, Italy displays lower trust in all media sources while France is located between the two other countries. Accordingly, we expect a stronger relation between the use of SNS and MIMS and the populist vote in Italy than in Germany, where digital media are less diffused and not very trusted. We do not have particular expectations regarding France because of the above-mentioned ambivalence, which has already been highlighted in previous studies. Consistently, we suggest the following research question:

(RQ3) Does the political use of SNS and MIMS increase the probability of voting for populist parties in Italy compared to Germany?

Research design

Data

We test our expectations using three original Computer Assisted Web Interviewing (CAWI) post-election surveys conducted in France (20 June 2017–9 July 2017), Germany (25 September 2017–2 October 2017) and Italy (5 March 2018–28 March 2018). For each country, samples of 1750 internet users aged 18–74 years were collected.[3] The samples are representative of the adult population with internet access and are based on quota sampling using age, gender, employment status, education and region of residence. Our surveys were designed to be comparable in terms of both modes of data collection and questionnaires, providing us with an opportunity to test the link between SNS and MIMS political use and the populist vote in different contexts.

Dependent variable

The dependent variable distinguishes voting choices in five categories: (a) voting for mainstream parties; (b) voting for populist parties; (c) voting for other parties (smaller parties with or without representation in national parliaments, or indicated by the respondents in response to an open-ended question); (d) abstainers; and (e) a residual category including spoilt votes, unidentifiable vote choices, ineligible voters and missing information.

There is quite considerable debate on how to classify populist parties (van Kessel, 2015). We consider the following parties to be populist: *Front National* (National Front) and *La France Insoumise* (France Unbowed) in France; *Alternative für Deutschland* (Alternative for Germany) and *Die Linke* (The Left) in Germany; *Lega* (The League) and the *Movimento 5 Stelle* (Five Star Movement) in Italy. This classification follows recent research on populist parties which attempts to categorise these actors according to a number of characteristics: the salience of the contrast between people and the elite, with one being seen in a positive and the other in a negative light; the idea that the people are part of a homogeneous group and that their interests should be defended against those of the elite; and popular sovereignty (Mudde, 2004; van Kessel, 2015). These characteristics constitute a minimal definition of populism and therefore we stress that additional characteristics which narrow the definition have not been considered.[4]

To address the second research question, we separate parties founded in the twentieth century, such as *Front National*, *Die Linke* and *Lega* (the 'old,' or 'digital immigrant,' populist parties), from those born during the Great Recession such as *La France Insoumise*, *Alternative für Deutschland* and *Movimento 5 Stelle* (the 'new,' or 'digital native,' populist parties). The former three parties were indeed founded much before the spread of digital media. The *Front National* was founded in 1972 and despite its long history and changes, it is still considered a 'classic populist party' (Surel, 2019). *Die Linke*, although founded in 2007, is a direct descendant of the post-1989 Party of Democratic Socialism, and thus it has its roots well before the 2010s decade and cannot be considered a 'genuinely new party' (Wuttke, 2020). The *Lega* was founded in 1991 and is the oldest party in the Italian political system. While its current leader, Matteo Salvini, has imprinted important changes to its organization, the *Lega* still presents the look of a traditional party (Biancalana, 2020). In contrast, *La France Insoumise* was founded in 2016 declaring itself being a populist party (Marlière, 2019). *Alternative für Deutschland* was founded in 2013 as a consequence of the financial, migration and Brexit crises hitting Germany (Lees, 2018). Eventually, the *Movimento 5 Stelle* is the oldest among the selected 'new' populist parties as it was founded in 2009, yet this party from the beginning of its history mainly used the internet as a means of communication (Mosca et al., 2015).

Independent variables

The independent variables of interest are two additive scales measuring comparable activities on SNS (such as Facebook, Twitter and YouTube) and MIMS (such as WhatsApp, Facebook Messenger, Telegram and the like). In the first case, we used dichotomous items asking the respondents whether or not in the previous 12 months, when using SNS, they: (a) sent a tweet to, or commented on, a post by a national party leader, politician or party; (b) discussed national political issues or the [last] general election; and (c) tried to convince someone to vote for a specific party leader, candidate or party. In the second case, respondents were asked whether or not in the previous 12 months, when using MIMS, they: (a) sent messages about politics, public affairs or the [last] general election; (b) discussed politics, public affairs or the [last] general election; (c) tried to convince someone to vote for a specific candidate or party. We applied a Mokken scale analysis to assess the reliability of the two scales (Van Schuur, 2003). The Loevinger's H for the SNS and the MIMS scales is 0.55 and 0.67 respectively, which indicates that both are strong. These are similar if we assess the scales for each country. Therefore, we built two summary indices measuring the political use of SNS and MIMS from 0 (no use) to 3 (full use).[5] We should underline that these scales capture the political use of SNS and MIMS and not the exposure to political information or the frequency by which political information is acquired. Nevertheless, it can be argued that being active on such platforms is the result of exposure to political information and messages (see Fletcher & Nielsen, 2018; Lee & Xenos, 2020) which might come from populist actors. Indeed, our strategy is in line with the literature arguing that the political use of social media platforms matters more than simple use for populist voting (see for instance Groshek & Koc-Michalska, 2017).

Controls

The models include a variable classifying respondents in four groups depending on the frequency with which they use media – whether 'traditional' (TV and newspapers) and/or 'digital' (internet and SNS) (Mosca & Quaranta, 2016) – for political information: (a) those who make infrequent use of both media; (b) those who prevalently use traditional media; (c) those who prevalently use digital media; and (d) those who frequently use both. The literature also shows that political (dis)trust is related to support for anti-establishment/populist parties (Schumacher & Roodujin, 2013). We use an index of political distrust measuring whether respondents are very confident, confident, not very confident or not at all confident in parties, government and parliament.[6] We then include other variables found to be important to the vote choice: political interest measured on a scale ranging from 1 (not at all interested) to 4 (very interested) and the left-right scale in categories (the reference category 'not located on the left-right scale/missing' and 'radical left,' 'left,' 'centre,' 'right' and 'radical right'). We also include gender, education (the reference category 'low' and 'medium' and 'high'), age (the reference category '18–24' and '25–34,' '35–44,' '45–54' and '55–74') and employment status (the reference category 'not employed' and 'employed'). Finally, we include country dummies to control for country heterogeneity.

Models

We use multinomial models to address the research questions. First, we include all the independent variables. With this model, we assess the expectation that political activities on SNS and MIMS are related to the populist vote. We then include, one at a time, interaction terms between the political activity scales and the country dummies. This allows us to assess whether the associations between political activity and the populist vote are heterogeneous across countries. Given that the coefficients of multinomial models are hard to interpret, especially in the presence of interaction terms (Long, 1997), we use average marginal effects.

Findings

Figure 1 shows the average marginal effects of SNS and MIMS political use on the probability of each vote choice.[7] The left-hand panel shows that an increase of one point on the SNS activity scale increases the probability of voting for a populist party by about three percentage points (henceforth p.p.) ($p \leq 0.001$). In contrast, SNS activity is not associated with the probability of voting for mainstream parties. Also, SNS activity is not associated with abstention or with other party choices. Another interesting finding is that the marginal effects of SNS activity on the probability of voting for populist and mainstream parties are different. In fact, a one-point increase on the SNS activity scale increases the probability of voting for a populist party vs a mainstream party by about 4.4 p.p. ($p \leq 0.001$). Therefore, this online political activity seems to be relevant to understanding the choice to vote for a populist party in contrast to mainstream ones. The right-hand panel shows the associations between MIMS use and the populist vote. In this case, we notice that political activities are only associated positively with the probability of voting for populist parties. A one-point increase on the scale corresponds to an increase in the probability of voting for a populist party of about 1.7 p.p. ($p \leq 0.05$). Instead, these political activities on MIMS are not associated with other vote choices. As before, we notice that there is a statistically significant difference between the marginal effects of MIMS activities on populist and mainstream vote choices. In fact, a one-point increase on the MIMS scale increases the probability of voting for a populist party vs a mainstream party by about 3 p.p. ($p \leq 0.05$).

These findings provide evidence addressing RQ1a and show that political activity on SNS and MIMS is associated with a populist vote rather than a mainstream vote. This implies that these forms of political activity and the related instruments may favour an exchange of information among individuals that tend to avoid expressing themselves politically in public, given that their ideas might be controversial or non-mainstream, like those of populist party supporters, and so find the digital space provided by SNS and

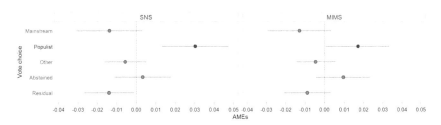

Figure 1. The average marginal effects of using SNS and MIMS for political activity on the probability of voting for mainstream or populist parties or making other vote choices, with 95% confidence intervals.

MIMS more comfortable for their political expression (Valeriani & Vaccari, 2018; Wojcieszak, 2010). Moreover, 'unlike legacy media, social media are built upon the logic of virality, which compels political actors to communicate primarily those messages that users like, comment on, promote, and share within their networks' (Ernst et al., 2017, p. 1349). However, we find that the role of MIMS is smaller than that of SNS as far as the populist vote is concerned, contrasting with RQ1b.

What about the effects of SNS and MIMS political use on voting for populist parties once we distinguish between 'old' and 'new' ones? To address this question, we turn our attention to Figure 2 which shows the average marginal effects of the two scales measuring activity on the probability of making the various vote choices. As before, we see that while the role of SNS and MIMS political use is not positively associated with other vote choices, it seems to be relevant to voting for 'new' populist parties but not for 'old' ones. In fact, a one-point increase on the SNS and MIMS use scales corresponds to increases in the probability of voting for 'new' populist parties of about 2.8 p.p. ($p \leq 0.000$) and 1.3 p.p. ($p \leq 0.05$) respectively. Furthermore, if we compare the roles of SNS and MIMS use in voting for 'old' or 'new' vs mainstream parties, we find that using SNS or MIMS does not increase the probability of voting for 'old' populist parties with respect to mainstream parties. Instead, using SNS and MIMS increases the probability of voting for 'new' populist parties vs mainstream parties by 4.2 p.p. ($p \leq 0.001$) and 2.6 p.p. ($p \leq 0.05$), respectively. These results seem to indicate that 'new' populist parties benefit more from digital media use, answering RQ2.

We now address RQ3, which asks whether there are country differences in the associations between SNS and MIMS political use and voting for populist parties. Figure 3 shows the average marginal effects of SNS and MIMS political use on the probability of voting for populist or mainstream parties in the three countries.[8] We see that an association between SNS political use and the populist vote is not present in all countries. In fact, in France and Italy a one-point increase on the SNS scale corresponds to increases in the probability of voting for populist parties of 3.4 ($p \leq 0.01$) and 4 p.p. ($p \leq 0.01$) respectively, while in Germany the association is not statistically significant. Regarding MIMS use, we notice that this association is only significant in Italy (3.8 p.p., $p \leq 0.01$), while in France and Germany it is not.

Finally, we explore the same differences while distinguishing between 'old' and 'new' populist parties. The average marginal effects are reported in Figure 4. Regarding the role of SNS use, in no country is this variable associated with the probability of voting for 'old'

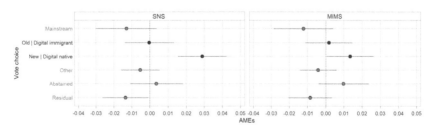

Figure 2. The average marginal effects of using SNS and MIMS for political activity on the probability of voting for mainstream, 'old' – 'digital immigrant' – or 'new' – 'digital native' – populist parties or making other vote choices, with 95% confidence intervals.

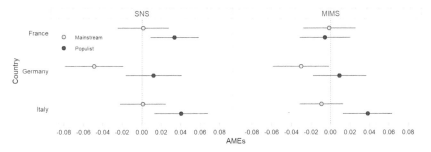

Figure 3. The average marginal effects of using SNS and MIMS for political activity on the probability of voting for mainstream or populist parties in France, Germany and Italy, with 95% confidence intervals.

populist parties, while in France and Italy it is associated with the probability of voting for 'new' populist parties but not in Germany. In fact, in France SNS use increases the probability of this vote choice by 2.6 p.p. ($p \leq 0.01$) and in Italy by 4.9 p.p. ($p \leq 0.000$). This finding suggests that also other factors might be at play in the relationship between SNS use and the populist vote, that have to do with the characteristics of *France Insoumise* and the *Movimento 5 Stelle*. Indeed, both parties have been labelled as 'digital parties.' As noted by Gerbaudo (2019) 'the term digital party attempts to capture the common essence seen across a number of quite diverse political formations that have risen in recent years, and which share the common attempt of using digital technology to devise new forms of political participation and democratic decision-making' (p. 7). They might attract voters more accustomed with digital platforms. Indeed, the above-mentioned parties introduced digital innovations allowing supporters and members to be more involved in their everyday life. There might thus be a special relationship between the voters who use SNS as a tool of political information and parties, such as these ones, which emphasize the role of digital platforms in politics. Nevertheless, this relationship seems to hold only for a subset of populist parties, so it cannot be generalized beyond these cases. Lastly, the role of MIMS use across the three countries is like that seen above: the variable is only associated with voting for 'new' populist parties in Italy (3.5 p.p., $p \leq 0.010$).

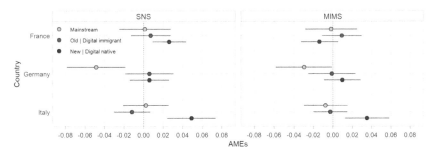

Figure 4. The average marginal effects of using SNS and MIMS for political activity on the probability of voting for mainstream, 'old' – 'digital immigrant' – or 'new' – 'digital native' – populist parties in France, Germany and Italy, with 95% confidence intervals.

Conclusion

To summarize, the empirical analysis has shown a relation between the political use of SNS and MIMS and populist voting, providing support to many scholarly claims (RQ1a). However, we have found that SNS use increases the likelihood of voting for populist parties more than MIMS use (RQ1b). This disconfirms our argument, which was built on the greater degree of intimacy afforded by MIMS vis-à-vis SNS. In this concluding section, we can only advance a tentative interpretation of this unexpected result.

First, because of financial constraints and restricted technical skills of their staff, populist parties (especially in Western countries) may be more inclined to invest in and concentrate their limited resources on SNS rather than MIMS. Second, since SNS tend to be visited by users for a longer period during the day than MIMS, the visibility of populist parties and leaders may be perceived to be greater on such platforms, pushing them to look after their presence there more. Third, because of interdependency mechanisms typical of hybrid media systems (Chadwick, 2013), contents published on SNS (often used by journalists as information sources) have a greater possibility of travelling 'from the desktop to the television screen' than those on MIMS (Bennett, 2003, p. 164). There are then potential indirect benefits in being present on SNS that are less likely to exist on MIMS since the virality and metrics of SNS contents can prove very important in attracting traditional media coverage (Klinger & Svensson, 2015).

Regarding our second research question (RQ2), we have only found partial evidence that digital media tend to only favour populist parties. In fact, only some of the parties we called 'digital natives' seem to benefit more from the political use of SNS and MIMS than 'older' populist parties, which have a longer history and originated in a different landscape where traditional media were absolutely dominant and central. In fact, out of three parties we classified as 'digital natives' only two display a clear relation with the political use of SNS and only one with the political use of MIMS. Accordingly, we should take into consideration alternative explanations downplaying the generational differences between the populist parties included in our study while focusing on their digital nature. From this point of view, we can notice that while *Alternative für Deutschland* is certainly very skilled in the use of social media (Serrano et al., 2019), differently from *La France Insoumise* and *Movimento 5 Stelle* the development of participatory platforms to involve its supporters in the life of the party is lacking. Unfortunately, our survey did not ask about the use of such platforms nor allows us to explore this relation in other digital parties active in the countries we considered.[9] From this point of view, the differences emerged between the populist parties we addressed could be related to the digital nature of these parties and the actual involvement of their supporters in their digital platforms.

Finally, we addressed country-specific differences with our third research question (RQ3). Our findings show that the relation between the political use of digital media and populist voting varies significantly across France, Italy and Germany. While Italy displays a stronger influence of SNS and MIMS on the populist vote, this relation is lighter in France and only holds for SNS, and it completely disappears in Germany for both types of platforms. As stated above, differences in institutional features, media systems and web regulations help interpreting this outcome. In a reinforcing pattern, government surveillance and concerns about privacy are culturally sensitive issues in Germany (Valeriani & Vaccari, 2018) coupled with a comparatively tougher regulation of the web, a less widespread use of digital media and a greater role of traditional media in the national media system. The Italian case could be put at Germany's antipodes: a relatively deregulated digital environment, wider diffusion of digital media and a lower degree of trust in different media outlets coupled with a very fragile and volatile party system (Chiaramonte & Emanuele, 2017) which is particularly open to challengers. The case of France – where SNS are relevant in influencing the populist vote but MIMS are not – is located between Italy and Germany, confirming Hallin and Mancini's classification (2004) of the country as one displaying a media system mixing features of the continental and Mediterranean types, to which Germany and Italy respectively belong.

Last, it is worth noticing that digital platforms are moving targets, which makes any observation provisional and highly subject to the passing of time. Because of the continually changing nature of SNS and MIMS, it is extremely difficult to study and interpret the linkage between digital platforms and the populist vote. For example, in recent times more constraints on the use of WhatsApp as a tool for political propaganda have been enacted by the application of the European General Data Protection Regulation (May 2018) and by the imposition of stricter limits on the forwarding function (from 20 to 5 recipients) by the platform itself to contrast the spread of fake news, thus reducing the virality of contents circulating on the platform and shifting it towards being a more private messaging app. Even stricter measures have been implemented as consequence of the Covid-19 crisis. To test how the platform works when the focus moves from popularity to contents, Instagram has recently hidden 'like' counts in a selected group of countries. Facebook might soon follow 'the like ban,' perhaps reducing the importance of virality for these platforms and their attractiveness in the eyes of traditional media outlets.

Despite ongoing changes in the platform ecosystem, our contribution seems to confirm the importance of digital media for a new breed of populist parties and shows, however, a pivotal role of SNS, a lighter but significant role of MIMS, the importance of contextual national characteristics in magnifying or limiting this linkage and the relevance of the features of the specific parties considered. Of course, the analysis shown here presents limitations that are related to the cross-sectional design of our surveys and the scope of the comparison. Thus, future research should look further into the link between digital media use and populist voting addressing such problems.

To conclude, it is worth mentioning that this study has some limitations that should be addressed in future research. Indeed, the measurement of the political use of SNS and MIMS does not allow us to assess the extent to which individuals find populist messages via selective or incidental exposure, thus directly affecting their voting preferences. That being said, it is also important to stress that research on the relation between the use of digital media and populist attitudes suffers from a clear myopia on the demand-side which needs to be seriously addressed in future studies. Despite this evident imbalance between supply and demand of populist ideas we believe roles of senders and receivers are increasingly blurred. While the reasons why populist actors tend to rely on digital platforms have been clarified, the motivations pushing citizens to use them needs to be further substantiated. One reason for this could be that digital platforms generate unconstrained and safe places where diverse actors can freely consume, share and exchange ideas that tend to be silenced in traditional media outlets (Hameleers, 2018). Further research is needed to shed light on this complex intertwining.

Notes

1. Standard Eurobarometer no. 88 (Autumn 2017) and Eurobarometer no. 464 (April 2018).
2. Data on access to and trust in different media outlets in the three countries are reported in the online appendix.
3. Due to rounding in the construction of the sample, 1751 internet users were interviewed in France. The models are estimated after list-wise deletion of missing values for the selected variables of interest (as also reported in Table A4 in the online appendix).
4. The classification of other voting choices is reported in the online appendix.
5. We report the estimates from additional models excluding from the scales the items measuring discussion in the online appendix. We do so as such items might be less close to the sphere of institutional politics. Results are consistent with those presented here.
6. Cronbach's alpha is 0.87 (similar scores are found in the separate samples).
7. The estimates of the models are reported in the online appendix.
8. The estimates of the models are reported in the online appendix. We omit the associations between SNS and MIMS use and other vote choices from the discussion.
9. For example, only nine respondents declared their vote for the German Pirate party in our survey.

Disclosure statement

No potential conflict of interest was reported by the author(s).

ORCID

Lorenzo Mosca http://orcid.org/0000-0002-3248-0489
Mario Quaranta http://orcid.org/0000-0003-4056-8998

References

Balbi, G., & Magaudda, P. (2018). *A history of digital media. An intermedia and global perspective*. Routledge.
Baldwin-Philippi, J. (2019). The technological performance of populism. *New Media & Society*, 21(2), 376–397. https://doi.org/10.1177/1461444818797591
Bennett, W. L. (2003). Communicating global activism. *Information, Communication & Society*, 6(2), 143–168. https://doi.org/10.1080/1369118032000093860a
Bennett, W. L., & Pfetsch, B. (2018). Rethinking political communication in a time of disrupted public spheres. *Journal of Communication*, 68(2), 243–253. https://doi.org/10.1093/joc/jqx017
Biancalana, C. (2020). Four Italian populisms. In P. Blokker, & M. Anselmi (Eds.), *Multiple populisms. Italy as democracy's mirror* (pp. 216–241). Routledge.
Bossetta, M. (2018). The digital architectures of social media: Comparing political campaigning on Facebook, Twitter, Instagram, and Snapchat in the 2016 U.S. Election. *Journalism & Mass Communication Quarterly*, 95(2), 471–496. https://doi.org/10.1177/1077699018763307

Boulianne, S. (2015). Social media use and participation: A meta-analysis of current research. *Information, Communication & Society*, 18(5), 524–538. https://doi.org/10.1080/1369118X.2015.1008542

Caiani, M., & Parenti, L. (2013). *European and American extreme right groups and the internet*. Ashgate.

Chadwick, H. (2013). *The hybrid media system*. Oxford University Press.

Chiaramonte, A., & Emanuele, V. (2017). Party system volatility, regeneration and de-institutionalization in Western Europe (1945–2015). *Party Politics*, 23(4), 376–388. https://doi.org/10.1177/1354068815601330

Cremonesi, C., Bobba, G., Legnante, G., Mancosu, M., Roncarolo, F., & Seddone, A. (2019). Political information exposure and populist attitudes in the laboratory of populism. An exploratory analysis of the 2018 Italian general election campaign. *Comunicazione Politica*, 1, 39–62. https://doi.org/10.3270/93028

Dodds, T. (2019). Reporting with WhatsApp: Mobile chat applications' impact on journalistic practices. *Digital Journalism*, 7(6), 725–745. https://doi.org/10.1080/21670811.2019.1592693

Engesser, S., Ernst, N., Esser, F., & Büchel, F. (2017). Populism and social media: How politicians spread a fragmented ideology. *Information, Communication & Society*, 20(8), 1109–1126. https://doi.org/10.1080/1369118X.2016.1207697

Ernst, N., Engesser, S., Büchel, F., Blassnig, S., & Esser, F. (2017). Extreme parties and populism: An analysis of Facebook and Twitter across six countries. *Information, Communication & Society*, 20(9), 1347–1364. https://doi.org/10.1080/1369118X.2017.1329333

Fawzi, N. (2019). Untrustworthy news and the media as 'enemy of the people?' How a populist worldview shapes recipients' attitudes toward the media. *The International Journal of Press/Politics*, 24(2), 146–164. https://doi.org/10.1177/1940161218811981

Fletcher, R., & Nielsen, R. K. (2018). Are people incidentally exposed to news on social media? A comparative analysis. *New Media & Society*, 20(7), 2450–2468. https://doi.org/10.1177/1461444817724170

Gerbaudo, P. (2018). Social media and populism: An elective affinity? *Media, Culture & Society*, 40(5), 745–753. https://doi.org/10.1177/0163443718772192

Gerbaudo, P. (2019). *The digital party. Political organisation and online democracy*. Pluto.

Gil de Zúñiga, H., Jung, N., & Valenzuela, S. (2012). Social media use for news and individuals' social capital, civic engagement and political participation. *Journal of Computer-Mediated Communication*, 17(3), 319–336. https://doi.org/10.1111/j.1083-6101.2012.01574.x

Groshek, J., & Koc-Michalska, K. (2017). Helping populism win? Social media use, filter bubbles, and support for populist presidential candidates in the 2016 US election campaign. *Information, Communication & Society*, 20(9), 1389–1407. https://doi.org/10.1080/1369118X.2017.1329334

Guess, A., Nyhan, B., & Reifler, J. (2018). *Selective exposure to misinformation: Evidence from the consumption of fake news during the 2016 US presidential campaign*. European Research Council.

Hallin, D., & Mancini, P. (2004). *Comparing media systems*. Cambridge University Press.

Hameleers, M. (2018). A typology of populism: Toward a revised theoretical framework on the sender side and receiver side of communication. *International Journal of Communication*, 12, 2171–2190. https://ijoc.org/index.php/ijoc/article/view/7456

Heiss, R., & Matthes, J. (2017). Who 'likes' populists? Characteristics of adolescents following right-wing populist actors on facebook. *Information, Communication & Society*, 20(9), 1408–1424. https://doi.org/10.1080/1369118X.2017.1328524

Jagers, J., & Walgrave, S. (2007). Populism as political communication style: An empirical study of political parties' discourse in Belgium. *European Journal of Political Research*, 46(3), 319–345. https://doi.org/10.1111/j.1475-6765.2006.00690.x

Jungherr, A., Schroeder, R., & Stier, S. (2019). Digital media and the surge of political outsiders. *Social Media + Society*, 5(3), 1–12. https://doi.org/10.1177/2056305119875439

Karpf, D. (2012). *The MoveOn effect. The unexpected transformation of American political advocacy*. Oxford University Press.

Klinger, U., & Svensson, J. (2015). Network media logic: Some conceptual considerations. In A. Bruns, G. Enli, E. Skogerbø, A. O. Larsson, & C. Christensen (Eds.), *The Routledge companion to social media and politics* (pp. 23–38). Routledge.

Kreiss, D., Lawrence, R. G., & McGregor, S. C. (2018). In their own words: Political practitioner accounts of candidates, audiences, affordances, genres, and timing in strategic social media use. *Political Communication*, *35*(1), 8–31. https://doi.org/10.1080/10584609.2017.1334727

Kriesi, H. (2014). The populist challenge. *West European Politics*, *37*(2), 361–378. https://doi.org/10.1080/01402382.2014.887879

Kruikemeier, S., van Noort, G., Vliegenthart, R., & de Vreese, C. H. (2014). Unravelling the effects of active and passive forms of political Internet use. *New Media & Society*, *16*(6), 903–920. https://doi.org/10.1177/1461444813495163

Lee, S., & Xenos, M. (2020). Incidental news exposure via social media and political participation: Evidence of reciprocal effects. *New Media & Society*, 1–24 . https://doi.org/10.1177/1461444820962121

Lees, C. (2018). The 'alternative for Germany': The rise of right-wing populism at the heart of Europe. *Politics*, *38*(3), 295–310. https://doi.org/10.1177/0263395718777718

Livingstone, S. (2017). Foreword. In E. Gee, L. M. Takeuchi, & E. Wartella (Eds.), *Children and families in the digital age: Learning together in a media saturated culture* (pp. X–XI). Routledge.

Long, J. S. (1997). *Regression models for categorical and limited dependent variables*. Sage.

Malka, V., Ariel, Y., & Avidar, R. (2015). Fighting, worrying and sharing: Operation 'protective edge' as the first WhatsApp war. *Media, War & Conflict*, *8*(3), 329–344. https://doi.org/10.1177/1750635215611610

Marlière, P. (2019). Jean-Luc Mélenchon and France Insoumise. The manifacturing of populism. In G. Katsambekis, & A. Kioupkiolis (Eds.), *The populist radical left in Europe* (pp. 93–112). Routledge.

Mosca, L., & Quaranta, M. (2016). News diets, social media use and non-institutional participation in three communication ecologies: Comparing Germany, Italy and the UK. *Information, Communication & Society*, *19*(3), 325–345. https://doi.org/10.1080/1369118X.2015.1105276

Mosca, L., & Tronconi, F. (2019). Beyond left and right: The eclectic populism of the Five Star movement. *West European Politics*, *42*(6), 1258–1283. https://doi.org/10.1080/01402382.2019.1596691

Mosca, L., Vaccari, C., & Valeriani, A. (2015). An internet-fuelled party? The Movimento 5 Stelle and the web. In F. Tronconi (Ed.), *Beppe Grillo's Five Star Movement* (pp. 127–151). Ashgate.

Mudde, C. (2004). The populist zeitgeist. *Government and Opposition*, *39*(4), 541–563. https://doi.org/10.1111/j.1477-7053.2004.00135.x

Newman, N., Fletcher, R., Kalogeropoulos, A., & Kleis Nielsen, R. (2019). *Digital news report*. Reuters Institute for the Study of Journalism.

Pappas, T. S., & Kriesi, H. (2015). Populism and crisis: A fuzzy relationship. In H. Kriesi, & T. S. Pappas (Eds.), *European populism in the shadow of the great recession* (pp. 303–325). ECPR Press.

Pettigrew, A. M. (1979). On studying organizational cultures. *Administrative Science Quarterly*, *24*(4), 570–581. https://doi.org/10.2307/2392363

Pew Research. (2018). *In Western Europe, public attitudes toward news media more divided by populist views than left-Right ideology*. https://www.journalism.org/2018/05/14/in-western-europe-public-attitudes-toward-news-media-more-divided-by-populist-views-than-left-right-ideology

Reinemann, C., Aalberg, T., Esser, F., Stromback, J., & de Vreese, C. H. (2017). Populist political communication: Toward a model of its causes, forms, and effects. In T. Aalberg, F. Esser, C. Reinemann, J. Stromback, & C. H. de Vreese (Eds.), *Populist political communication in Europe* (pp. 12–25). Routledge.

Schaub, M., & Morisi, D. (2019). Voter mobilization in the echo chamber: Broadband internet and the rise of populism in Europe. *European Journal of Political Research*, *59*(4), 752–773. https://doi.org/10.1111/1475-6765.12373

Schulz, A. (2019). Where populist citizens get the news: An investigation of news audience polarization along populist attitudes in 11 countries. *Communication Monographs*, *86*(1), 88–111. https://doi.org/10.1080/03637751.2018.1508876

Schumacher, G., & Roodujin, M. (2013). Sympathy for the 'devil'? Voting for populists in the 2006 and 2010 Dutch general elections. *Electoral Studies*, *32*(1), 124–133. https://doi.org/10.1016/j.electstud.2012.11.003

Schumann, S., Boer, D., Hanke, K., & Liu, J. (2019). Social media use and support for populist radical right parties: Assessing exposure and selection effects in a two-wave panel study. *Information, Communication & Society*, 1–20. https://doi.org/10.1080/1369118X.2019.1668455

Serrano, J. C. M., Shahrezaye, M., Papakyriakopoulos, O., & Hegelich, S. (2019). The rise of Germany's AfD: A social media analysis. In *SMSociety '19: Proceedings of the 10th International Conference on Social Media and Society* (pp. 214–223).

Stier, S., Kirkizh, N., Froio, C., & Schroeder, R. (2020). Populist attitudes and selective exposure to online news: A cross-country analysis combining web tracking and surveys. *The International Journal of Press/Politics*, *25*(3), 426–446. https://doi.org/10.1177/1940161220907018

Surel, Y. (2019). How to stay populist? The Front National and the changing French party system. *West European Politics*, *42*(6), 1230–1257. https://doi.org/10.1080/01402382.2019.1596693

Valeriani, A., & Vaccari, C. (2018). Political talk on mobile instant messaging services: A comparative analysis of Germany, Italy, and the UK. *Information, Communication & Society*, *21*(11), 1715–1731. https://doi.org/10.1080/1369118X.2017.1350730

van Kessel, S. (2015). *Populist parties in Europe: Agents of discontent?* Palgrave Macmillan.

Van Schuur, W. H. (2003). Mokken scale analysis: Between the Guttman scale and parametric item response theory. *Political Analysis*, *11*(2), 139–163. https://doi.org/10.1093/pan/mpg002

Waterloo, S. F., Baumgartner, S. E., Peter, J., & Valkenburg, P. M. (2018). Norms of online expressions of emotion: Comparing Facebook, Twitter, Instagram, and WhatsApp. *New Media & Society*, *20*(5), 1813–1831. https://doi.org/10.1177/1461444817707349

Wojcieszak, M. (2010). 'Don't talk to me': Effects of ideologically homogeneous online groups and politically dissimilar offline ties on extremism. *New Media & Society*, *12*(4), 637–655. https://doi.org/10.1177/1461444809342775

Wuttke, A. (2020). New political parties through the voters' eyes. *West European Politics*, *43*(1), 22–48. https://doi.org/10.1080/01402382.2019.1603940

Zhuravskaya, E., Petrova, M., & Enikolopov, R. (2020). Political effects of the internet and social media. *Annual Review of Economics*, *12*, 415–438. https://doi.org/10.1146/annurev-economics-081919-050239

Still 'fire in the (full) belly'? Anti-establishment rhetoric before and after government participation

Andrea Ceron [iD], Alessandro Gandini [iD] and Patrizio Lodetti

ABSTRACT
Scholars argued that anti-establishment parties use a populist rhetoric that appeals to the worst instincts of people. Indeed, populist politicians are often viewed as charismatic leaders that have fire in their belly. While in the past these parties heavily relied on anti-establishment platforms and communication rhetoric, their increasing electoral success along with the growing duties linked with government membership transform them into more established parties, rather than pure outsiders, and cast doubts on the feasibility of keeping a populist rhetoric. This paper compares right-wing and non-right-wing populism, investigating whether populist leaders change their rhetorical strategy once in office, decreasing the level of negativity and adopting a more forward-looking and inclusive style of communication, with a stronger focus on fulfilling the policy proposal made during the electoral campaign rather than blaming political rivals. For this purpose, we collected a new corpus of political speeches extracted from video messages posted on Facebook by four anti-establishment party leaders in three countries (Austria, Italy and Spain), from 2016 to 2018, i.e., immediately before and immediately after their access to power. Overall, 30 h of recorded audio from 215 videos (amounting to around 140 million visualizations) have been analyzed using topic models and well-established semantic psycholinguistic dictionaries. The results highlight slight changes in the rhetoric of populist leaders once in power, mostly for non-right-wing populists, as their language becomes less negative, less assertive and more focused on government duties.

Introduction

For a long time, the relevance of populism in Europe has been negligible. Populist parties were seen as anti-establishment challengers, small in size, extremist in views, and confined into niche areas of the political space. Sporadically some populists managed to grasp media attention due to their striking electoral performance (often reached behind the shield of a charismatic leader). This happened, for instance, to the Swiss People's Party in Switzerland (particularly after 1995), to the List Pym Fortuyn in the Netherlands (2002) and to the

Supplemental data for this article can be accessed at https://doi.org/10.1080/1369118X.2020.1776373

Freedom Party of Austria (FPö), which managed to enter into a government coalition in 1999.

Over time, the relevance of populist parties has markedly increased in several European countries, particularly in the latest years. Nowadays, a number of them is getting more and more electorally successful and several parties managed to offer external support to a ruling cabinet or to get direct access to the government office, either alone or in coalition with other populist or non-populist parties.

Out of 33 European countries surveyed, the number of governments supported by populist parties increased from 3 in 2010, when the Party for Freedom in the Netherlands granted external support to a minority center-right government, to 8 in 2015, when in Greece the Coalition of the Radical Left (SYRIZA) formed a populist cabinet jointly with the right-wing Independent Greeks, up to 12 in 2018, when a populist coalition was formed in Italy involving Salvini's League (LN) and the Five Stars Movement (M5S), while in Spain Podemos externally supported the Sanchez I cabinet and in Austria the FPö had just restored the center-right coalition jointly with the Austrian People's Party.[1]

Anti-establishment parties tend to adopt an emotional style of communication based on criticism and negativity and use a populist rhetoric that appeals to the worst instincts of people (Engesser et al., 2017). Indeed, populist politicians are often viewed as charismatic leaders that have fire in their belly. While in the past these parties heavily relied on anti-establishment platforms and communication rhetoric, their increasing electoral success along with the growing duties linked with government membership make them more established parties (Krause & Wagner, 2019); this makes populists less able to present themselves as pure outsiders of the political system and casts doubts on whether keeping a similar rhetoric would be a feasible strategy in the near future.

Pointing to the chameleonic nature of populism (Mudde & Rovira Kaltwasser, 2013), we argue that populist parties strategically change their rhetorical approach. Indeed, we present reasons suggesting that, once in office, populist parties could decrease the level of negativity and adopt a more forward-looking and inclusive style of communication, with a stronger focus on fulfilling the policy proposal made during the electoral campaign rather than blaming political rivals for their negative qualities in terms of character-based valence issues.

To test whether, once in office, anti-establishment leaders change their political language we exploit a new corpus of political speeches pronounced by anti-establishment party leaders. Textual data have been gathered from the audio of video messages posted on Facebook, focusing on those that reached a wider audience. From 2016 to 2018, 4 political leaders in 3 countries have been monitored for two months (before the election and after government formation): Luigi Di Maio (M5S, Italy), Pablo Iglesias (Podemos, Spain), Matteo Salvini (LN, Italy), and Heinz-Christian Strache (FPö, Austria). On the whole, 215 videos (watched almost 140 million of times) have been analyzed, for a total amount of 30 h of recorded audio.

We investigate our research questions taking advantage of several techniques of text analysis. In particular, we combine well-established psycholinguistic dictionaries (Linguistic Inquiry and Word Count, LIWC) and topic models in order to investigate the sentiment, the emotion (negativity, in particular) connected to the message spread by politicians but also the political content broadcast to assess whether, once in office, anti-establishment leaders start to address other topics compared to those emphasized during the electoral campaign. Following the idea that not all populists are equal to each other, we explore the differences between right-wing and non-right-wing populists (Mudde & Rovira Kaltwasser, 2013).

The results points to a partial effect of government participation on the rhetoric of anti-establishment leaders, particularly for non-right-wing populists, and on the content of their speeches. The findings have implications for the literature on electoral campaigns, government responsiveness, and for the study of populist rhetoric.

Populist content and style: theoretical framework

Populism was a contested concept and the academic literature has long been debating on its definition. A plurality of scholars now seems to agree on a minimal definition of this concept, which identifies populism as a 'thin ideology that believes society to ultimately be separated into two homogenous and antagonistic groups – "the pure people" versus the "corrupt elite" – and which argues that politics should be an expression of the general will of the people' (Mudde, 2004, p. 543), so that populist parties tend so self-proclaim themselves as the sole representatives of the common people.

Three key notions of populism are usually identified. The first refers to 'people-centrism', i.e., the glorification of the own people, often with the use of ethnic terms and with an emphasis on the myths of a glorious past (Rydgren 2017); the second appeal concerns 'anti-elitism', i.e., criticizing and condemning the allegedly corrupt elites; the third involves 'popular sovereignty' and the claim for its restoration. The use of such key messages, however, is part of a strategy based on clear communication patterns (Ernst et al., 2019).

Wodak (2015, p. 3) points out that the populist communication 'combines and integrates form and content' and provides 'a dynamic mix of substance and style' so that it is worth examining both ideological key messages and peculiar stylistic elements (Bracciale & Martella, 2017; Stockemer & Barisione, 2017). Therefore, for the operationalization of populism, one can rely on the analysis of political communication (Bernhard & Kriesi, 2019) focusing on two main aspects of it, namely the content (topics and ideas promoted by these parties) as well as the style and the specific discourse patterns through which such contents are expressed.

Scholars shed light on the populist rhetoric emphasizing some peculiar traits that are common to many populist messages. These traits can be summarized into three main areas, i.e., negativity, emotionality and sociability. Let us start from the first one. Negativity sends back to the populists' aptitude to paint society in 'dark'. They ascribe negative traits to the elites, discuss about the dangers faced by the society, condemn negative choices made by their rivals, and emphasize negative societal outcomes blaming the establishment as the sole responsible for such crises. By doing that, the populists also adopt a crisis rhetoric, underpinned by the usage of words with a negative tone that point to immorality, scandals and conditions of emergency (Bracciale & Martella, 2017; Engesser et al., 2017).

Focusing on populist voters, scholars found that 'populism is hardly ever considered to be a positive voting choice' (Hooghe & Oser, 2016, p. 27); several studies shown that negative evaluations of democratic institutions and hostile attitudes against the political elite are in fact one of the main reasons to explain the electoral success of populists (Spierings

& Zaslove, 2017). The literature highlights the affinity between populism and negativism, suggesting that such stylistic element is one of the core strategies used by the populists to spread their key messages. Indeed, a content analysis of social media and talk shows statements across six countries (Ernst et al., 2019) found that negativity represented the main element of a populism-related communication: more than half of all populist messages made use of a negative style (19.9% out of a 38% of populist statements).

This can also be linked with negative campaigning, i.e., a strategy based on criticizing the opponents by focusing on the flaws of their policy program or of their character-based valence attributes, such as incompetence, disunity, immorality, dishonesty and corruption (Ceron & d'Adda, 2016). Opposition parties usually resort more to negative campaigning. As long as populist parties are in opposition, we can expect them to exploit negative campaigning, rather than positive campaign, and to communicate their messages using a negatively connoted style. In this regard, studies found that populist parties do tend to engage more in negative campaigning (Nai, 2018), unless they are in power (Van Kessel & Castelein, 2016).

If populists win the elections getting access to the government (or obtaining a full control on it, as in Greece, Hungary or Italy), they become part of the establishment they used to criticize. If so, behaving as in a 'permanent campaign' framework and maintaining a harsh anti-elitist rhetoric to target established parties becomes more and more an unfeasible strategy. Some studies argued that in that case populists could moderate their anti-establishment appeals by toning down their rhetoric (Akkerman, 2016; for a review: Krause & Wagner, 2019).

The same argument could apply to the adoption of a crisis rhetoric. When painting the world in 'black', by blaming the wrong choices took by the establishment which generated a crisis, populists will not only adopt a negative style. They will also share a backward-looking perspective, that is more oriented on past events, rather than on what has to be done in the near future. Once in office for populist parties it will be harder to only blame the former elite for the mistakes made in the past. Conversely, they ought to employ a rhetoric that is focused more on the future to explain what they will do to rule the country and solve the problems.

To the contrary, other studies suggest that anti-elite criticism did not completely disappear from the discourses of ruling populist parties (Aslanidis & Rovira Kaltwasser, 2016; Batory, 2016). Populists can in fact look for other (possibly external) enemies, targeting them instead of the national political elite that was previously in power. This reasoning suggests that the rhetoric of negativity might persist. What can change is the target of such negativity. The list of new potential enemies includes the European Union or other supranational and intergovernmental institutions (e.g., the World Trade Organization or the United Nations), foreign countries, multinational corporations, non-governmental organizations, but also foreign capitalists, opulent millionaires, small niches of people representing economic and cultural elites, the mass media, or non-elected national democratic institutions that might limit the effectiveness of government.

RQ1: When populists get into office do they adjust their rhetoric style by decreasing negativity and adopting a forward-looking discourse or do they simply change the target of their negativity?

Apart from negativity, emotionality is a second stylistic element deemed crucial in populist communication. The best way to get in touch with the common people is to share emotions and reveal feelings. Beside negative emotions, in fact, populists can also express positive emotions directed to the people or the populist leader himself. Populists can express a positive communication also in patriotic terms to emphasize (and idealize) the qualities of their own country and the myths of the distant past. In addition, within the boundary of emotionality scholars also argue that populists tend to speak with un unflattering assertive tone, avoiding hesitations (Engesser et al., 2017; Ernst et al., 2019). As such, populist actors can resort to a more emotional language (Bracciale & Martella, 2017; Engesser et al., 2017; Hameleers et al., 2017) so that the share of emotional words and contents will be overall higher than that of other parties. Content analysis of politicians' statements suggests that emotionality is the second style used in populism-related communication: Ernst et al. (2019) classified almost one third of the populist statements in this category (12.2% out of 38%).

Once in office, however, due to the commitments linked with government responsibilities, even populist parties might want to adopt a less emotional language, in favor of a more analytic discourse. In addition, the need for negotiations and compromises (Akkerman, 2016), particularly in coalition governments, suggests that populists can adopt a lesser rate of exclusive words and a more inclusive language, reducing their propensity to paint the society in black and white terms (Ernst et al., 2019). However, some positive emotions can still be conveyed to celebrate the successful electoral performance and to depict this victory as a revolution that succeeded in dissolving the hated political establishment to install the 'government of change'.

The third stylistic element of populist communication has to do with sociality, and can be partially related to the previous one. Scholars argue that the populists tend to reduce complexity by adopting a colloquial language, using simple words and dialects in order to reach an audience of ordinary citizens (Bracciale & Martella, 2017; Engesser et al., 2017). Analogously, to show their friendly nature, populists are prone to use an intimization style, discussing about their personal life in order to be perceived as common citizens easily reachable by the voters (Bracciale & Martella, 2017). This element seems less relevant as empirical analyses (Ernst et al., 2019) found a marginal use of sociability compared to other populist-related styles of communication (only 4.8% of politicians' statements follow this stylistic approach).

> RQ2: When populists get into office do they lower the level of emotionality in favor of a more complex and less personal language, adopting fewer excluding words, or do they keep using a sociability style and emphasize the emotions linked with the electoral victory and the political change?

Finally, according to the academic literature, there is a fourth element linked with communication for which we might foresee a change when comparing populists before and after the electoral success. In fact, when populist parties are in opposition, beside an anti-elite rhetoric they also focus their strategy on offering a clear set of policy promises during election campaigns (Akkerman, 2016; Krause & Wagner, 2019). Being in the opposition, free from any government responsibility, populists might offer unfeasible policy claims and make promises that they would not be able to fulfill later. Populist parties are often deemed unable to deliver once in office (Heinisch, 2003; Kitschelt, 2007). To cope with this, when populist parties seize power, they should make an effort to present themselves as credible political agents that can successfully implement policies and fulfill promises, being responsive toward the demands of voters.

By doing that, the populists can detach themselves from the former political elite, which was accused to lack responsiveness and to ignore the voters' wills. Additionally, this strategy is crucial to preserve their electoral support and to avoid a valence loss, linked with the deterioration of their image of credible agents of policy change (Krause & Wagner, 2019). Indeed, for such parties that are often considered as policy-seeker, succeeding in policy implementation and fulfilling election pledges becomes crucial to enhance the likelihood of their survival (Akkerman & de Lange, 2012). Accordingly, after joining the cabinet, one can expect a stronger emphasis of populists' communication on the core issues and the main policy pledges discussed during the electoral campaign. If the reasoning leading to our first research question suggested that we should observe less negativity (including less negative campaigning) along with a forward-looking lexicon, this latter discussion points in a similar direction, indicating that we can expect a stronger emphasis on the core policies that will have to be (profitably) addressed by the new populist government.

> RQ3: When populists get into office do they increase the share of policy-related statements to prove their ability to fulfill electoral pledges?

Noticeably, while populism is a wide phenomenon that includes both right-wing and left-wing variants, not all populist parties are equal to each other and the literature distinguishes between right-wing and left-wing populists. Both retain anti-establishment views, being similar on the so-called anti-elitist (vertical) dimension of populism; however, concerning the nativist (horizontal) dimension of it, right-wing populists are deemed exclusionary in nature (Heiss & Matthes, 2020) while left-wing populists follow a more inclusionary logic (Mudde & Rovira Kaltwasser, 2013).

As discussed above, relying on anti-elitist populism can become more unfeasible once in office (since the elite was defeated); conversely, exclusionary populist arguments related to the nativist/patriotic dimension of populism can still be used, and right-wing populists can foster in-group/out-group dynamics claiming that they are defending the interests of the in-group against several out-groups (Heiss & Matthes, 2020). Furthermore, the exclusionary nature of right-wing populists suggests that they are less adaptable and less prone to meet the need for negotiations and compromises in coalition governments (Akkerman, 2016).

Therefore, one can argue that right-wing populists are less prone to get fully embedded into institutions: they try to partially preserve their purity and keep one foot in and one foot out of institutions, to avoid becoming part of the system, especially 'in terms of the linguistic register adopted' by their leaders (Albertazzi & McDonnell, 2005, p. 959).

As such, throughout the paper we will answer our broad research questions on a variety of outcomes and from multiple facets, paying attention also to the potential differences between right-wing and non-right-wing populists.

Case selection and data collection

Moving beyond the analysis of textual Twitter data, in the present paper we will investigate the communication of populist leaders using videos posted on Facebook.

The choice to focus on videos fits well with the study of populism. Compared to a written text, in a video a charismatic leader has the opportunity to establish a direct link with the audience showing his face and a slice of his real life, and using his voice and visual nonverbal cues to strengthen the efficacy of the contents and words expressed in the speech. The content broadcast on video is also more usable, compared to a written text, as it requires a lower effort from the consumer, who can just listen (even passively) instead of reading (actively). Due to its efficacy and to its ability to become viral, reaching a wider audience, this source of data will be very relevant in the upcoming future. Indeed, the consumption of branded video content is rapidly increasing: on Facebook it grew by 258% from 2016 to 2017.[2]

In turn, focusing on Facebook, instead of other social media (e.g., Twitter), seems appropriate and coherent with our research design. For populist purposes, Facebook has several advantages compared to Twitter (Ernst et al., 2019, p. 5): it offers more reciprocal message exchanges and 'it has higher levels of proximity and the connection between Facebook users is generally more intensive, personal, and intimate'. Furthermore, due to the socio-demographic features of Twitter users (such as education, socioeconomic status, or political interest), political actors consider Twitter less suitable for spreading populism (Jacobs & Spierings, 2019) compared to Facebook, which is a platform that allows also ordinary citizens to interact with politicians (Kalsnes et al., 2017). Indeed, populist citizens tend to use Facebook as a source of political information (Schulz, 2019), and empirical content analyses of political messages show that political actors prefer Facebook (over Twitter or televised debates) as an outlet for their populist-related communication (Ernst et al., 2019). All these reasons indicate that Facebook is more suitable for populist communication. Last but not least, Facebook remains the most widely used social media in all the countries considered in the analysis; its penetration and market share are strikingly high so that an audience of millions of voters is potentially exposed to the video content broadcast there by populist leaders. In the period considered, the potential audience on Facebook amounted to almost 22 million of users in Italy (36% of the population),[3] more than 19 million in Spain (41% of the population)[4], and around 4 million in Austria (46% of the population).[5]

Our aim is to investigate whether and to what extent populist parties have changed their rhetorical strategies after seizing power, exploring any potential difference between right-wing and non-right-wing populists. To do that, we focus on the communication of populist parties that have recently shifted from the opposition to a ruling position. Given that the data collection is based on video content spread on Facebook, we restrict the time frame of our analysis to the latest years in which videos started to play a prominent role in social media communication, i.e., starting after 2016. For this reason, we do not consider SYRIZA in Greece (2015), the Danish People's Party (which supported the center-right cabinet in 2015), or the Slovak National Party that joined the cabinet in early 2016. The volume of video data concerning these three parties would be too low to perform any analysis. Consequently, we focus on four populist parties that switched their status, from government to opposition, later than 2016: the Freedom Party, in Austria, which got involved in the coalition government in December 2017, soon after the general election held in October; the League and the M5S, which formed a coalition in June 2018 (after the Italian election held in March) and the Spanish Podemos, which contributed to the dismissal of the center-right cabinet led by Mariano Rajoy voting a motion of no-confidence, jointly with the Spanish Socialist Workers' Party (PSOE) and with regionalist parties in June 2018. This motion resulted in the downfall of Rajoy (who was in office after the 2016 election) and in the PSOE leader Pedro Sánchez becoming new Prime Minister of Spain. According to the Spanish Constitution, Sánchez was automatically deemed to have the confidence of the legislature as the motion of no-confidence reached a majority, therefore, Podemos provided an external support to the socialist cabinet led by Sánchez.

While scholars have long neglected the analysis of left-wing populism, recent studies have started to investigate populism distinguishing between left and right (Bernhard & Kriesi, 2019; Ernst et al., 2017, 2019; Krause & Wagner, 2019; Rooduijn & Akkerman, 2017; Schmuck & Hameleers, 2019). Accordingly, in the present paper we investigate two right-wing populist parties, i.e., the LN and the FPö, and two non-right-wing populist parties, i.e., the left-wing Podemos and the Italian M5S. Notably, scholars are unsure about the political location of the M5S. Its leadership defines itself beyond left and right (Hooghe & Oser, 2016; Mosca, 2014). Some studies point to its eclectic or polyvalent nature (Mosca & Tronconi, 2019; Pirro, 2018), while others consider it as a moderate (Ernst et al., 2019) left-of-centre party (Ernst et al., 2017), or as a radical left party (Bernhard & Kriesi, 2019; Ceron, 2017a; Conti & Memoli, 2015). Overall, the M5S seems to combine left-of-centre positions on economy and welfare with vague, elusive and mixed (sometimes progressive, sometimes conservative) views on socio-cultural issues (Ceron, 2017b; Mosca & Tronconi, 2019). Nevertheless, 2018 data based on manual coding of its party manifesto,[6] or of M5S parliamentary speeches during the Conte I investiture debate,[7] suggest that this party is overall leaning more toward the left than toward the right. These data refer to documents collected immediately before (manifesto) and immediately after (investiture debate) M5S access to power, therefore they are suitable, being temporally close to the period of our analysis. Accordingly, we will consider the M5S as a non-right-wing populist party.

From this perspective, our sample is balanced. The literature on digital politics has often focused on communication patterns during electoral campaigns, while non-election periods have been investigated less (with some exceptions: Ceron, 2017b; Ernst et al., 2019; Schmuck & Hameleers, 2019). Conversely, in the present study we will compare the communication during the electoral campaign (focusing on data concerning the last month before the election), with what happens in times of 'ordinary politics', i.e., one month after the new cabinet has been installed. Per each party in each country we analyze two months of data, focusing on the official account of the party leader, which can be the most suitable to investigate populism in light of the growing personalization of politics. Many scholars suggest that right-wing populist communication appears centered on the person of the leader (e.g., Krämer, 2017); fewer studies address non-right-wing populists (Bracciale & Martella, 2017; Ernst et al., 2017), but leaders are deemed important even in these parties: typically, the leaders of Podemos and the M5S personify the party, pushing scholars to discuss about their 'hyperleadership' (Gerbaudo, 2019).

Accordingly, the following political leaders have been considered: Luigi Di Maio (M5S, Italy), Pablo Iglesias (Podemos, Spain), Matteo Salvini (LN, Italy), and Heinz-Christian Strache (FPö, Austria). Interestingly, while some parties are older than others and already had experience in office during their life (LN and FPö), this is not true for their political leaders. Indeed, none of them was in office before, nor was leading the party during prior coalition government experiences.

Following these criteria, using a custom-built, ad hoc script, we downloaded 354 videos. To enhance the comparability of the documents, we excluded videos falling in the 25th percentile in terms of visualization (few visualization, i.e., less interesting content accessed by few users) and falling above the 75th percentile in terms of length (very long videos, which might contain multiple breaks or off topic contents). We manually checked the content to keep only videos in which the leader was directly speaking or spreading the party line; off topic videos were excluded (e.g., videos without audio or with a very bad audio, TV reports unrelated to the leader or the party, videos not related to the party leader but to other persons). As a result, 215 videos have been analyzed (this is our unit of analysis): 126 in the last month of election campaign and 89 in the first month after government formation, with an overall balance between right-wing (118) and non-right-wing (97) videos (see Table A1 in the Online Appendix for details).

The total length amounts to 1,748 min of audio, i.e., almost 30 h videotaped (with an average of 7.84 min per video) and the content has been cumulatively watched 138,300,000 times (average number of visualizations: 620,277). The audio has been converted into text using the Google Speech API and manually cleaned when necessary, producing a dataset that contains overall 158,623 words, though the length is higher for Salvini and especially for Di Maio.

Facebook videos do not only report original content, thought to be addressed to the Facebook audience. To the contrary, populist leaders broadcast on Facebook contents form a variety of sources that includes interviews in news programs, declaration released during televised talk shows, press releases, speeches delivered at political rallies, and professional advertisements or self-produced video messages in the form of video-selfies (that were later broadcast also on TV by news programs).

From a qualitative inspection, we notice that the content of Facebook's video seems perfectly representative of the communication style of these populist leaders. For instance, we find videos introducing the viral prize contest 'Vinci Salvini' ('you win Salvini'), a gamification strategy for mobilization and personal data collection purposes, along with selected declarations released on TV or Facebook Live videos recorded directly from the minister's desk or while driving between one electoral campaign rally and the following one.

We proceed with the empirical analysis focusing on the topics, first, using automated topic models to perform an exploratory analysis, and then on the linguistic style using the software LIWC, a well-established psycholinguistic tool that implements semantic analysis through predefined dictionaries.

Analysis and results

Topic models analysis

For the topic model analysis, we revert to an unsupervised non-probabilistic algorithm, the Non-negative Matrix Factorization, which has some advantages compared to other traditional topic model techniques (see the Online Appendix for references and methodological details). We kept constant the number of topics (5) set ex-ante for all the politicians. We reduced the sparsity removing rare words and selecting only words that appeared more than once in each text, though the substantive results are similar when removing this filter.

Two main patterns seem to emerge from this analysis (see Section 2 of the Online Appendix for extensive details and results). First, we notice a widespread use of valence issues and attacks to rival politicians before the election, while after government formation their new institutional roles bring populists to focus more on policies and government duties. Before the election Di Maio referred to valence issues (corruption, competence and costs of politics) in 4 topics out of 5, while later he spent more effort (3 topics) discussing social policy and economic development ('*sviluppo economico*'); Iglesias shifted from valence issues (2 topics) to government duties and concrete policies in the fields of devolution, immigration and welfare (4 topics overall); the same pattern applies to Strache (3 valence related topics before the elections, 4 topics about social policy and government duties later). Salvini too devoted more attention to immigration policy once in office (this occurs in 3 topics).

In detail, before the election, several topics concerning the League and the M5S (but also Podemos and the FPö) contain attacks against the leader of the incumbent party ('*Renzi*' or '*Rajoy*'), or refer to the need to face existing 'problems' ('*probleme*'), in line with a crisis rhetoric, and include mentions to 'corruption' ('*corruzione*') and to rival politicians ('*De Luca*') involved in corruption scandals. Conversely, after government formation we notice references to respecting 'campaign commitments' ('*wahlversprechen*'), for instance in the videos of Strache. Similarly, Di Maio discusses about the implementation of public policies in line with the declarations released during the campaign (e.g., the so called *reddito di cittadinanza*: minimum citizenship income); Strache, makes reference to the 'future' ('*zukunft*') and to social policies for the families ('*familienbeihilfe*'). Iglesias points to new 'proposition' ('*proposición*') to be put on the '*agenda*', including public services ('*servicios públicos*') and immigration policy ('*puerto*'). In turn, Salvini widely focused on immigration policy (boats, '*navi*'; borders, '*confini*'; immigrants, '*immigrati*'; '*Tunisia*'), but he also refers to the European Union ('*europa*'), which can potentially become a new enemy to be attacked using a populist rhetoric.

Indeed, the topic models reveal a second pattern that points to some differences between right-wing and non-right-wing populism. We notice that after government formation the two right-wing leaders still devote attention to very peculiar topics linked with a populist rhetoric, such as patriotism and paternalism. This seems an attempt to preserve a more distinct populist language even once in office. Specifically, Strache makes reference to the issue of traditions (Topic 3, Table A9, Online Appendix) and Salvini adopts a language based on patriotism (Topic 3, Table A5, Online Appendix) and paternalism (Topic 1, Table A5, Online Appendix). This preliminary evidence will be further investigated with a statistical analysis of semantic occurrences.

Semantic analysis

For the semantic analysis we employ LIWC, i.e., a text analysis program that counts words belonging to psychologically meaningful categories; remarkably, 'empirical results using LIWC demonstrate its ability to detect meaning in a wide variety of experimental settings, including to show attentional focus, emotionality, social relationships, thinking styles, and individual differences' (Tausczik & Pennebaker, 2010, p. 24).

We revert to 2001 and 2007 dictionaries in Italian, German and Spanish. LIWC is particularly suitable for our purpose as it allows to investigate the style of communication of populist leaders by looking at their words usage and by comparing words falling into alternative categories that can be directly linked with our research questions.

Accordingly, to answer RQ1 and RQ2, we created 8 dependent variables (Positive Tone, Forward Looking, Total Emotions, Inclusive/Exclusive, I/We, Complex Words, Personal, Social) that provide a picture of the three stylistic facets of populist rhetoric described above. All these variables theoretically range from 0 to 100 (see Table A10 and A11 in the Online Appendix).[8] We analyzed each variable through a linear regression with random effects to account for the nested structure of the data (we have repeated observations, i.e., videos, within politicians).[9]

Our main independent variable is a dummy equal to 1 when the video is recorded after government formation (and 0 otherwise). To investigate similarities and differences between populists, we interact this variable with a dummy equal to 1 for right-wing populists (and 0 otherwise). Figure 1 displays the results on all the 8 dependent variables; we report the change in the outcome when a video is published after government formation for all populist leaders (left panel) or separately for right-wing and non-right-wing populist leaders (right panel). The latter representation also allows to detect if the effects hold true for only one of the two groups (Brambor et al., 2006).[10]

Overall, we notice an impact only on a few outcomes. We observe a stronger focus on the future rather than on the past and the present (+2.64), a more complex language (+3.01),[11] which partially runs against the populist stylistic element of sociability (in terms of colloquialism), and an evolution toward a less assertive language, which employs relatively more words denoting inclusion than exclusion (+9.35). Conversely, we do not see differences in the tone, the share of emotional words or words related to social processes (references to friends, babies and human beings) and personal concerns (both linked with the logic of sociability and intimization: Ernst et al., 2019).

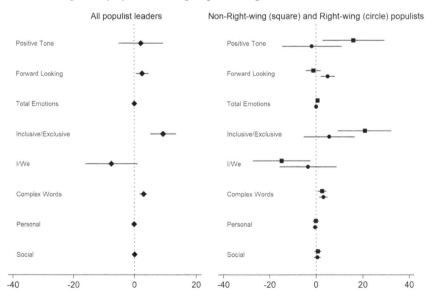

Figure 1. Change in populists' language after government formation (with 95% confidence interval).

Interestingly, when running separate analyses to distinguish right-wing populists from non-right-wing ones, we notice some additional changes and generally the findings tend to hold true more for the latter than for the former. Once in office, non-right-wing populists tend to use a more positive tone (+16.04); their language gets more complex (+2.60) and less assertive, with a lower emphasis on the first-person singular rather than plural ('we' instead of 'I'; −14.79) and more words denoting inclusion rather than exclusion (+20.80). Conversely, when considering right-wing populists alone, we only find a more complex (+3.16) and forward-looking (+5.00) language after government formation, while no additional change is detected with respect to the other stylistic elements considered.

Discussion

Our results point to some slight changes in the rhetoric of populist leaders once in power, particularly for non-right-wing populist leaders. The language becomes relatively less negative, more future oriented, and less assertive (more inclusive and less personalized). Despite this, some elements, peculiar of populist communication, are still in place, including a persistent intimization and emotional words are still used, arguably to express satisfaction for the success of the 'populist revolution' and outlining positive expectations in terms of policy change.

This latter finding is also reflected in the topic model analysis, which showed a stronger emphasis on the concept of change, as well as on the actual policy proposals presented during the electoral campaign, at the expense of reduced emphasis on valence attributes and on anti-establishment and anti-elite discourse. This latter strategy remains only partially present, becoming addressed now to other potential enemies such as the European Unions and the multinational corporations instead of the former ruling elite.

Overall, the evidence of a partial adaptation to their new roles is coherent with the idea that anti-establishment leaders might feel to have a 'full belly': the satisfaction due to government membership can alter their communication strategies reducing the recourse to harsh criticism.

While recent studies show that both populists and non-populists parties are more likely to adopt populist communication before the election than afterward (Schmuck & Hameleers, 2019), our results hold true mainly for non-right-wing populist leaders. This can imply that, at least in the very short term, right-wing populists tend to adopt a 'one foot in, one foot out strategy' (Albertazzi & McDonnell, 2005); they adapt less to their new governmental role and keep a rather populist style that is more in line with election campaign dynamics. Remarkably, this finding represents a very strong evidence against the idea of the moderation of right-wing populists once in office.

To the contrary, non-right-wing populists do modify their language and seem more ready to get institutionalized passing from harsh criticism to more constructive viewpoints. These findings seem to align with the constructive behavior showed by Podemos in Spain and the M5S in Italy, which repeatedly proved their willingness to enter into office; conversely, both the League and the FPö have suddenly rejected their government posts (although for different reasons).

On the one hand, after the successful performance of the League in the 2019 European elections, Salvini called for snap elections showing his propensity to exploit his consensus among voters instead of promoting the stability of the Conte I cabinet;[12] similarly, after a political scandal involving Strache, the FPö opted for a mass resignation and withdrew its ministers from the Kurz I cabinet, leading to its termination.[13]

On the other hand, in Italy the M5S tried to bargain either with the center-left Democratic Party or the right-wing League immediately after the 2018 general election to end political instability and form a new cabinet; after Salvini's request for early elections, in the summer of 2019, the M5S moved from an alliance with the League to a new coalition government (Conte II) formed jointly with the Democratic Party and the left-wing party Free and Equal to preserve its cabinet membership.[14] Analogously, in Spain Podemos has repeatedly invited the socialist party to form a formal coalition government that includes both parties, as a sign of its willingness to get into office in a new Sánchez II cabinet (which was finally formed in January 2020).[15]

Beside the limitations of the present study (such as the selection of populist parties only), we should also consider two possible alternative explanations that can apply to our findings. First, the two right-wing populists are junior parties in the government coalition and might need to differentiate themselves from their partner, while the M5S was the largest party in parliament and Podemos was a supporting partner with an incentive to show allegiance to the coalition and prove its reliability (Van Kessel & Castelein, 2016). This can be true, though in the Italian case the League immediately closed the gap with the M5S in the voting intention polls (already in June 2018) and was more than just a junior partner (Marangoni & Verzichelli, 2019): Salvini led its own agenda and was deemed 'the most influential leader in the Conte government' (Fabbrini & Zgaga, 2019, p. 290); this could have fostered the incentive to adjust the language accordingly (something that we did not observe).

Secondly, both the LN and the FPö had already been in government before. From their previous experience they could have learnt the benefit of keeping a sharp profile. While this is reasonable, we must consider that our paper focuses on party leaders and on their personal communication style; notably, none of them was directly in office before, nor was the party leader during prior coalition government experiences.[16]

Nevertheless, future research could disentangle these concerns, investigating more in depth the differences between right-wing and non-right-wing populists net of any potential confounding factor that we cannot account for in this study. Unfortunately, the cabinets formed with the contribution of these four populist parties lasted only few months; accordingly, future research could possibly investigate changes in the long run. Future studies can also analyze the communication patterns of populists from a qualitative point of view: taking advantage of the increasing relevance of online videos, scholars can grasp whether, beside language, other elements of non-verbal communication change when anti-establishment parties get into office.

Notes

1. Timbro Authoritarian Populism Index, https://populismindex.com/ (last accessed 21st June 2019).
2. https://www.wyzowl.com/video-social-media-2019/
3. https://www.statista.com/statistics/568802/forecast-of-facebook-user-numbers-in-italy/
4. https://www.statista.com/statistics/568845/forecast-of-facebook-user-numbers-in-the-spain/

5. https://www.statista.com/statistics/568740/forecast-of-facebook-user-numbers-in-austria/
6. See the well-known Manifesto Project dataset: https://manifesto-project.wzb.eu/
7. https://www.lavoce.info/archives/54161/rischi-di-un-governo-bipolare/
8. There are few missing cases concerning some variables when the LIWC software did not detect any word belonging to the categories included in the numerator or denominator of our index. Additionally, the category Personal is not available in the Spanish LIWC dictionary.
9. This option was suggested by the Hausman test (except when analyzing Personal and Social). Using fixed effects (Table A13, Online Appendix) or a fractional logit does not alter our findings. The results hold even when including basic control variables, such as the type of video (interview on news media, advertisement, institutional speech or propaganda speech) or the intensity of the speech (rate of words). The findings are substantively similar to a simple mean comparison t-test.
10. The full models are reported in the Online Appendix (Table A12, A14 and A15).
11. While it is not possible to evaluate language complexity using standard measures based on the length of the sentences (since any punctuation is lost with the audio transcription), we rely on the rate of complex words composed of more than six letters under the idea that the length of the words reflects their complexity.
12. https://www.bbc.com/news/world-europe-49287219
13. https://www.bbc.com/news/world-europe-48335316
14. https://www.ft.com/content/346cc922-ce69-11e9-99a4-b5ded7a7fe3f
15. https://www.euronews.com/2019/09/04/podemos-insist-on-formal-coalition-as-price-for-saving-sanchez
16. Strache became leader of the FPö in 2005, after a party split promoted by Jörg Haider, whose new party replaced the FPö as junior partner of the ruling coalition.

Acknowledgements

The authors wish to thank the anonymous reviewers, the editors as well as the discussant and the participants at the conference 'Social Movements and Parties in a Fractured MediaLandscape', Florence, 1-2 July 2019.

Disclosure statement

No potential conflict of interest was reported by the author(s).

ORCID

Andrea Ceron http://orcid.org/0000-0002-6686-5969
Alessandro Gandini http://orcid.org/0000-0002-7705-7625

References

Akkerman, T. (2016). Conclusions. In T. Akkerman, S. L. de Lange, & M. Rooduij (Eds.), *Radical right-wing populist parties. Into the mainstream?* (pp. 268–282). Routledge.

Akkerman, T., & de Lange, S. L. (2012). Radical right parties in office: Incumbency records and the electoral cost of governing. *Government and Opposition, 47*(4), 574–596. https://doi.org/10.1111/j.1477-7053.2012.01375.x

Albertazzi, D., & McDonnell, D. (2005). The Lega Nord in the second Berlusconi government: In a league of its own. *West European Politics, 28*(5), 952–972. https://doi.org/10.1080/01402380500310600

Aslanidis, P., & Rovira Kaltwasser, C. (2016). Dealing with populists in government: The SYRIZA-ANEL coalition in Greece. *Democratization, 23*(6), 1077–1091. https://doi.org/10.1080/13510347.2016.1154842

Batory, A. (2016). Populists in government? Hungary's 'system of national cooperation'. *Democratization, 23*(2), 283–303. https://doi.org/10.1080/13510347.2015.1076214

Bernhard, L., & Kriesi, H. (2019). Populism in election times: A comparative analysis of 11 countries in Western Europe. *West European Politics,* https://doi.org/10.1080/01402382.2019.1596694

Bracciale, R., & Martella, A. (2017). Define the populist political communication style: The case of Italian political leaders on Twitter. *Information, Communication & Society, 20*(9), 1310–1329. https://doi.org/10.1080/1369118X.2017.1328522

Brambor, T., Clark, W. R., & Golder, M. (2006). Understanding interaction models: improving empirical analyses. *Political Analysis, 14*(1), 63–82. https://doi.org/10.1093/pan/mpi014

Ceron, A. (2017a). Intra-party politics in 140 characters. *Party Politics, 23*(1), 7–17. https://doi.org/10.1177/1354068816654325

Ceron, A. (2017b). *Social media and political Accountability: Bridging the gap between citizens and politicians.* Palgrave Macmillan.

Ceron, A., & d'Adda, G. (2016). E-campaigning on Twitter: The effectiveness of distributive promises and negative campaign in the 2013 Italian election. *New Media & Society, 18*(9), 1935–1955. https://doi.org/10.1177/1461444815571915

Conti, N., & Memoli, V. (2015). The emergence of a new party in the Italian party system: Rise and fortunes of the five star movement. *West European Politics, 38*(3), 516–534. https://doi.org/10.1080/01402382.2014.996377

Engesser, S., Fawzi, N., & Larsson, A. O. (2017). Populist online communication: Introduction to the special issue. *Information, Communication & Society, 20*(9), 1279–1292. https://doi.org/10.1080/1369118X.2017.1328525

Ernst, N., Blassnig, S., Engesser, S., Büchel, F., & Esser, F. (2019). Populists prefer social media over talk shows: An analysis of populist messages and stylistic elements across Six countries. *Social Media+Society,* https://doi.org/10.1177/2056305118823358

Ernst, N., Engesser, S., Büchel, F., Blassnig, S., & Esser, F. (2017). Extreme parties and populism: An analysis of Facebook and Twitter across six countries. *Information, Communication & Society, 20*(9), 1347–1364. https://doi.org/10.1080/1369118X.2017.1329333

Fabbrini, S., & Zgaga, T. (2019). Italy and the European Union: The discontinuity of the Conte government. *Contemporary Italian Politics, 11*(3), 280–293. https://doi.org/10.1080/23248823.2019.1642657

Gerbaudo, P. (2019). *The digital party: Political organisation and online democracy.* Pluto Press.

Hameleers, M., Bos, L., & de Vreese, C. (2017). "They did it": The effects of emotionalized blame attribution in populist communication. *Communication Research, 44*(6), 870–900. https://doi.org/10.1177/0093650216644026

Heinisch, R. (2003). Success in opposition – failure in government: Explaining the performance of right-wing populist parties in public office. *West European Politics, 26*(3), 91–130. https://doi.org/10.1080/01402380312331280608

Heiss, R., & Matthes, J. (2020). Stuck in a nativist spiral: Content, selection, and effects of right-wing populists' communication on Facebook. *Political Communication, 37*(3), 303–328. https://doi.org/10.1080/10584609.2019.1661890

Hooghe, M., & Oser, J. (2016). The electoral success of the Movimento 5 Stelle: An example of a left populist vote? *Österreichische Zeitschrift Für Politikwissenschaft*, *44*(4), 25–36. https://doi.org/10.15203/ozp.1049.vol44iss4

Jacobs, K., & Spierings, N. (2019). A populist paradise? Examining populists' Twitter adoption and use. *Information, Communication & Society*, *22*(12), 1681–1696. https://doi.org/10.1080/1369118X.2018.1449883

Kalsnes, B., Larsson, A. O., & Enli, G. S. (2017). The social media logic of political interaction: Exploring citizens' and politicians' relationship on Facebook and Twitter. *First Monday*, *22*, 2. https://doi.org/10.5210/fm.v22i2.6348

Kitschelt, H. (2007). Growth and persistence of the radical right in postindustrial democracies: Advances and challenges in comparative research. *West European Politics*, *30*(5), 1176–1206. https://doi.org/10.1080/01402380701617563

Krämer, B. (2017). Populist online practices: The function of the Internet in right-wing populism. *Information, Communication & Society*, *20*(9), 1293–1309. https://doi.org/10.1080/1369118X.2017.1328520

Krause, W., & Wagner, A. (2019). Becoming part of the gang? Established and nonestablished populist parties and the role of external efficacy. *Party Politics*, https://doi.org/10.1177/1354068819839210

Marangoni, F., & Verzichelli, L. (2019). Goat-stag, chimera or chameleon? The formation and first semester of the Conte government. *Contemporary Italian Politics*, *11*(3), 263–279. https://doi.org/10.1080/23248823.2019.1645998

Mosca, L. (2014). The Five Star Movement: Exception or Vanguard in Europe? *The International Spectator*, *49*(1), 36–52. https://doi.org/10.1080/03932729.2013.875821

Mosca, L., & Tronconi, F. (2019). Beyond left and right: The eclectic populism of the Five Star Movement. *West European Politics*, *42*(6), 1258–1283. https://doi.org/10.1080/01402382.2019.1596691

Mudde, C. (2004). The populist zeitgeist. *Government and Opposition*, *39*(4), 541–563. https://doi.org/10.1111/j.1477-7053.2004.00135.x

Mudde, C., & Rovira Kaltwasser, C. (2013). Exclusionary vs. Inclusionary populism: Comparing contemporary Europe and Latin America. *Government and Opposition*, *48*(2), 147–174. https://doi.org/10.1017/gov.2012.11

Nai, A. (2018). Fear and loathing in populist campaigns? Comparing the communication style of populists and non-populists in elections worldwide. *Journal of Political Marketing*, 1–32. https://doi.org/10.1080/15377857.2018.1491439

Pirro, A. (2018). The polyvalent populism of the 5 Star Movement. *Journal of Contemporary European Studies*, *26*(4), 443–458. https://doi.org/10.1080/14782804.2018.1519484

Rooduijn, M., & Akkerman, T. (2017). Flank attacks: Populism and left-right radicalism in Western Europe. *Party Politics*, *23*(3), 193–204. https://doi.org/10.1177/1354068815596514

Rydgren, J. (2017). Right-Wing populism in Europe & USA. *Journal of Language and Politics*, *16*(4), 485–496. https://doi.org/10.1075/jlp.17024.ryd

Schmuck, D., & Hameleers, M. (2019). Closer to the people: A comparative content analysis of populist communication on social networking sites in pre- and post-election periods. *Information, Communication & Society*, 1–18. https://doi.org/10.1080/1369118X.2019.1588909

Schulz, A. (2019). Where populist citizens get the news: An investigation of news audience polarization along populist attitudes in 11 countries. *Communication Monographs*, *86*(1), 88–111. https://doi.org/10.1080/03637751.2018.1508876

Spierings, N., & Zaslove, A. (2017). Gender, populist attitudes, and voting: Explaining the gender gap in voting for populist radical right and populist radical left parties. *West European Politics*, *40*(4), 821–847. https://doi.org/10.1080/01402382.2017.1287448

Stockemer, D., & Barisione, M. (2017). The "new" discourse of the front national under Marine Le Pen: A slight change with a big impact. *European Journal of Communication*, *32*(2), 100–115. https://doi.org/10.1177/0267323116680132

Tausczik, Y. R., & Pennebaker, Y. W. (2010). The psychological meaning of words: LIWC and computerized text analysis methods. *Journal of Language and Social Psychology, 29*(1), 24–54. https://doi.org/10.1177/0261927X09351676

Van Kessel, S., & Castelein, R. (2016). Shifting the blame. Populist politicians' use of Twitter as a tool of opposition. *Journal of Contemporary European Research, 12*(2), 594–614.

Wodak, R. (2015). *The politics of fear: What right-wing populist discourses mean.* Sage.

Does populism go viral? How Italian leaders engage citizens through social media

Roberta Bracciale ⓘ, Massimiliano Andretta ⓘ and Antonio Martella ⓘ

ABSTRACT
This study explores populism in terms of communication while distinguishing between its ideological and stylistic dimensions. We examine the social media communication of the three main Italian political leaders during the last national electoral campaign to underline the differences and similarities in their use of populist communication in terms of ideology and style and assess how it affects Facebook and Twitter engagement. Our analysis shows that the three leaders all adopt populist communication styles but in slightly different ways. In all cases, populist style elements have a stronger impact on online engagement than populist ideology. The main difference between social media seems to be related less to the leaders' communication elements than to their platform-specific audiences' positive reactions to populist communication strategies.

Introduction

The electoral consent gained by many political movements and leaders characterized by populist references has increased the importance of understanding populism as a political and social phenomenon (Albertazzi & McDonnell, 2008; Kriesi, 2014).

Scholarly interest in the several interpretations of the populist phenomenon (e.g., ideology, communication style, strategy, etc.) has grown recently because it clearly affects political communication and the ways in which political actors represent themselves (Aalberg & de Vreese, 2017; Blassnig et al., 2019).

Modern political communication is strongly characterized by the use of social network sites, which have emerged as extremely conducive to the spread of populism (Ernst et al., 2017; Ernst et al., 2019; Mazzoleni & Bracciale, 2018), as they allow political actors to directly address (Bartlett, 2014) and mobilize their audiences (Kriesi, 2014). Populist communication seems to represent a winning strategy for political actors on social media for many reasons. First, the personalization of politics fostered by social media fits well with the self-presentation of the leader as one of the people ('one of us') – one of the 'ordinary hard-working citizens, victimized by an economic and political

Supplemental data for this article can be accessed https://doi.org/10.1080/1369118X.2021.1874472

establishment' (Gerbaudo, 2015, p. 78). Second, the widespread polarization within social network sites (Conover et al., 2011) offers a fertile ground for the typical populist 'us-against-them' construction, in both the vertical dimension, against political elites (van Kessel & Castelein, 2016), and the horizontal dimension, against ostracized social subsectors (Bartlett, 2014; Ernst et al., 2018).

We seek to grasp the differences amongst political leaders' use of social media and understand how populism affects citizens' social media engagement following the two main approaches in the literature: examining populism as both a 'thin'-centered ideology (Mudde, 2004) and as a communication style (Jagers & Walgrave, 2007). We adopt a communication-centric approach (Stanyer et al., 2017), positing that any political actor (even a non-populist one) can use populist communication to activate audiences and maximize consent among voters (Blassnig & Wirz, 2019). Building on the work of scholars who focused on populism as a broader communication strategy (Bracciale & Martella, 2017; Ernst et al., 2019), we analyze populist styles and ideology separately to verify their interdependence as 'communicative tools used for spreading populist ideas are just as central as the populist ideas themselves' (de Vreese et al., 2018, p. 425).

This study examines political leaders' communication strategies on social network sites to, first, provide a wider and more precise systematization of stylistic elements related to populist communication; second, to compare the populist communication patterns (style and ideology) of political leaders; and, third, to shed light on whether populist 'success' (in terms of public activation) depends on content (ideology) or form (style).

The remainder of this article is structured as follows. In the next section, we discuss the interpretation of populism as a 'thin' ideology to identify the main aspects of the concept. Then, we discuss the importance of approaching populism from a communication point of view and describe the main aspects of this approach. Next, we detail our case study and analytical method. Then, we present and discuss our results. In the final section, we summarize the study's main results, discuss their theoretical implications, and suggest avenues for further research.

Analyzing social media populism

Populism as thin ideology

The notion of populism as a thin ideology is one of the most popular interpretations among researchers in the field (Moffitt, 2016). As theorized by Mudde (2004) and later by several other scholars (Aalberg et al., 2017; Abts & Rummens, 2007; Albertazzi & McDonnell, 2008; Mudde & Kaltwasser, 2017), this view of populism defines it as a thin-centered ideology that considers society to be ultimately separated into two homogeneous and antagonistic groups—the 'pure people' and the 'corrupt elite' who manipulate them (Mudde, 2004, p. 543)—as well as (sometimes) the 'others' who threaten the pure people (Albertazzi & McDonnell, 2008). Three fundamental elements of the ideology emerge based on this conceptualization of populism: (i) the people, (ii) the elites, and (ii) the dangerous others.

The concept of 'people' can be used to define a population as a whole or part of it depending on various perspectives, such as that of the 'nation,' 'citizens,' 'voters', etc. (Rooduijn, 2014). The notion of 'elites' comprises many categories (e.g., political, economic, media, intellectual; Jagers & Walgrave, 2007), and they are often depicted as corrupt actors who ignore the people in favor of their own interests (Albertazzi & McDonnell, 2008; Mudde, 2004). The concept of 'dangerous others' is based on the identification and isolation of population subgroups with characteristics that differ from those of the so-called 'people' (Albertazzi & McDonnell, 2008).

Populist ideology in social media appears in fragmented and nebulous forms due to its thin nature and 'inherent incompleteness' (Engesser, Ernst, et al., 2017). Consequently, populist ideology is not always easy to detect, as populist references are often implicit and vague and do not necessarily co-occur. Scholars have argued that populism is a matter of degree measured by the selective adoption of populist ideology-driven references in political messages (Blassnig & Wirz, 2019; Mazzoleni & Bracciale, 2018).

Many studies have identified social media as a favorable channel for the spread of populist ideology (Blassnig et al., 2020; Engesser, Fawzi, et al., 2017; Ernst et al., 2017; Gerbaudo, 2018). Among these media, Facebook has emerged as the platform preferred by populist actors—probably due to its facilitation of political communication and user demographics (Jacobs & Spierings, 2019)—and by populist citizens as a source of political information (Schulz, 2019). As the widespread adoption of populist references in political discourse seems to be a communication strategy designed to gain audiences' attention, we can hypothesize that political leaders differentiate their messages according to channel characteristics. We thus propose the following:

H1: Messages with populist ideology fragments are more frequent on Facebook than on Twitter.

Among studies focusing on populism and social media engagement, Ceccobelli et al. (2020) found that populist leaders were more effective than others in fostering 'likes' and shares among their followers on Facebook. Bobba and Roncarolo (2018) showed that posts conveying populist ideology gained more likes than non-populist posts on Facebook. They found that only 'complete' and 'excluding' populism types were significantly correlated with the number of likes. Bobba (2019) also found that Facebook engagement with Matteo Salvini was strictly related to the presence of populist ideology fragments in his posts: On average, the number of likes for populist posts was almost double the number for non-populist ones.

In the same vein, Blassnig and Wirz (2019) found that populist Facebook posts were more likely to engage users with a populist attitude and affiliation and that recipients were more likely to react to posts sent by typically populist actors, regardless of post content. However, the authors did not consider rhetoric based on 'dangerous others' as a key populist message, which has been proven to be an efficient driver on Facebook in Italy (Bobba, 2019; Bobba & Roncarolo, 2018).

Therefore, the ability of populist content and leaders to both attract attention and elicit user reaction as reported in the literature suggests that populism contributes to content popularity (Blassnig & Wirz, 2019). Content popularity is a key factor in how political actors propose specific content and how users select which content to promote to their peers (Porten-Cheé et al., 2018). Consequently, content popularity fosters message spread across social media, allowing messages to reach wider audiences and triggering the network media logic (Klinger & Svensson, 2015). Thus, we propose the following:

H2. Online messages characterized by populist ideology fragments generate more engagement.

Another important question is whether social media type filters the impact of populist messages on user engagement. Blassnig et al. (2020) found that populism was generally more 'engaging' on Facebook than on Twitter, likely due (as mentioned) to the different functions the two platforms perform in political communication. We thus propose the following:

H3. Populist ideology fragments are more engaging on Facebook than on Twitter.

Studies on the Italian context have found that anti-immigrant rhetoric, strongly related to the concept of 'dangerous others,' has become widespread among the Italian public in recent years (Tarchi, 2015). This leads to the next hypothesis:

H4. Populist ideology fragments related to the ostracism of others are more likely to engage online audiences.

Populism as a political communication style

Populism has been linked to several specific communication aspects, including the adoption of a highly emotional language (Canovan, 1999; Mazzoleni et al., 2003), simple and straightforward speech (Mudde, 2007; Taggart, 2000), and the use of a taboo-breaking discourse (Mudde, 2004). However, such specific communication stylistic elements are rarely included in the operationalization of populism as a communication style or systematized as part of populist communication (Aalberg et al., 2017; Cranmer, 2011; Jagers & Walgrave, 2007). Thus, following scholars who have analyzed both the form and content of populism as a communication style (Bracciale & Martella, 2017; Ernst et al., 2019; Moffitt, 2016), we argue that populist communication blends populist ideology and populism-related stylistic elements together and that they must be kept analytically separate in any empirical assessment of whether the two dimensions are connected. Following Kriesi (2018) and Ernst et al. (2019), we consider these stylistic elements to be not exclusively related to populist actors or populist communication but to be 'expressions of the same communication strategy that can also lead to the use of populist key messages' (Ernst et al., 2019, p. 3).

Empirically identifying populist communicative styles requires an inductive approach based on the populist-related stylistic elements discussed in the literature. First, many scholars have identified appeals to emotion as a recurrent characteristic of populist speech, language, and style (Alvares & Dahlgren, 2016; Bossetta, 2017; Ernst et al., 2019; Moffitt, 2016), which has been key to communication effectiveness (Hameleers et al., 2016; Wirz, 2018). Emotions can be 'positive,' such as pride, enthusiasm, and hope; or 'negative,' such as fear and anger (Caiani & Graziano, 2016; Ernst et al., 2018). Both have been found to be key strategic styles for gaining attention.

Moreover, the figure of the 'leader' has grown significantly on social media due to the personalization process that characterizes the hybrid media system (Enli & Skogerbø, 2013). Several authors (Kriesi, 2018; Urbinati, 2014) have shown that the personalization of politics is not an 'accident in populism' but is probably its 'destiny,' for several reasons. First, the personalization of politics encourages political leaders to share 'private' aspects and moments (Karlsen & Enjolras, 2016; Stanyer, 2012) in order to be perceived as 'authentic' and ordinary. Second, personalization relates to the rhetorical construction of charismatic leadership, which has been identified as a fundamental trait of populist communication (Bobba, 2019; Bos et al., 2012; Caiani & Graziano, 2016; Canovan, 1999). This rhetoric can be performed either through a 'decision-making' language intended to represent the leader's strong problem-solving ability by recurring to a black/white logic (Bordignon, 2014; Ernst et al., 2019); or through so-called 'missionary politics' language, which presents the leader as the savior of the nation (Moffitt, 2016; Zúquete, 2013).

Simplification and increasingly frequent references to 'popular wisdom' are also communication strategies strongly connected to populist communication (Engesser, Ernst, et al., 2017; Moffitt, 2016; Oliver & Rahn, 2016). The first is based on the oversimplification of complex problems, leading to quick, ready-made, and easy solutions (Alvares & Dahlgren, 2016; Caiani & Graziano, 2016). Appeals to popular wisdom can be conceptually placed between simplification and popularization. Here, continuous references to proverbs, stereotypes, clichés, and 'common sense' (Moffitt, 2016; Tarchi, 2015) allow political leaders to represent themselves as ordinary people, and simplifies the debate with reference to a common imaginary.

Finally, the strong polarization, which is often amplified on social media (Conover et al., 2011; Guimaraes et al., 2017), combines with an adversarial use of online platforms to create another typical trait of populist communication (van Kessel & Castelein, 2016; Waisbord & Amado, 2017). The adversarial use of social media is also linked to the exploitation of news and consists of the application of 'cherry-picking' logic (Kepplinger et al., 1991; Krämer, 2014) to facts or events, which polarizes the audience. Table 1.

Based on the literature's identification of the strong connection between these stylistic aspects and populist ideology, we hypothesize as follows:

H5. Social media messages with populist ideology fragments are more likely to include populist-style features.

Table 1. Populist ideology elements (literature review).

Ideology fragment	Categories	Definitions
Appeal to the people	Socio-economic	Specific sub-set of the people based on socio-economic factors, or ordinary people (Aalberg et al., 2017; Abts & Rummens, 2007; Ernst et al., 2017; Mudde & Kaltwasser, 2017).
	National identity	Defence of national identity, national community, or referring to native population in ethnic or nationalistic terms (Albertazzi & McDonnell, 2008; Alvares & Dahlgren, 2016).
	Norms and values	Identifying people from traditional norms, values, and religion, or depicting a segment of people as a temporary 'people' based on shared values (i.e., moral, cultural, etc.) (Aalberg et al., 2017; Taggart, 2000).
Attack to élites	Blame shifting, discrediting, and delegitimising	Elites are all corrupted and deemed responsible for causing the people's problems. Elites are distant from the people and take care only of their interests (Bos et al., 2012; Ernst et al., 2018; van Kessel & Castelein, 2016)
Ostracism	Dangerous others	Identifying groups within the people as an internal enemy: stigmatising and excluding them. Representing the others as parasites or spongers, as addicts or deviants, as disorderly or dangerous, as undeserving of benefits and unworthy of respect (Abts & Rummens, 2007; Albertazzi & McDonnell, 2008; Jagers & Walgrave, 2007).

Populist ideology and communication styles have been described as efficient communicative tools for maximizing user attention in social media (Engesser, Fawzi, et al., 2017) because of their ability to attract attention, polarize debates, and stir emotions. These aspects are fundamental for activating the network media logic online (Klinger & Svensson, 2015) and for spreading messages beyond immediate followers, causing them to go viral and reach secondary audiences (Vaccari & Valeriani, 2015). Emotional content is known to increase user engagement on social media (boyd et al., 2010), along with providing additional information (URLs) and engaging in community practices (e.g., hashtags; Suh et al., 2010). A recent study by Ceccobelli et al. (2020) found, surprisingly, that references to the personalization of politics (encompassed by the 'popularization' category) did not help content spread through social media. Table 2.

Based on our previous hypotheses (H2 and H4) on the relationship between populist ideology and content popularity, and since many communicative elements have been proven to foster social media engagement (e.g., emotions, personalization), it seems reasonable to expect that both stylistic and ideological elements affect users' attention and content selection on social media. However, very few studies on populism and social media engagement have analyzed both the aspects of populist communication to determine which elements are more likely to increase online engagement across different social media platforms. Thus, we pose the following research question:

RQ1. Which elements of populist communication (populist ideology or populist style) are most engaging?

Finally, we have hypothesized that leaders prefer Facebook as a way to spread populist content (H1), that populist ideology elements elicit more user reactions (H2 and H4) and that, consequently, populist ideology is more successful on Facebook (H3), as found in Blassnig et al. (2020). However, other studies have shown that populist actors seem to prefer Twitter as a platform for attacking competitors and for adversarial behaviors (van Kessel & Castelein, 2016; Waisbord & Amado, 2017) and that they adopt particular

Table 2. Populist style elements (literature review).

Categories	Style Elements	Definition
Appeal to emotions	Negative	fear, anger, emergency, and insecurity feelings (Alvares & Dahlgren, 2016; Caiani & Graziano, 2016; Hameleers et al., 2016)
	Positive	enthusiasm, pride, hope (Blassnig, Engesser, Ernst, & Esser, 2019; Wirz, 2018)
Leader's figure	Personal leader	referring to private life events and talking about personal emotions (Bracciale & Martella, 2017; Stanyer, 2012)
	Charismatic leader	referring to charismatic traits such as the ability to make quick and effective decisions, or the leader's missionary function (Bordignon, 2014; Kriesi, 2018; Moffitt, 2016; Zúquete, 2013)
	Professional leader	referring to distinct skills, such as professional qualities, or by emphasizing own actions (Karlsen & Enjolras, 2016; Van Aelst & Stanyer, 2012)
Adversarial behaviours	Attacking	attacking the competitors with critiques, blames and the use of bad manners (Hameleers et al., 2016; van Kessel & Castelein, 2016; Waisbord & Amado, 2017)
	Instrumental actualization	instrumentalizing facts and events to polarize the public opinion (Bordignon, 2014; Kepplinger et al., 1991; Krämer, 2014)
Problem solving	Simplification	simplifying complex problems (Alvares & Dahlgren, 2016; Caiani & Graziano, 2016; Canovan, 1999)
	Popular wisdom	relying on the popular wisdom using proverbs, referring to common sense, etc. (Moffitt, 2016; Tarchi, 2015)

communication elements for their populist ideology suitable for the platform. Therefore, another research question arises:

> RQ2. Does populism conceived as a communication style provoke more engagement on Twitter or on Facebook?

Research design and method

Case study

We analyzed the Facebook and Twitter messages of Italy's three main political leaders during the 2018 general election campaign. The leaders were selected according to their significance in Italian politics, ideologies, and party types. Matteo Renzi was leader of the Democratic Party (PD) during the election. This is a center-left party with a mass party tradition and was the biggest party in the governing coalition before the 2018 election. His party obtained about 19% of the vote in 2018, down 6% from the party's 2013 general election result. Luigi Di Maio is the leader of the Five Stars Movement (5SM) founded by comic Beppe Grillo, a new post-ideological and anti-establishment party (Bordignon & Ceccarini, 2013). In 2018, the 5SM obtained 33% of the vote, the largest electoral share. Finally, Matteo Salvini is the leader of the Salvini League (SL), formerly the 'Northern League,' an extreme-right party; it went from a mere 4% of the vote in 2013–15% in 2018. Salvini transformed his party by giving it a nationalist orientation through sovereigntist, Eurosceptic, and anti-immigrant rhetoric (Caiani & Graziano, 2016). Under his leadership, the League gained the most Italian votes (about 40%) in the 2019 European elections.

Dataset

The Facebook (FB) and Twitter (TW) timelines of the three leaders – Luigi Di Maio (5SM), Matteo Renzi (PD), and Matteo Salvini (SL) – were downloaded via Facebook Graph API and Twitter REST API covering February 4 to March 4, 2018, the last month of the election campaign (inclusive of election day).

Method

A total of 866 Facebook posts and 907 Tweets (see Table 3) were codified through content analysis by two trained coders,[1] who drew on an intensive literature review to identify the populist ideological elements and populist communication styles in the data.

Each variable was operationalized as a dummy. Following the literature, we performed a negative binomial regression model for each leader and social media platform in order

Table 3. Main data on tweets and posts by leader.

Leader	Facebook	no. fan*	Twitter	no. followers*
Luigi Di Maio	310	1,229,420	58	281,889
Matteo Renzi	88	1,115,199	109	3,365,525
Matteo Salvini	468	2,025,681	740	648,669

* Updated to February 18, 2018

to test how populist ideology fragments and communication styles impacted audience activation (Vergeer, 2017; Vergeer & Hermans, 2013).

We tested whether the impact of the leaders' messages was driven by content type or informativeness (Ceccobelli et al., 2020; Suh et al., 2010) by adding two control variables to the model: a) references to a specific policy issue (i.e., any reference to a specific issue, such as the economy, welfare, institutions and bureaucracies, immigration, and public order); and b) the use of media content in posts and tweets (photos or videos). The target variable for each model represents the number of retweets/shares.

A populist-driven communication?

The data on the Italian leaders' social communication during the electoral campaign show that appeal to the people was the most frequently used populist ideology fragment. In Di Maio's messages, this fragment often went together with attacks on elite: depicting Italians against mainstream political parties (accounting for 17% and 16%, respectively, of the elements on Facebook and about 9% and 16% of them on Twitter). This result confirms the literature in showing a typical rhetorical contraposition between the people and the elites (or *casta*) framed by the 5SM (Bordignon & Ceccarini, 2015). Very few messages were characterized by ostracism.

The only populist ideology fragment adopted by Renzi was appeal to the people (18.3% of Facebook posts and 14.8% of tweets), confirming his characterization as a soft populist in the literature (Ceccarini & Bordignon, 2017; Mazzoleni & Bracciale, 2018). The people depicted by Renzi were most often associated with his community and were invoked to stimulate a sense of belonging among party members.

Not surprisingly (Bobba, 2019), Salvini adopted populist ideology elements most frequently, and with almost no differences between the social media platforms. Appeal to the people was used in around 40% of his posts and tweets, often framed in national identity terms through the use of the slogan 'Italians First!' which relates to the ostracism of immigrants (appearing in about 30% of his posts).

Although Facebook was expected to be a better fit with the adoption of populist ideology fragments (H1), our data show that the three leaders preferred Twitter for this purpose. About 65% of the messages that contained at least one populist element were tweeted. Moreover, a clear pattern emerged: Salvini used all the populist fragments frequently (the people = 38%; elites = 6%; ostracism = 28%), while Di Maio focused on appeal to the people (16%) and the elites (16%), and Renzi only used appeal to the people (17%).

Regarding communication style, the leaders all preferred to share positive emotions, especially on Facebook, while negative emotions were more frequent on Twitter. A similar pattern was found regarding personal emotions and private lives, which appeared more frequently on Facebook, while adversarial behavior was more frequent on Twitter. All leaders were quite aggressive, but Renzi and Salvini tended to personalize the most by sharing private emotions and lives, while Di Maio tended to emphasize his professional and charismatic personality. He, along with Salvini, was also more prone to simplify political discourses.

Particularly interesting is the way the leaders combined their populist ideology with their communication style. Figure 1 shows how populist communication style elements

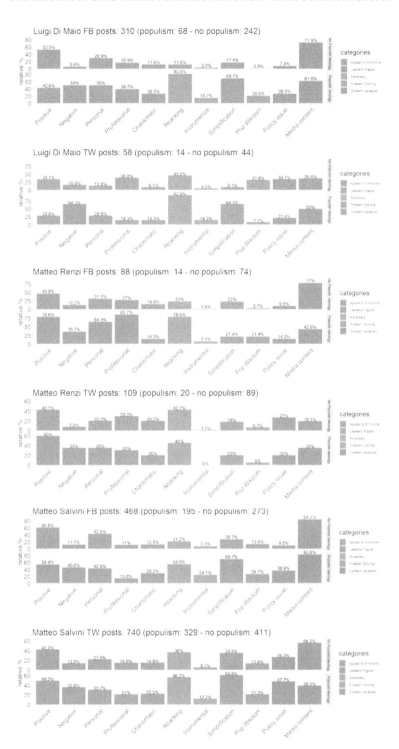

Figure 1. Communication styles by leader, use of populist ideology, and platform.

appeared in posts characterized by the presence of at least one populist ideology fragment. The populist ideology of Di Maio and Salvini was embedded in a more general communication strategy based on negative emotions, attacking, simplification, emphasis on their charismatic leadership, and instrumentalization, with no relevant differences observed between platforms.[2] In both cases, policy issues were framed within this coherent populist discourse as much as were references to popular wisdom, although Di Maio did this more often on Facebook. Renzi's communication strategy was far less coherently populist. He also used negative emotions and attacked his competitors—especially when making reference to his 'people'– but he was more prone to use positive emotions, while the other communication styles seem to be more freely distributed across ideological and non-ideological populist messages.

Salvini's and Di Maio's use of social communication strategies reveals that populist communication style elements, such as attacking, simplification, emotionalization, and emphasizing the leader's charisma serve to make the populist ideology more vibrant. Contrariwise, the use of populist ideological elements may allow for the exaltation of specific communication styles. These results seem to confirm H5's proposition that social media messages with populist ideology fragments are more likely to include populist-style features. However, specific discourse/communication styles do not seem to be associated with specific platform types, or at least not in the expected directions and with no clear patterns.

Does populism go viral?

Figure 2 shows the results of negative binomial regression analyses assessing the impact of populist ideology and communication styles on online audiences' engagement in sharing the leaders' messages on the two platforms.[3]

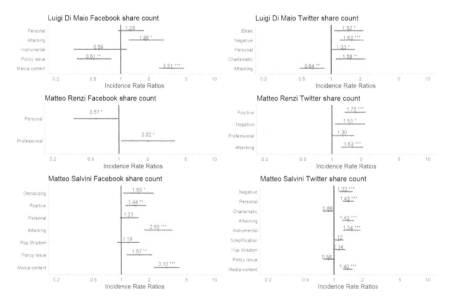

Figure 2. Significant predictors of engagement.

It seems at first glance that, for each leader, the style elements affecting online engagement differ depending on the social media platform used. For example, the regression models show that appeals to negative emotions (fear and anger) engaged only Twitter audiences. The use of populist ideology elements, seldom predictors of the number of shares, engaged Di Maio's Twitter audience when he attacked the elite, while Salvini engaged his Facebook followers when he ostracized the others. These results confirm the importance of a specific analysis for each online community (FB and TW).

For instance, for Renzi's Facebook, the model shows that his community preferred a communicative style based on an emphasis of Renzi as a professional leader and reacted negatively to the sharing of personal emotions or moments from his private life (Personal leader).

For Twitter, the model shows a more complex and richer pattern. The emphasis on Renzi as a professional still has a significant impact, but emotions and attacks are more decisive. Populist styles engage the other two leaders' audiences much more strongly, however.

On Facebook, as well as by the presence of videos and photos (Media Content), Di Maio's followers were activated strongly by attacks on his competitors and the sharing of personal feelings and moments (Personal), while his references to policy issues and his instrumental actualization have negative effects on engagement. The regression model for his Twitter feed shows a slightly different pattern: besides the personal elements and negative emotions, the Twitter community's preferred style was related to 'championship of the people' (Bracciale & Martella, 2017), aimed at presenting a strong leader (Charismatic) attacking the elites. The negative relation between attacking and online engagement seems to suggest that aggressive behavior triggers engagement almost exclusively when the targets are elites. Thus, the most effective communication strategy for the 5SM leader was apparently populist attacks against elites based on negative feelings and his self-depiction as a charismatic and 'close-to-the-people' leader (Personal and Charismatic).

Salvini's online community engaged for different reasons, and the range of engaging populist style elements was even broader. His Facebook audience seemed to engage more strongly when specific populist communication styles, such as attacking were used for policy issues, especially immigration. As mentioned, Salvini often used a communication strategy based on attacks on others, ostracism, and references to common sense (Popular Wisdom) to discuss policy issues. On the other hand, Salvini's posts also included references to positive feelings and personal moments, which affected the number of shares. Therefore, except for the use of simplification (which was very common in his messages but was not significantly engaging), his communication strategy appears effective for inducing positive reactions to a leader who represents himself as being 'close to the people' by sharing personal feelings, referring to 'common sense,' criticizing unpopular policies, attacking others, and identifying culprits among the 'dangerous others.' Moreover, having a vital media presence is extremely important for politicians; thus, together with sharing URLs, using pictures and Facebook Live were fundamental drivers in sharing Salvini's messages.

An even wider range of populist styles engaged Salvini's audience on Twitter. References to policy issues and charismatic aspects surprisingly attracted fewer retweets, whereas media content, sharing of personal moments, attacks on competitors, use of negative emotions, instrumental actualization, simplification, and references to popular wisdom all engaged his followers.

Overall, our data show that populist ideology engaged more online audiences (H2) only for Di Maio (on TW) and Salvini (on FB). Therefore, H3 is partially rejected because we did not find a clear association between ideology and engagement on Facebook. Salvini induced much more engagement on Facebook by ostracizing immigrants (H4), and Di Maio's attacks on elites engaged more of his audience on Twitter. Therefore, the expected effect of populist ideology on engagement seems to depend on several factors including the leader's ideology and constituency/user type.

In any case, stylistic aspects were much more effective than ideology elements in engaging social media audiences (RQ1). Several populist style aspects were effective in audiences' activation for all three leaders: sharing of personal feelings and moments, use of emotions, and attacks on competitors. However, the leaders who had more frequent recourse to a populist ideology (and who, we assume, attracted populist audiences) had a wider range of engaging stylistic elements, such as the emphasis on charismatic traits for Di Maio and simplification, appeal to popular wisdom, and instrumental actualization for the bold populist Salvini. It is not an accident that the only leader who was able to engage his audience by appealing to his professional skills, decision-making ability, and past achievements (Professional leader) was Renzi, whose audience might prefer a less-populist style. Therefore, with regard to RQ1, we find that populist communication style elements were more engaging than ideology elements.

Finally, the analysis revealed differences in the way the communication styles engaged audiences across the two social media platforms, along with the differences in the impacts of the ideological fragments. For instance, Di Maio's attacking style triggered more engagement on Facebook than on Twitter, Renzi's emotional mobilization worked on Twitter but not on Facebook, and simplification activated Salvini's audience on Twitter but not on Facebook. Appeals to negative feelings clearly worked for all leaders on Twitter, and references to charismatic leadership were effective for Salvini's and Di Maio's Twitter audiences. Otherwise, the differences we found do not follow a clear pattern and cannot be explained by the technological features of the two social media platforms (RQ2).

Conclusions

Social media communication is becoming a powerful tool by which political leaders can gain momentum in electoral campaigns. Leaders are using social media to influence mainstream media, implement agendas, make their issues central to political debate, obtain public support by spreading their message, and get supporters involved in campaigning. The e-campaigning conducted by Italian party leaders before the last national election supports the view argued in the literature that populism is not only a thin ideology but is, above all, a communication strategy. The leaders examined in our analysis differ in terms of party identity and position, but they all adopted populist communication elements, albeit in different ways.

The leaders employed and mixed populist style elements in different ways and at different intensities, but the overall differences were slight: all appealed to the emotions; all emphasized their professional, personal, and charismatic nature; and all attacked their opponents. However, our results confirmed the relationship between style elements and populist ideology in populist communication (Kriesi, 2018), since their use was significantly higher when the leaders adopted populist references.

Moreover, regarding the impact of populism on online engagement, we found that ideological elements were much less significant than communication styles. This suggests that populism's growing leverage in electoral campaigns has much more to do with the use of individualized, personalized, aggressive, and emotional communication strategies than with its thin ideology. Interestingly, however, populist styles engaged Salvini's and Di Maio's audiences significantly more strongly. These results seem to be related to the blending of populist ideology and style elements: a more frequent and wider adoption of populist ideology fragments seems to have led to a more frequent and wider adoption of many populist style elements, leading to a stronger impact on audience mobilization. Indeed, our analysis reveals that the online success of populism is related to style elements and their entanglement with populist ideology in populist communication. If populism fosters online content popularity (Blassnig et al., 2020) and works with network media logic to induce message spread, we can shed some light on how this unfolds on social media. First, we observed that both adoption rates and users' approval of populist ideology affected challenger/extreme leaders and their audiences more strongly than they did incumbents (Renzi) and their audiences, confirming prior results (Ernst et al., 2019). Second, given the frequent co-presence of stylistic elements and populist ideology, populist communication should be addressed as a whole when seeking to identify its effects on online engagement. Populist ideology emerged as the discriminating factor in stylistic element adoption rates, regardless of leader characteristics, but not as the fundamental predictor of online engagement. This behavior intersects with platform specificity, in addition to the political differences between leaders. Facebook was perceived as the more intimate environment, especially from the supply side, as political actors shared more positive and personalized posts on the platform (Ernst et al., 2019). Twitter was more closely associated with negative campaigning for both message senders and recipients, who shared more tweets characterized by adversarial behavior and negative feelings. Therefore, the popularity and success of populism on social media is clearly the result of multiple factors, including political positioning (challenger vs. incumbent), platform characteristics (demographics and uses), and communication strategies (adopted to 'perform' populist ideology).

Keeping all these elements separate helped us better understand their relationships and effects and discover that populist ideology contributes to online popularity not in itself but along with other factors that are strongly related to how and in which context ideology is 'performed' through key communication elements (Kriesi, 2018; Moffitt, 2016).

Limitations and further research

Although we hope this study makes some contributions to the flourishing literature that conceives populism as a communication-centered phenomenon, it has limitations that point to future research possibilities.

First, we found that a populist communication strategy can be adopted regardless of support for a populist ideology, but it remains unclear how populist fragments are strategically embodied by communication styles. Future studies could also investigate the extent to which leaders adopt a populist ideology for strategic reasons or adopt specific communication strategies to support a populist ideology.

Notes

1. The Krippendorff α calculated for each variable coded by the two coders ranged from 0.68 to 0.82, considered highly satisfactory values according to field norms (Hayes & Krippendorff, 2007). Detailed information for each variable coded is provided in the supplementary material.
2. The differences in the use of those communication styles between messages that contained at least one populist ideological fragment and those that contained no populist ideology element are all significant at the .001 level.
3. Figure 2 shows only the significant predictors transformed according to the formula exp(b). The significance codes are as follows: " " = $p < 0.1$; * = $p < 0.05$; ** = $p < 0.01$; *** = $p < 0.001$. The full models can be found in the supplementary material.

Disclosure statement

No potential conflict of interest was reported by the author(s).

Data availability statement

The data that support the findings of this study are available upon reasonable request from the corresponding author. The data are not publicly available due to social media TOS.

Funding

This work was supported by the Università di Pisa PRA (Athenaeum Research Project) under Grant *Populismo in Italia: attori e processi in tempi di crisi* (PRA_2018_10).

ORCID

Roberta Bracciale ⓘ http://orcid.org/0000-0002-7567-4785
Massimiliano Andretta ⓘ http://orcid.org/0000-0002-7078-4635
Antonio Martella ⓘ http://orcid.org/0000-0003-3378-1782

References

Aalberg, T., & de Vreese, C. H. (2017). Introduction: Comprehending populist political communication. In T. Aalberg, F. Esser, C. Reinemann, J. Stromback, & C. H. de Vreese (Eds.), *Populist political communication in Europe* (pp. 3–11). Routledge.

Aalberg, T., Esser, F., Reinemann, C., Stromback, J., & de Vreese, C. H. (2017). *Populist political communication in Europe*. Routledge.

Abts, K., & Rummens, S. (2007). Populism versus democracy. *Political Studies*, 55(2), 405–424. https://doi.org/10.1111/j.1467-9248.2007.00657.x

Albertazzi, D., & McDonnell, D. (2008). *Twenty-first century populism: The spectre of Western European democracy*. Palgrave Macmillan.

Alvares, C., & Dahlgren, P. (2016). Populism, extremism and media: Mapping an uncertain terrain. *European Journal of Communication*, 31(1), 46–57. https://doi.org/10.1177/0267323115614485

Bartlett, J. (2014). Populism, social media and democratic strain. In G. Lodge, & G. Gottfried (Eds.), *Democracy in Britain: Essays in honour of James Cornford* (pp. 91–96). Institute for Public Policy Research.

Blassnig, S., Büchel, F., Ernst, N., & Engesser, S. (2019). Populism and informal fallacies: An analysis of right-wing populist rhetoric in election campaigns. *Argumentation*, 33(1), 107–136. https://doi.org/10.1007/s10503-018-9461-2

Blassnig, S., Engesser, S., Ernst, N., & Esser, F. (2019). Hitting a nerve: Populist news articles lead to more frequent and more populist reader comments. *Political Communication*, 36(4), 629–651. https://doi.org/10.1080/10584609.2019.1637980

Blassnig, S., Ernst, N., Engesser, S., & Esser, F. (2020). Populism and social media popularity: How populist communication benefits political leaders on Facebook and Twitter. In R. Davis, & D. Taras (Eds.), *Power shift? Political leadership and social media: Case studies in political communication* (pp. 97–111). Routledge.

Blassnig, S., & Wirz, D. S. (2019). Populist and popular: An experiment on the drivers of user reactions to populist posts on Facebook. *Social Media + Society*, 5(4), 1–12. https://doi.org/10.1177/2056305119890062

Bobba, G. (2019). Social media populism: Features and "likeability" of Lega Nord communication on Facebook. *European Political Science*, 18(1), 11–23. https://doi.org/10.1057/s41304-017-0141-8

Bobba, G., & Roncarolo, F. (2018). The likeability of populism on social media in the 2018 Italian general election. *Italian Political Science*, 13(1), 51–62.

Bordignon, F. (2014). Matteo Renzi: A "leftist Berlusconi" for the Italian Democratic Party? *South European Society and Politics*, 19(1), 1–23. https://doi.org/10.1080/13608746.2014.887240

Bordignon, F., & Ceccarini, L. (2013). Five stars and a Cricket. Beppe Grillo shakes Italian politics. *South European Society and Politics*, 18(4), 427–449. https://doi.org/10.1080/13608746.2013.775720

Bordignon, F., & Ceccarini, L. (2015). The Five-Star Movement: A hybrid actor in the net of state institutions. *Journal of Modern Italian Studies*, *20*(4), 454–473. https://doi.org/10.1080/1354571X.2015.1066112

Bos, L., van der Brug, W., & de Vreese, C. H. (2012). An experimental test of the impact of style and rhetoric on the perception of right-wing populist and mainstream party leaders. *Acta Politica*, *48*(2), 1–17. https://doi.org/10.1057/ap.2012.27

Bossetta, M. (2017). Fighting fire with fire: Mainstream adoption of the populist political style in the 2014 Europe debates between Nick Clegg and Nigel Farage. *The British Journal of Politics and International Relations*, *19*(4), 715–734. https://doi.org/10.1177/1369148117715646

boyd, d., Golder, S., & Lotan, G. (2010). Tweet, Tweet, Retweet: Conversational aspects of retweeting on Twitter. In 2010 *43rd Hawaii International Conference on System Sciences* (pp. 1–10). IEEE.

Bracciale, R., & Martella, A. (2017). Define the populist political communication style: The case of Italian political leaders on Twitter. *Information, Communication & Society*, *20*(9), 1310–1329. https://doi.org/10.1080/1369118X.2017.1328522

Caiani, M., & Graziano, P. R. (2016). Varieties of populism: Insights from the Italian case. *Italian Political Science Review/Rivista Italiana Di Scienza Politica*, *46*(02), 1–25. https://doi.org/10.1017/ipo.2016.6

Canovan, M. (1999). Trust the people! populism and the two faces of democracy. *Political Studies*, *47*(1), 2–16. https://doi.org/10.1111/1467-9248.00184

Ceccarini, L., & Bordignon, F. (2017). Referendum on Renzi: The 2016 vote on the Italian constitutional revision. *South European Society and Politics*, *22*(3), 281–302. https://doi.org/10.1080/13608746.2017.1354421

Ceccobelli, D., Quaranta, M., & Valeriani, A. (2020). Citizens' engagement with popularization and with populist actors on Facebook: A study on 52 leaders in 18 Western democracies. *European Journal of Communication*, 1-18. https://doi.org/10.1177/0267323120909292

Conover, M., Ratkiewicz, J., Francisco, M., Goncalves, B., Flammini, A., & Menczer, F. (2011). Political polarization on Twitter. *Proceedings of the Fifth International AAAI Conference on Weblogs and Social Media*, *5*(1), 89–96.

Cranmer, M. (2011). Populist communication and publicity: An empirical study of contextual differences in Switzerland. *Swiss Political Science Review*, *17*(3), 286–307. https://doi.org/10.1111/j.1662-6370.2011.02019.x

de Vreese, C. H., Esser, F., Aalberg, T., Reinemann, C., & Stanyer, J. (2018). Populism as an expression of political communication content and style: A new perspective. *The International Journal of Press/Politics*, *23*(4), 423–438. https://doi.org/10.1177/1940161218790035

Engesser, S., Ernst, N., Esser, F., & Büchel, F. (2017). Populism and social media: How politicians spread a fragmented ideology. *Information, Communication & Society*, *20*(8), 1109–1126. https://doi.org/10.1080/1369118X.2016.1207697

Engesser, S., Fawzi, N., & Larsson, A. O. (2017). Populist online communication: Introduction to the special issue. *Information, Communication & Society*, *20*(9), 1279–1292. https://doi.org/10.1080/1369118X.2017.1328525

Enli, G. S., & Skogerbø, E. (2013). Personalized campaigns in party-centred politics. *Information, Communication & Society*, *16*(5), 757–774. https://doi.org/10.1080/1369118X.2013.782330

Ernst, N., Blassnig, S., Engesser, S., Büchel, F., & Esser, F. (2019). Populists prefer social media over talk shows: An analysis of populist messages and stylistic elements across six countries. *Social Media + Society*, *5*(1), 1–14. https://doi.org/10.1177/2056305118823358

Ernst, N., Engesser, S., Büchel, F., Blassnig, S., & Esser, F. (2017). Extreme parties and populism: An analysis of Facebook and Twitter across six countries. *Information, Communication & Society*, *20*(9), 1347–1364. https://doi.org/10.1080/1369118X.2017.1329333

Ernst, N., Esser, F., Blassnig, S., & Engesser, S. (2018). Favorable opportunity structures for populist communication: Comparing different types of politicians and issues in social media, television and the press. *The International Journal of Press/Politics*, *24*(2), 165–188. https://doi.org/10.1177/1940161218819430

Gerbaudo, P. (2015). Populism 2.0: Social media activism, the generic Internet user and interactive direct democracy. In D. Trottier, & C. Fuchs (Eds.), *Social media, politics and the state: Protests, revolutions, riots, crime and policing in the age of Facebook, Twitter and YouTube* (pp. 67–87). Routledge.

Gerbaudo, P. (2018). Social media and populism: An elective affinity? *Media, Culture & Society*, *40*(5), 745–753. https://doi.org/10.1177/0163443718772192

Guimaraes, A., Wang, L., & Weikum, G. (2017). Us and them: Adversarial politics on Twitter. *2017 IEEE International Conference on data Mining Workshops (ICDMW)*, *5*, 872–877. https://doi.org/10.1109/ICDMW.2017.119

Hameleers, M., Bos, L., & de Vreese, C. H. (2016). "They did it": The effects of emotionalized blame attribution in populist communication. *Communication Research*, *44*(6), 870–900. https://doi.org/10.1177/0093650216644026

Hayes, A. F., & Krippendorff, K. (2007). Answering the call for a standard reliability measure for coding data. *Communication Methods and Measures*, *1*(1), 77–89. https://doi.org/10.1080/19312450709336664

Jacobs, K., & Spierings, N. (2019). A populist paradise? Examining populists' Twitter adoption and use. *Information, Communication & Society*, *22*(12), 1681–1696. https://doi.org/10.1080/1369118X.2018.1449883

Jagers, J., & Walgrave, S. (2007). Populism as political communication style: An empirical study of political parties' discourse in Belgium. *European Journal of Political Research*, *46*(3), 319–345. https://doi.org/10.1111/j.1475-6765.2006.00690.x

Karlsen, R., & Enjolras, B. (2016). Styles of social media campaigning and influence in a hybrid political communication system: Linking candidate survey data with Twitter data. *The International Journal of Press/Politics*, *21*(3), 338–357. https://doi.org/10.1177/1940161216645335

Kepplinger, H. M., Brosius, H.-B., & Staab, J. F. (1991). Instrumental actualization: A theory of mediated conflicts. *European Journal of Communication*, *6*(3), 263–290. https://doi.org/10.1177/0267323191006003002

Klinger, U., & Svensson, J. (2015). The emergence of network media logic in political communication: A theoretical approach. *New Media & Society*, *17*(8), 1241–1257. https://doi.org/10.1177/1461444814522952

Krämer, B. (2014). Media populism: A conceptual clarification and some theses on its effects. *Communication Theory*, *24*(1), 42–60. https://doi.org/10.1111/comt.12029

Kriesi, H. (2014). The populist challenge. *West European Politics*, *37*(2), 361–378. https://doi.org/10.1080/01402382.2014.887879

Kriesi, H. (2018). Revisiting the populist challenge. *Politologický Časopis - Czech Journal of Political Science*, *25*(1), 5–27. https://doi.org/10.5817/PC2018-1-5

Mazzoleni, G., & Bracciale, R. (2018). Socially mediated populism: The communicative strategies of political leaders on Facebook. *Palgrave Communications*, *4*(1), 50. https://doi.org/10.1057/s41599-018-0104-x

Mazzoleni, G., Stewart, J., & Horsfield, B. (2003). *The media and neo-populism: A contemporary comparative analysis*. Preager.

Moffitt, B. (2016). *The global rise of populism: Performance, political style, and representation*. Stanford University Press.

Mudde, C. (2004). The populist zeitgeist. *Government and Opposition*, *39*(4), 542–563. https://doi.org/10.1111/j.1477-7053.2004.00135.x

Mudde, C. (2007). *Populist radical right parties in Europe (Vol. 91)*. Cambridge University Press.

Mudde, C., & Kaltwasser, R. C. (2017). *Populism: A very short introduction*. Oxford University Press.

Oliver, J. E., & Rahn, W. M. (2016). Rise of the Trumpenvolk. *The ANNALS of the American Academy of Political and Social Science*, *667*(1), 189–206. https://doi.org/10.1177/0002716216662639

Porten-Cheé, P., Haßler, J., Jost, P., Eilders, C., & Maurer, M. (2018). Popularity cues in online media: Theoretical and methodological perspectives. *Studies in Communication and Media, 7*(2), 208–230. https://doi.org/10.5771/2192-4007-2018-2-80

Rooduijn, M. (2014). The mesmerising message: The diffusion of populism in public debates in Western European media. *Political Studies, 62*(4), 726–744. https://doi.org/10.1111/1467-9248.12074

Schulz, A. (2019). Where populist citizens get the news: An investigation of news audience polarization along populist attitudes in 11 countries. *Communication Monographs, 86*(1), 88–111. https://doi.org/10.1080/03637751.2018.1508876

Stanyer, J. (2012). *Intimate politics*. Polity Press.

Stanyer, J., Salgado, S., & Stromback, J. (2017). Populist actors as communicators or political actors as populist communicators. In T. Aalberg, F. Esser, C. Reinemann, J. Stromback, & E. H. de Vreese (Eds.), *Populist political communication in Europe* (pp. 353–364). Routledge.

Suh, B., Hong, L., Pirolli, P., & Chi, E. H. (2010). Want to be Retweeted? Large Scale Analytics on Factors Impacting Retweet in Twitter Network. *2010 IEEE second International Conference on social Computing*, 177–184. https://doi.org/10.1109/SocialCom.2010.33

Taggart, P. (2000). *Populism*. Open University Press.

Tarchi, M. (2015). Italy: The promised land of populism? *Contemporary Italian Politics, 7*(3), 273–285. https://doi.org/10.1080/23248823.2015.1094224

Urbinati, N. (2014). *Democracy disfigured*. Harvard University Press. https://www.jstor.org/stable/j.ctt6wpndf

Vaccari, C., & Valeriani, A. (2015). Follow the leader! Direct and indirect flows of political communication during the 2013 Italian general election campaign. *New Media & Society, 17*(7), 1025–1042. https://doi.org/10.1177/1461444813511038

Van Aelst, Peter, Sheafer, Tamir, & Stanyer, James. (2012). The personalization of mediated political communication: A review of concepts, operationalizations and key findings. *Journalism: Theory, Practice & Criticism, 13*(2), 203–220. https://doi.org/10.1177/1464884911427802

van Kessel, S., & Castelein, R. (2016). Shifting the blame: Populist politicians' use of Twitter as a tool of opposition. *Journal of Contemporary European Research, 12*(2), 594–614. http://jcer.net/index.php/jcer/article/view/709/578

Vergeer, M. (2017). Adopting, networking, and communicating on Twitter. *Social Science Computer Review, 35*(6), 698–712. https://doi.org/10.1177/0894439316672826

Vergeer, M., & Hermans, L. (2013). Campaigning on Twitter: Microblogging and online social networking as campaign tools in the 2010 general elections in the Netherlands. *Journal of Computer-Mediated Communication, 18*(4), 399–419. https://doi.org/10.1111/jcc4.12023

Waisbord, S., & Amado, A. (2017). Populist communication by digital means: Presidential Twitter in Latin America. *Information, Communication & Society, 20*(9), 1330–1346. https://doi.org/10.1080/1369118X.2017.1328521

Wirz, D. S. (2018). Persuasion through emotion? An experimental test of the emotion-eliciting nature of populist communication. *International Journal of Communication, 12*, 1114–1138. https://doi.org/1932-8036/20180005

Zúquete, J. P. (2013). Missionary politics: A contribution to the study of populism. *Religion Compass, 7*(7), 263–271. https://doi.org/10.1111/rec3.12048

Why study media ecosystems?

Ethan Zuckerman

ABSTRACT
Much as ecology emerged from biology as scientists began studying the complex interactions between organisms in their environments, a shift is happening in communication and media studies regarding analysis of social media. The complex relationships between user-generated social media and professionally created news media are best understood as a complex media ecosystem with its own emergent behaviors that only become visible when studied from a perspective broader than considering a single medium in isolation. Some of the key debates regarding social media's effects in spreading mis- and disinformation can be studied in richer ways by applying quantitative methods that integrate information across multiple types of media using a media ecosystem model. Understanding these characteristics of media ecosystems could help political parties, activists and others who depend on media to advance their messages.

The invention of the ecosystem

Arthur Tansley was one of Britain's foremost scholars of ecology. Sherardian Professor of Botany at the University of Oxford, chair of the British Ecological Society and founding editor of the Journal of Ecology, Tansley's opinions carried great weight in scientific societies, and especially around the complex and 'polymorphic science' (Cooper, 1957) of ecology (McIntosh, 1986).

His 1935 paper, 'The use and abuse of vegetational terms and concepts' (Tansley, 1935) = introduced the term 'ecosystem', which he defines as

> ... the whole system (in the sense of physics), indicating not only the organism-complex, but also the whole complex of physical factors forming what we call the environment of the biome – the habitat factors in the widest sense. Though the organisms may claim our primary interest, when we are trying to think fundamentally, we cannot separate them from their special environment, with which they form one physical system.

In offering this definition, Tansley pushed his colleagues to view their field's horizons more broadly than those of the disciplines ecology emerged from: natural history, botany, zoology. Ecology's special role was the consideration of these broad systems, understood through the movement of materials and energy through living communities. Scholars would continue to examine individual species of plants and animals, Tansley believed, but 'the systems we isolate mentally are not only included as parts of larger ones, but they also overlap, interlock and interact with one another. The isolation is partly artificial but is the only possible way in which we can proceed' (Tansley, 1935).

While Tansley's definition was influential within ecology, discussions of 'ecosystems' did not reach broader audiences until the 1960s when a wave of activism around ecological issues, particularly Rachel Carson's *Silent Spring* (Carson, 2002), began a widespread conversation about systemic threats to the environment as a whole. Carson's documentation of the risks to human and environmental health that could come from the bioaccumulation of DDT within food webs introduced a new way of thinking about human impact on the environment to millions of readers. Environmental activist Bill McKibben credits Carson as 'the very first person to knock some of the shine off modernity' (Griswold, 2012), confronting readers with the uncomfortable truth that the celebrated lab-produced chemicals that characterized modern life could alter an entire ecosystem, eventually threatening human life itself.

If Carson's call to arms was the key event bringing the idea of ecosystems to wide popular understanding, a trio of related events in 2016 may serve as the Silent Spring moment to inspire a broad study of media ecosystems. In June 2016, Britain stunned much of the world in voting to leave the European Union. In November 2016, the United States elected the supremely unqualified Donald Trump to the presidency, shocking political prognosticators globally. Journalists began to focus on political disinformation and its possible effects as a way to explain the surprise of the Brexit and US presidential elections. This narrative gained traction in 2018 with news of a massive leak of Facebook profile data by Cambridge Analytica, a political consulting firm that had worked for Leave. EU and also the Trump 2016 presidential campaign. The emergent narrative about the dangers of social media ecosystems is summarized in a phrase uttered by everyone from Roger McNamee (Tucker, 2020), an early investor in Facebook, to Derrick Johnson, the president of the NAACP (Thornbecke, 2020): 'Facebook is a threat to democracy'.

This line of thought about the power of a media system leads directly back to ideas articulated in the 1960s by Marshall McLuhan and Neil Postman. Postman adopted McLuhan's term 'media ecology' and established the Program in Media Ecology at NYU in 1971, positing that 'Media ecology looks into the matter of how media of communication affect human perception, understanding, feeling, and value; and how our interaction with media facilitates or impedes our chances of survival' (Postman, 1970). That perspective informed Postman's best known work, *Amusing Ourselves to Death* (Postman, 1985), in which he argues that the shortcomings of television as a medium make rational argumentation difficult or impossible.

It is dangerous to extend Postman' work to include technologies invented after his death, but it is likely he would have echoed those worried about Facebook and democracy, as he was sufficiently skeptical of a computation future to tell the German Informatics Society in 1990, 'Through the computer, the heralds say, we will make education better, religion better, politics better, our minds better – best of all, ourselves better. This is, of course, nonsense, and only the young or the ignorant or the foolish could believe it' (Postman, 1990). Postman would not have been surprised to see a narrative emerge in which social media made politics and civic dialog worse and might have gone further to argue that these tools make some forms of responsible political discussions impossible.

Yet while McLuhan and Postman argue for 'media ecology' as the practice of understanding media's effects on society more broadly, the concept of a 'media *ecosystem*' as a complex but quantitatively analyzable set of relationships and flows, offers a lens to understand our Facebook/Cambridge Analytica/disinformation moment. Media is the environment in which we understand, feel and value, and Postman and McLuhan might agree that ads and content microtargeted to us based on previously expressed preferences have the power to shift our political positions.

But it is Tansley who gives us the tools to understand the anxieties and suspicions of social media and their effects on contemporary society. It is not just the ways individuals have received propaganda and misinformation on Facebook that should give us concern for democracy: it is the complex interactions between digital media, conventional media, politicians, voters, advertisers and platforms that we need to investigate to understand the contemporary moment. Much as the weakening of condor eggshells implicated not just DDT, but the broader project of better living through chemistry, the 2016 Facebook/Cambridge Analytica/misinformation scandal suggests a need not just to look closely at Facebook but at the complex relationships between digital media and citizenship.

The concept of the media ecosystem is not a new one – we see references to the changing media ecosystem in studies of the relationship between blogs and mainstream media in the early 2000s, and the term is applied particularly to the structure of media in specific geographic areas, i.e., the Muslim world (Eickelman & Anderson, 2003). Recent work exploring the different behaviors that occur within a single social media platform, using ethnographic and historical techniques, presents a deeply helpful foundation to build upon for broader studies of relationships between platforms and networks (Burgess & Baym, 2020; Mailland & Driscoll, 2017).

In this sense, earlier discussions of media ecosystems parallel the use of ecosystem to describe physical environments, applying first to specific geographical areas before discussing the environment, in totality, on scales up to the planetary. The term has gained significant traction in the past ten years, as the rising power of platforms like Facebook, YouTube and Twitter and the waning influence of newspapers and television have forced a re-examination of the complex relationships between pre-digital media, digital native media and their collective interactions with public opinion formation, voting and other civic behaviors.

What we study when we study media ecosystems

In positing ecosystems as a study of 'the whole system (in the sense of physics)', Tansley encourages us to think in terms of large-scale flows: how energy and nutrients flow through an ecosystem from photosynthesis to consumption, to predation, to decay. Media ecosystems operate on flows as well: the flow of attention. The pioneer in identifying attention as the key currency of the media ecosystem was the wildly interdisciplinary thinker, Herbert Simon.

Simon won both the Nobel for economics in 1978 and the Turing Award for computer science in 1975. Simon's expertise was diverse, and he was sought out as a collaborator in many fields.

That Simon was so widely celebrated and in demand may explain his interest in the limits of human attention. In 1969, Simon gave a lecture to the Brookings Institute titled

'Designing Organizations for an Information-Rich World' (Simon, 1969). Simon opens the lecture with a story about his neighbors, who bought a pair of rabbits for their daughters as a Christmas present. One was male and one female, and the neighbors now have many rabbits. Too many? Simon answers the question in ecological terms: ' … we might judge the world as rabbit rich or rabbit poor by relating the number of rabbits to the amount of lettuce and grass (and garden flowers) available for them to eat' (Simon, 1969, p. 6). A surplus of rabbits exists if there is a surfeit of grass, and vice versa.

'What information consumes is the attention of its recipients. Hence a wealth of information creates a poverty of attention, and a need to allocate that attention efficiently among the overabundance of information sources that might consume it' (Simon, 1969, p. 7). Designing Organizations for an Information-Rich World Simon uses this idea of surplus and scarcity to encourage us to understand information not in terms of bits and bytes, but in terms of time: 'We can measure how much scarce resource is consumed by a message by noting how much time the recipient spends on it' (Simon, 1969, p. 7). In those terms, subscribing to a daily newspaper is an extremely expensive habit: we pay not only the subscription cost but the time we need to read and comprehend it.

Simon did not believe we could multitask our way free of this problem. Instead, he offers as a solution the careful use of market mechanisms to ensure that 'free' information does not overwhelm the finite capacities of organizations to consume, analyze, compress and pass on relevant information to those who might need it. Simon warns that this is far harder than it might seem – simply computerizing systems accelerates the flow of information without addressing our finite capacity to understand the information flowing back and forth.

Unfortunately, very little of the technology assessment Simon prescribed has been applied to media technologies. Innovators in the space have worked to make it easier to create and disseminate 'content' – new information – with little consideration for the scarcity of attention to encounter and understand that information. Different waves of innovation have made the problem worse. The breakthrough technology of Simon's day, the photocopier, led to an explosion in the production of text, and a wave of 'information overload' concerns in the American workplace. Word processing and desktop publishing allowed individuals to create sophisticated-looking publications without the involvement of a print shop or a publisher. Email and the early web allowed content to be published to a theoretically global audience. The 'social media' paradigm turned the process of socializing with friends into a publication activity, creating waves of content intended for small audiences, but with the possibility of 'going viral' to a vast crowd.

One effect of these technological changes – and the increased scarcity of attention brought about by this surfeit of digital rabbits – is a tendency to overfocus on the importance of these new technologies at the expense of older ones. Despite the rise of cable television news, the birth of countless digitally native news publications and the emergence of platforms like Facebook as powerful disseminators of news, print-based newspapers continue to be the most important producers of investigative journalism in many countries. Local television news broadcasts and talk radio remain enormously influential in American politics, despite the rise of countless other spaces for political and civic conversation (Mitchell et al., 2016).

An understanding of media as an ecosystem helps us overcome this tendency: we can see how often the topic of digital discussions are the reporting conducted by 'elite' media outlets, and how powerful those digital discussions can be in cueing offline journalists towards what topics deserve their attention. Ecosystem approaches let us look beyond flows of attention between different media types and towards larger-scale shifts: from fixed-time media (the morning newspaper, the 10 o'clock news) to asynchronous media (streaming video, text posted on the web); from professional content creators to amateurs; from a text-centric media to a video-centric one.

Understanding how media ecosystems operate offers a set of powerful new tools for political parties and activist movements who learn to navigate and manipulate these new spaces. Social change is, in part, a battle for attention: media attention makes the issues a movement advocates for visible to the public, raises the profile of a movement's leaders, can help raise funds for a movement and can help inject movement issues into political debate (Andrews & Caren, 2010). Political parties similarly compete for attention, both in traditional and digital media (Cogburn & Espinoza-Vasquez, 2011), seeking 'earned media' to complement advertising, and seeking signals from media as to public opinion on controversial issues (Green-Pedersen & Stubager, 2010). As a consequence, the dynamics of contemporary media ecosystems are of deep interest to scholars and practitioners of social movements and political parties.

Here is one of several possible models we might use to understand a media ecosystem where attention is the central commodity, as 'energy' is central to an ecological food web. (I outline this model in more detail in a 2018 essay (Zuckerman, 2019)).

In a pre-digital information ecosystem, the power to direct attention was controlled primarily by entities that could disseminate information to large audiences: printers and broadcasters. These entities created vertically integrated businesses that produced news and entertainment, solicited advertising, and delivered an integrated package of content – some explicitly requested, some along for the ride – to their audiences. By delivering this content, they claimed a huge swath of attention. In the 1980s and 1990s, the top performing news and entertainment programming on US television networks claimed audiences of more than 20 million people watching simultaneously (https://en.wikipedia.org/wiki/Nielsen_ratings#Top-rated_programs_in_the_U.S.). Sixty million households subscribed to at least one daily newspaper. By renting part of that attention to local and national advertisers, publishers and broadcasters operated businesses that were often wildly profitable. In the mid-1990s, publicly traded newspapers boasted close to a twenty percent margin at a time when the margin for the average US manufacturing business was 7.6% (Nieman Reports, 1999). In the following decade, broadcasters and cable providers operated wildly profitable businesses, with cable operators running at 38% profit and television broadcasters at 16% (Ernst and Young, 2011).

That position of economic power came from the concentration of attention. A local newspaper offered perhaps the only way to tell people in a specific geographic area that peaches were on sale at the local supermarket. That local newspaper – always a combination of news and entertainment – is now a less reliable way to reach that audience, particularly because there are so many more demands on their attention, including both other news sites and hybrid spaces like YouTube and TikTok. What newspapers and local broadcasters had going for them as businesses were their near monopoly on attention – if you wanted to get in front of local audiences, they were the only game in town.

There is significant power that comes from this position of concentrated attention. Newspapers and broadcasters were not just brokers of attention. The profits of that business allowed them to produce news and information that made it possible for their audiences to participate in society as informed citizens. In the process, newspapers and broadcasters got to determine what issues and questions were most appropriate for discussion. As Max McCoombs and Don Shaw found in their seminal 1972 study, 'The Agenda-Setting Function of Mass Media', there was strong correlation between what issues local media in a small town (Chapel Hill, North Carolina) reported on most often and what citizens identified as the key issues in an upcoming election. The authors quote a memorable take from Bernard Cohen a decade earlier, who noted that the press 'may not be successful much of the time in telling people what to think but is stunningly successful in telling its readers what to think *about*' (McCombs & Shaw, 1972).

With an explosion of media options available to audiences, newspapers and broadcasters no longer hold this monopoly position as brokers of attention. We are paying attention to Facebook, to Twitter, to a thousand different websites, all of which are trying to further broker our attention, to the advertisers who support their platforms. In such a divided landscape, power over directing attention – and the political power associated with that attention – falls to 'discovery engines', tools that help us discover interesting and relevant content, either through choices we make or through carefully engineered serendipity.

Google is one of the most powerful of these discovery engines, using our search queries to direct our attention to their varied web properties as well as countless other websites. Facebook is another, directing our attention to posts made by our friends, but also pages across the web they recommend – the logic of Facebook's discovery engine is that we will be interested in what our friends are interested in, while with Google, we tell the search engine what we want to know about. It is no surprise that these two discovery engines are now enormously economically successful, aggregating ad space and data about user behavior on their own properties, and on vast networks of other websites. Jointly, Google and Facebook now represent 70% of the global digital ad market (Marketwatch, 2020).

This shift in power from publishers and broadcasters as brokers of attention to discovery engines has several consequences for the broader media ecosystem. As broadcasters and print publishers lose their supply of concentrated attention, their revenues are falling. Print newspapers in the US had 59 million daily subscribers in 2000 and fewer than 29 million in 2018 – revenues have fallen accordingly, with $48.6 billion in advertising revenue in 2000 and $14.3 billion in 2018 (Pew Research Center, 2019). The drop in revenue has been even more stark than the decline in subscription because online advertising has pushed down ad prices in print. As a result, the newspaper industry employed almost 72,000 people in newsroom jobs in 2004, and only 38,000 in 2018. These reduced staffs cover fewer stories in less detail, leading to warnings that accountability journalism, especially outside of major cities, may be threatened.

As newspapers and broadcasters lose their gatekeeping and agenda-setting capacity, an interesting phenomenon unfolds. If discovery engines saw themselves as successors to publishers, choosing topics and sources of information to favor over others, they would inherit the agenda-setting capabilities of newspapers and broadcasters. Instead, Google, Facebook and others portray themselves as neutral platforms, making as few judgements as possible about what information should be featured or suppressed. This stance comes in part from vagaries of US law: Section 230 of the 1996 Communications Decency Act limits the liability of these discovery services, stating 'No provider or user of an interactive computer service shall be treated as the publisher or speaker of any information provided by another information content provider'. Google is not liable for pointing users to information published on another site, and Facebook is not liable for information a Facebook user posts – that user instead is liable. Platforms are reluctant to take actions that make them look like publishers, favoring some content over others, for fear of taking on this liability.

Instead, platforms use algorithms to favor content, deciding what items appear in your Facebook feed or search results. By relying on opaque technical processes, these platforms hope to insulate both from liability and from accusations of political bias. (This often fails – Facebook is criticized by the right in the US for 'censoring' their speech and by the left for amplifying extremist voices).

By moving the power of agenda-setting from human publishers to algorithms, individual users gain power in two interesting ways. The algorithms that govern discovery services depend on feedback from users. If friends 'like' your post on Facebook, Facebook's feed will conclude your post is interesting and feature it in more of your friends' feeds. As a result, users of these systems gain a new power: they can direct attention to pieces of content by amplifying and sharing them. At scale, this process causes content to 'go viral', but it is a powerful dynamic even for content that never reaches mass audiences. The effect has a second order as well. If users share a piece of news content, for instance, helping it reach a wider audience, they signal to a publisher that users might be interested in additional content like this, spurring creation of similar content.

This power has been harnessed by social movements as well, through processes called 'brigading', where groups work in concert to amplify or suppress specific pieces of content, often on platforms like Reddit where user voting determines what content gains recognition and attention (Carman et al., 2018). Reddit expressly forbids brigading as a form of 'vote manipulation', recognizing its power (Reddit, n.d.).

In addition to amplifying (or suppressing) information by signaling relevance to discovery engines, individuals create their own content in response to content already circulating online. That content enters into the ecosystem much the same ways content from a professional publisher does competing for attention, amplification and recommendation.

Rather than a linear model in which writers create news, publishers' package and deliver it to audiences, who have limited influence over the production cycle, this understanding of media includes two feedback loops, shown in Figure 1. Feedback loops are one of the characteristics of complex systems, systems that can exhibit unpredictable, disparate behavior given very similar starting conditions (Sterman, 1994). The challenges we experience unpacking why one bit of content goes viral and another flops, why one user becomes an influencer, and another disappears from view may reflect the difficulties of making predictions in a model where feedback loops can amplify weak signals through positive feedback.

This model for understanding the flow of attention in a media ecosystem looks a bit like a food web, a graphical representation of what eats what within an ecosystem (Elton, 2001). This is not by accident – a food web is at heart a visualization of how energy moves

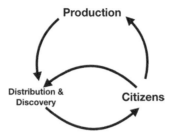

Figure 1. A model of attention flows.

through an ecosystem – from the sun to plants to herbivores to predators to decomposers. Attention moves in similar paths in our web: producers of content – often inspired by content elsewhere on the web – seek attention for the content they have created. Discovery engines feed on this content and direct attention from their vast audiences to this newly created content. Consumers of that content amplify or dampen it, sending signals back to the discovery engine (and via second-order effects to the content creator) about its popularity. Some may go beyond paying attention to the content and amplifying it by creating their own content in response, re-entering the attention web at the top of the cycle.

Food webs help ecologists diagnose problems within an ecosystem: a declining fox population might reflect a scarcity of rabbits due to insufficient lettuce. Similarly, our model suggests insights about some of the problems that affect contemporary media ecosystems, shown in Figure 2.

'Bots', computer programs that 'like' or amplify content en masse, seek to hijack the feedback cycle between citizens and discovery engines. They are common online – academic studies find between 10% and 66% of links on Twitter were posted by bots (The wide variation is explained by different methodologies in these studies.) (Rauchfleisch & Kaiser, 2020). If 5000 people like my post, perhaps, Twitter concludes that it is popular and worthy of attention. If those 5000 people are created by a program controlled by a Russian bot farm, the attention artificially directed to my content is a form of attention hijacking. Brigading, mentioned above, accomplishes the same goal as bots, using coordinated human action rather than computer programs. Brigading has been used by political movements, notably by the Digg Patriots, who coordinated downvoting of liberal-leaning articles on the Digg website, to promote conservative points of view (Peterson, 2016), and Twitter reported that 4.25% of all tweets promoting Donald

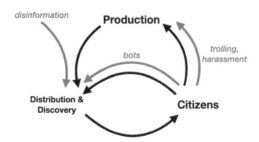

Figure 2. Vulnerabilities of the attention feedback model.

Trump in the last weeks of his 2016 political campaign came from Russian-linked bot accounts (O'Sullivan, 2018).

Other vulnerabilities of this ecosystem focus on dampening, not amplifying, signals. Posting content often opens an author to hostile reactions. Performative hostility, sometimes termed trolling, is a longstanding tradition in some online spaces. But sustained harassment has the effect of driving users offline, or at minimum, making them less likely to share their opinions. A recent study of online harassment in Norway found that while men experienced some form of harassment online even more often than women, women, in particular, reacted to sustained harassment by silencing themselves (Nadim & Fladmoe, 2021). Given the cycle through which some readers respond to content by creating their own content, this can act as dampening a feedback cycle. In many complex systems, dampening of feedback loops helps make systems more stable and predictable; in this case, the effect may be that those unwilling to engage in speech in hostile environments drop out, leaving only those who can tolerate – or enjoy! – combative speech in the conversation.

Discovery engines are a particularly vulnerable node in this attention web. Disinformation – information created specifically to misinform – can be presented to discovery engines and may be amplified and spread by readers who believe it to be true. (The definitions of disinformation, misinformation and malinformation offered by Claire Wardle and Hossein Derakhshan make clear that mis and disinformation are interdependent – the same piece of information could be either depending on the intent of the person spreading it, Wardle & Derakhshan, 2017).

Discovery engines have become much more aggressive in weeding out disinformation during the COVID-19 pandemic, taking down a video titled 'Plandemic' that advised viewers not to wear masks, within three days of publication (Frenkel et al., 2020). Generally, the platforms have been less willing to eliminate political disinformation, fearing accusations of political bias. President Trump's assertions of voter fraud in the wake of the US presidential election in 2020 were allowed to stand on Twitter with warnings that the claims they make are disputed until the attack on the US Capitol on 6 January 2021. The debates over platform responsibility for disinformation are a reminder of the sensitivity of this part of the attention ecosystem. Asking corporations to decide what speech is acceptable is uncomfortable. But so is asking governments to moderate speech or accepting the unchecked spread of disinformation.

A hope for this (simple, incomplete) model of attention flows is that it might apply independent of the affordances of any particular tool or platform. Flows of attention are understood as unfolding across many different media channels simultaneously. Content from the New York Times is amplified and commented on across social media. Snarky tweets on Twitter might inspire a blogger to write a response, or offer feedback to the Times on whether peas are ever appropriate in guacamole (Anderson, 2015). Ideas first posted on social media inspire reactions from traditional press or television as well as commentary online. Since there is no consistent answer to the question 'which came first, the article or the tweet?' we are best served thinking in terms of cycles: this time, the idea started online and spread through traditional media; the next time, the cycle began in print or broadcast.

This need to understand media holistically, particularly through quantitative analysis of flows from one part of an ecosystem to another, may ultimately result in a Tansleyian shift in media. In particular, while we will and should continue to study individual species – Twitter, YouTube, Facebook, broadcast television, talk radio – we also need to study them in the context of 'the habitat factors in the widest sense' to understand their effects on social movements and political parties.

Researching media ecosystems

As the internet became a mainstream technology and millions of users began adopting email, social scientists realized they had a massive new source of data on which they could test existing theories, replicating Stanley Milgram's 'six degrees' experiment with email, for example (Dodds et al., 2003). The massive adoption of social media combined with the fact that data was already digitized promised a new era for computational social science.

It is likely that the level availability of data from various platforms has contributed to their popularity as a topic for study. Twitter, in particular, has become an enormously popular medium to research, despite having a much smaller online audience than platforms that are less well studied. Between 2008 and 2019, Google Scholar indexes an average of 577,167 papers per year that mention Twitter, just slightly more than mention Facebook (552,917 papers per year on average). What is remarkable is that Twitter has only 330 million monthly users (Twitter, 2020) while Facebook has roughly eight times the audience, around 2.7 billion monthly users (Statista, 2020). The only social media site that challenges Facebook's user numbers is YouTube, with a reported two billion monthly users (YouTube, 2020). Yet YouTube is vastly less studied, averaging 308,167 papers per year between 2008 and 2019, or 53% of the papers Twitter inspired.[1]

Scholars love Twitter because it is easy to study – it is the drosophila of social media. Shortly after it launched, Twitter opened an API for researchers that allowed scholars to collect a 10% sample of all tweets posted. Because tweets were under 140 characters, even an enormous collection of tweets was relatively small. Network theorists were able to build graphs of Twitter communities, looking to see who followed each other, and who retweeted or quoted each other. Hashtags made it easy to study the emergence of topics and indexing the text of tweets made it easy to quickly identify what users were talking about what subjects. While Twitter has restricted access to researchers over the years, it remains perhaps the easiest social media platform to study.

Facebook, by contrast, provides very little data to researchers, activists and others who would seek to understand it, citing its privacy model. Most Facebook posts are not public – they are shared with a person's friends, not with the general public. To protect the privacy of users' speech, Facebook's tools primarily allow researchers to study Pages, public-facing collections of posts mostly maintained by brands and celebrities. Of course, some scholars found ways to study Facebook by joining the 'Facebook ecosystem' as app developers, using their status to collect data on users – the Cambridge Analytica scandal unmasked a scholar violating research norms by collecting data for academic study and transferring it to a political consultancy (Wong et al., 2018). More recently, scholars have entered into complex negotiations to access carefully constrained and anonymized sets of data from Facebook.[2]

YouTube presents different challenges for researchers and activists. While well-developed tools exist to study text, many researchers are unprepared to study large sets of videos. Videos are large, which makes it difficult to store them, and extracting text from them is expensive, whether conducted via automated tools or via transcription. While YouTube provides an API that allows researchers to query the entire site, the results available are limited and make it difficult to assemble large data sets.

Each platform within the broader media ecosystem presents different barriers to study and studying the spread of ideas or trends across multiple platforms magnifies the technical difficulties associated with research. Reddit, which Alexa's traffic comparison service sees as having much higher engagement than Twitter, was difficult to study quantitatively until 2015, when Jason Baumgartner launched Pushshift.io, a comprehensive archive of posts made to the service (Baumgartner et al., 2020). Other important services have no dedicated indices or archives or are technically challenging to collect data from. Chat-like services like Whatsapp advertise end to end encryption, which should make it impossible even for the platform operator to study the content of conversations through fully automated methods. Some researchers have had success studying publicly advertised WhatsApp groups, declaring their presence as researchers, though half of the groups they joined refused to participate (Narayanan et al., 2019).

Despite these barriers, ambitious work that tracks phenomena across multiple platforms is emerging. Some is ethnographic, focusing on phenomena like extremist speech, which flows across many platforms and sometimes demands that a researcher go 'undercover' to infiltrate these groups. In her book, *The Rage*, Julia Ebner (2017) infiltrates right-wing extremist groups and tracks their discussions across closed platforms like Telegram onto more traditional, public social media platforms. Her colleagues at ISD Global, which monitors Islamic extremists as well as white nationalist groups, routinely use cross-platform ethnographic and quantitative methods to trace ideas like the 'holohoax' across Facebook, Twitter, YouTube, and Reddit. This and other work demonstrate the ways disinformation spreads between platforms and how platform policies regarding speech can chase dialogs from one platform to another (Guhl & Davey, 2020). The idea of a Digital Influence Machine developed at Data & Society (Nadler et al., 2018) makes clear the ways attention flows between extremists and media outlets is a system that is actively gamed and manipulated.

Other work uses quantitative methods to demonstrate linkages between attention in digital media and traditional news coverage. Deen Freelon and colleagues demonstrated that the intensity of Twitter traffic focused on the Black Lives Matter (BLM) movement correlated with increased attention to the deaths of unarmed people of color in mainstream news (Freelon et al., 2016). Freelon's team demonstrated the power of correlating multiple timelines to show possible causality – a spike in Twitter attention preceding a wave of news coverage suggests that one may cause the other. Based on Freelon's work and the broader successes of BLM in bringing attention to under-covered issues of police violence, it is reasonable to predict that social movements will study BLM's use of social media as a possible model for attention-driven social change.

Timelines have proven a popular way of demonstrating the unfolding of social phenomena across multiple media, looking for ecosystem effects as different media focus on an unfolding story. Keith Collins and Kevin Roose, reporters for the New York Times, have turned cross-media attention patterns into a powerful visualization to understand the flow of an idea across different media over time. In one examination, they follow the phrase 'Jobs Not Mobs' from a video shared on Twitter to amplification in pro-Trump Reddit groups, to widespread visibility on Facebook and in mainstream media. By tracking the attention paid to different posts, the authors are able to demonstrate how a phrase becomes a meme, and then later a central theme of how Republicans differentiated Trump's policies from those of Democrats (Collins & Roose, 2018). The visualization, a vertically scrolled timeline illustrated with multicolored bubbles has become a feature for the Times as they visualize online campaigns and their influence on broader dialogs.

While Collins and Roose studied a single case using quantitative methods, the iDrama team (a large research collective) tracked URLs shared on Twitter, Reddit and a subset of 4chan image boards to examine the spread of information from 'alternative news sources', including sites that feature conspiracy theories and Russian disinformation. They find that this news is often shared first on Twitter, perhaps because bots appear to be highly active in promoting this content. 4chan, often celebrated as a powerful source of subcultural memes, is well behind Twitter and Reddit in spreading most of this political content, suggesting that conventional wisdom about the roles of different services in amplifying content requires re-examination (Zannettou et al., 2017).

Timelines are only one way to study the complexities of internet ecosystems. In the wake of the 2016 US presidential election, Yochai Benkler and his team at Harvard University conducted ambitious quantitative research that offered a comprehensive analysis of media roles in that surprising contest (Benkler et al., 2018). Benkler and team used Twitter to identify news media most often shared by political partisans on the left and the right. They identify partisans based on their retweeting of visible political figures in their parties, then examined what media outlets those partisans amplified. They constructed a classification of hundreds of English-language media sources favored by different political groups, demonstrating which ones were popular on Twitter.

What emerged was evidence of two disconnected media ecosystems, one followed by the far left through the center right, the other followed entirely by the far right. Attention to media when ranked from far left to center-right followed a normal distribution, with higher attention to sources favored by the center and center-left than those favored by the far left or center right. Far-right media followed an entirely different distribution, with disproportionate attention to media most favored by the far-right, especially Breitbart, which played a critical role in the media ecosystem leading up to the 2016 election. Benkler and team called this phenomenon 'asymmetric polarization' and suggested that while left-center media was behaving in normal and predictable ways, this new right-wing media ecosystem displayed new and important dynamics.

Through both network analysis and case studies, Benkler and team illustrated a path from far-right media like Gateway Pundit that amplified conspiracy theories, through Breitbart, which served to 'clean up' and legitimate these stories, to Fox News, which demanded these stories receive broader attention. Often mainstream news sources like CNN or the New York Times would respond to these prompts, if only to demonstrate their falsity. Using Media Cloud to analyze stories at scale, the team was able to demonstrate that narratives favored by far-right media – notably stories about Hillary Clinton's email server – dominated overall media coverage of the 2016 election.

Benkler and team's work is important because it considers social media not as a proxy for public opinion – where it is an imperfect proxy at best – but as a channel for injecting ideas into the public sphere and 'upcycling' them from the fringe to the mainstream. As the Republican party reorganizes around Trump's claims to have won the 2020 election, this has become a deliberate strategy by activists within the Republican Party and will likely affect political party relationships with media going forward.

My team in conjunction with (anonymized for review) replicated Benkler's work to study whether similar dynamics were emerging from the French media ecosystem. We used similar methods to develop a map of the ecosystem and identified clusters of elite and mainstream media similar to what the Benkler team found on the left and center, and a cluster of extremist and conspiracy theory media that was disconnected from the mainstream dialog.

But similarities ended there – in the French media ecosystem, ideas from the more extreme parts of the web seldom, if ever, crossed into mainstream media dialog. The critical difference was the gatekeeping function of elite media, which linked to left – and right-leaning elite media sources, but never to the conspiratorial outsiders. This elite firewall has advantages and disadvantages. While it means that French media is less vulnerable to the injections seen in US media, it also means that elite media may be blind to popular movements that begin online. We found evidence that French elite media was late in their understanding of the Yellow Vests movement, which was better and more thoroughly understood in regional and local media, while elite media understood it almost entirely in terms of implications for the government in Paris.[3],[4]

These projects of understanding the broad structure of a nation's media ecosystem suggest the intriguing possibility that the same social media platforms may have different effects in different contexts. Fabio Giglietto and colleagues are using similar methods to understand the Italian media ecosystem's responses to coordinated disinformation efforts during elections in 2018 and 2019 (Giglietto et al., 2020). We are likely to discover that it is unwise to generalize about the effects of any given platform as the ways each works in the context of a nation's ecosystem is likely to be different from how they work in the United States. Indeed, studies of national ecosystems have already demonstrated their value in overturning established wisdom. A deep dive into the Chinese media ecosystem by Harsh Taneja and Angela Wu suggests that an overfocus by western researchers on the effects of censorship on Chinese internet users blinds us to the simple truth that language barriers likely shape online behavior more than the Great Firewall (Taneja & Wu, 2014).

Some of the most ambitious recent work seeks to understand ecosystems that cross national borders, united by ideology rather than language or geography. A team at the Freie Universität Berlin has investigated links between alternative right-wing news sources in Germany, Austria, the UK, US, Denmark and Sweden, finding shared agendas across the different nations, with large US sites serving as hubs for information (Heft et al., 2021). An investigation by anti-extremism thinktank ISD Global confirmed the centrality of US far-right sites in extremist media circles in France and Germany, but suggests that extremist media is more likely to influence mainstream media in the US than in Europe (ISD Global, 2020). This work suggests we might understand extreme right-wing media as a transnational ecosystem interacting with local media ecosystems in unique and specific ways and offers a route to study other international movements.

What we need to understand media ecosystems

This incomplete overview of Media Ecosystem research suggests that considering media as an integrated ecosystem can lead to novel and unexpected results. However, this sort of multiplatform research is challenging to conduct. As we understand from the heavy research focus on some platforms over others, media ecosystem research is likely to struggle for viability until tools and methods improve significantly.

If the shift from studying individual media organisms to studying integrated ecosystems through quantitative methods is the right one, we will need at least four developments to make the method more viable. We need archives, search engines and other tools that help us understand a broader range of media. Projects like Pushshift that have made Reddit, Telegram, Gab and others searchable by researchers deserve widespread support and funding to allow them to expand. Efforts like the Internet Archive Television offer the possibility for more thorough linkages between digitally native and traditional media (Internet Archive, n.d.). Efforts by Deb Roy and other scholars to collect and transcribe talk radio offer the possibility to study ephemeral but broadly influential media (Beeferman et al., 2019).

But in recognizing these efforts, there is a grave need for tools that enable better research on critical parts of the new media ecosystem. YouTube is an enormously important and influential platform and remains difficult to research at scale. Platforms like WhatsApp are likely critical in understanding political dynamics in many nations, and the encrypted nature of conversations means that we face significant privacy and technical challenges in archiving and studying material. (Mosca & Quaranta, in this issue) We need both better tools to understand some platforms, and methods that accept that some important data will never be accessible to researchers.

We need better tools that allow scholars and other researchers to examine words, phrases, URLs and ideas across multiple platforms at the same time. Media Cloud enables comparisons of terms across different collections of media, allowing researchers to see how terms appear in newspapers, digital publications and talk radio, for example. Some commercial tools allow comparison across different social media platforms. For research to be accessible to people unable to afford commercial data sets and tools, open-source systems like Media Cloud will need to expand to incorporate new data sets and encourage cross-comparison.

We need a clearer understanding of how different social media platforms report data about information shared on their systems. Facebook, for example, makes information available about 'high engagement' pages through its Crowdtangle tool, but insists that this information is not reflective on what most users see in their newsfeed (Schultz, 2020). Putting aside how confusing this is – Facebook is telling researchers that their own tool does not provide an accurate picture of what is popular on their platform – this reflects a larger problem researchers encounter when they conduct studies across platforms. Can we compare the visibility of a URL on Twitter, where most posts are public, to that visibility on Facebook, where most are restricted to a small set of users? How do we consider a platform like 4chan, where most content is ephemeral? Could tools designed to help advertisers determine if they are reaching their audiences help researchers better estimate audiences for social media content?

As media ecosystem studies go forward, we need to find ways to integrate tools that investigate individual users' experience of social media with the broad view offered by search engines and archives. Such work builds on existing audits conducted using panels of users (Sandvig et al., 2014) to study search engines (Robertson et al., 2018), Facebook ads (Silva et al., 2020), or YouTube videos (Chen et al., 2021). Mozilla's Project Rally data donation program (Mozilla, n.d.) offers one way this data might become available to researchers, through the cooperation of users who opt into a study. The Markup is taking a different approach, recruiting a panel of representative users to power their 'citizen browser' program, auditing the behavior of platform algorithms (The Markup, 2020).

In addition to these technical changes, we need a shift in attitudes and approaches. For media ecosystem studies to gain prominence, we need an increased understanding from the field that data that comes only from one platform, or even just from social media, has limitations. Yet, this work is also foundational. The deep understanding of a single platform, or of the use of multiple platforms by a single subculture or community, developed through quantitative or qualitative methods, provides a basis for understanding global cross-platform flows. But this valuable work should be complemented with tools and techniques that seek to analyze flows of attention across many platforms and communities.

My hope is that we can build on the discoveries made of particular linguistic or national media ecosystems and start to better understand fundamental dynamics and patterns that recur in different contexts. The 'upcycling' that Benkler and team identified in their election study is likely to be tried in different linguistic or national ecosystems – can we identify attempts to use this technique and examine their successes or failures? Can we identify other patterns that recur across different linguistic and national ecosystems? Can we begin to understand how ideas spread from one ecosystem to another, across lines of language and culture? Could identifying those common patterns bring us closer to an understanding of media dynamics that is closer to physics than our current piecemeal understanding?

Beyond these scholarly questions is a broader question about political parties, activist movements and other civic and social actors: how will increased understanding of media ecosystem dynamics change political participation? Will the phenomena that appear novel abuses of the system be stamped out by platform moderation and rule changes, or will armies of trolls, bots and brigades become as much a part of political campaigns as television ads and door knocking?

Arthur Tansley's call to focus on ecology, ' … the whole system (in the sense of physics)', led to a fundamental shift in biology, allowing for the scholarly consideration of complex systems. Could understanding media ecosystems be a fundamental shift in how we understand our complex media environments? We need such a shift if we want to understand pressing topics, like the harnessing of conspiratorial thinking for political gain, as we are seeing in the United States. So long as those who govern are powerful media manipulators, understanding the complex dynamics of media ecosystems will be fundamental to understanding our political, social and economic systems as well as our communications.

Notes

1. I searched Google Scholar for the terms "Facebook", "Twitter" and "YouTube", restricting results to a specific year between 2008 and 2019. I also noted the most cited paper for each

year, which shows a pattern similar to the total number of papers, with YouTube underperforming Twitter and Facebook.
2. See Social Science One, https://socialscience.one.
3. Anonymized for review.
4. Anonymized for review.

Disclosure statement

No potential conflict of interest was reported by the author(s).

References

Anderson, L. V. (2015, July 2). What was Peagate? Slate. https://slate.com/culture/2015/07/new-york-times-pea-guacamole-controversy-a-deep-analysis-of-the-tweet-that-outraged-america.html

Andrews, K. T., & Caren, N. (2010). Making the news: Movement organizations, media attention, and the public agenda. *American Sociological Review*, *75*(6), 841–866. https://doi.org/10.1177/0003122410386689

Baumgartner, J., Zannettou, S., Keegan, B., Squire, M., & Blackburn, J. (2020, May). The pushshift reddit dataset. In *Proceedings of the International AAAI Conference on Web and Social Media* (Vol. 14, pp. 830–839.

Beeferman, D., Brannon, W., & Roy, D. (2019). RadioTalk: A large-scale corpus of talk radio transcripts. *arXiv preprint arXiv:1907.07073*.

Benkler, Y., Faris, R., & Roberts, H. (2018). *Network propaganda: Manipulation, disinformation, and radicalization in American politics*. Oxford University Press.

Burgess, J., & Baym, N. K. (2020). *Twitter: A biography*. NYU Press.

Carman, M., Koerber, M., Li, J., Choo, K. K. R., & Ashman, H. (2018, August). Manipulating visibility of political and apolitical threads on Reddit via score boosting. In *2018 17th IEEE International Conference on Trust, Security and Privacy in Computing and Communications/12th IEEE International Conference on Big Data Science and Engineering (TrustCom/BigDataSE)* (pp. 184–190). IEEE.

Carson, R. (2002). *Silent spring*. Houghton Mifflin Harcourt.

Chen, A., Nyhan, B., Reifler, J., Robertson, R., & Wilson, C. (2021). Exposure to alternative & extremist content on YouTube. Anti-defamation league research publication. https://www.adl.org/resources/reports/exposure-to-alternative-extremist-content-on-youtube

Cogburn, D. L., & Espinoza-Vasquez, F. K. (2011). From networked nominee to networked nation: Examining the impact of Web 2.0 and social media on political participation and civic engagement in the 2008 Obama campaign. *Journal of Political Marketing*, *10*(1–2), 189–213. https://doi.org/10.1080/15377857.2011.540224

Collins, K., & Roose, K. (2018, November 4). Tracing a meme from the internet's fringes to a Republican slogan. *The New York Times*. https://www.nytimes.com/interactive/2018/11/04/technology/jobs-not-mobs.html

Cooper, W. S. (1957). Sir Arthur Tansley and the science of ecology. *Ecology*, *38*(4), 658–659. https://doi.org/10.2307/1943136

Dodds, P. S., Muhamad, R., & Watts, D. J. (2003). An experimental study of search in global social networks. *Science*, *301*(5634), 827–829. https://doi.org/10.1126/science.1081058

Ebner, J. (2017). *The rage: The vicious circle of Islamist and far-right extremism*. Bloomsbury Publishing.

Eickelman, D. F., & Anderson, J. W. (2003). *New media in the Muslim world: The emerging public sphere*. Indiana University Press.

Elton, C. S. (2001). *Animal ecology*. University of Chicago Press.

Ernst & Young. (2011, March 14). New study shows profitability and growth in media & entertainment. Press release. https://www.prnewswire.com/news-releases/new-study-shows-profitability-and-growth-in-media–entertainment-117927419.html

Freelon, D., McIlwain, C. D., & Clark, M. (2016). *Beyond the hashtags: #Ferguson, #Blacklivesmatter, and the online struggle for offline justice*. Center for Media & Social Impact, American University. https://cmsimpact.org/resource/beyond-hashtags-ferguson-blacklivesmatter-online-struggle-offline-justice/

Frenkel, S., Decker, B., & Alba, D. (2020, May 21). How the 'Plandemic' movie and its falsehoods spread widely online. *The New York Times*.

Giglietto, F., Righetti, N., Rossi, L., & Marino, G. (2020). It takes a village to manipulate the media: Coordinated link sharing behavior during 2018 and 2019 Italian elections. *Information, Communication & Society*, *23*(6), 867–891. https://doi.org/10.1080/1369118X.2020.1739732

Green-Pedersen, C., & Stubager, R. (2010). The political conditionality of mass media influence: When do parties follow mass media attention? *British Journal of Political Science*, *40*(3), 663–677. https://doi.org/10.1017/S0007123410000037

Griswold, E. (2012, September 21). How "Silent Spring" ignited the environmental movement. *The New York Times*. https://www.nytimes.com/2012/09/23/magazine/how-silent-spring-ignited-the-environmental-movement.html

Guhl, J., & Davey, J. (2020, August 10). Hosting the 'Holohoax': A snapshot of Holocaust denial across social media. *ISD Global* [Whitepaper]. https://www.isdglobal.org/wp-content/uploads/2020/08/Hosting-the-Holohoax.pdf

Heft, A., Knüpfer, C., Reinhardt, S., & Mayerhöffer, E. (2021). Toward a transnational information ecology on the right? Hyperlink networking among right-wing digital news sites in Europe and the United States. *The International Journal of Press/Politics*, *26*(2), 484–504. https://doi.org/10.1177/1940161220963670

Internet Archive. (n.d.). Internet Archive TV News. https://archive.org/details/tv

ISD Global. (2020). Transatlantic journeys of far-right narratives through online-media ecosystems. *ISD Global* [whitepaper]. https://www.isdglobal.org/wp-content/uploads/2020/12/TransAtlanticJourneysofFar-RightNarratives_v4.pdf

Mailland, J., & Driscoll, K. (2017). *Minitel: Welcome to the internet* (Platform studies). MIT Press.

Marketwatch. (2020, April 28). Plummeting digital Ad market may complicate life for Google, Facebook. https://www.marketwatch.com/story/as-demand-for-digital-advertising-plummets-google-and-facebook-could-have-shrinking-revenues-2020-04-28

The Markup. (2020, October 16). The Citizen browser project – Auditing the algorithms of discrimination. https://themarkup.org/citizen-browser

McCombs, M. E., & Shaw, D. L. (1972). The agenda-setting function of mass media. *Public Opinion Quarterly*, *36*(2), 176–187. https://doi.org/10.1086/267990

McIntosh, R. P. (1986). *The background of ecology: Concept and theory*. Cambridge University Press.

Mitchell, A., Gottfried, J., Barthel, M., Shearer, E. (2016, July 7). The modern news consumer. *Pew Research Center Report*. https://www.journalism.org/2016/07/07/pathways-to-news/

Mozilla. (n.d.). About Mozilla Ion. https://support.mozilla.org/en-US/kb/about-mozilla-ion

Nadim, M., & Fladmoe, A. (2021). Silencing women? Gender and online harassment. *Social Science Computer Review*, *39*(2).

Nadler, A., Crain, M., & Donovan, J. (2018). *Weaponizing the digital influence machine*. Data & Society report. https://datasociety.net/wp-content/uploads/2018/10/DS_Digital_Influence_Machine.pdf

Narayanan, V., Kollanyi, B., Hajela, R., Barthwal, A., Marchal, N., & Howard, P. N. (2019). News and information over Facebook and WhatsApp during the Indian election campaign. Data Memo, 2.

Nieman Reports. (1999, June 15). Newspapers arrive at economic crossroads. https://niemanreports.org/articles/newspapers-arrive-at-economic-crossroads/

O'Sullivan, D. (2018, January 27). Russian bots retweeted Trump nearly 500,000 times in final weeks of 2016 campaign. *CNN*. https://money.cnn.com/2018/01/27/technology/business/russian-twitter-bots-election-2016/index.html

Peterson, C. (2016). Case study: "Bury until they change their ways"– The Digg Patriots and/as user-generated censorship. In Gordon, E., & Mihailidis, P. (Eds.). (2016). Civic media: Technology, design, practice. MIT Press.

Pew Research Center. (2019, July 9). Newspaper Fact Sheet. https://www.journalism.org/fact-sheet/newspapers/

Postman, N. (1970). The reformed English curriculum. In A. C. Eurich (Ed.), *High school 1980: The shape of the future in American secondary education* (pp. 8). Pitman Publishing.

Postman, N. (1985). *Amusing ourselves to death*. Viking.

Postman, N. (1990, October 11). Informing ourselves to death [Speech to the German Informatics Society]. Transcript. https://web.williams.edu/HistSci/curriculum/101/informing.html

Rauchfleisch, A., & Kaiser, J. (2020). *The false positive problem of automatic bot detection in social science research*. Berkman Klein Center Research Publication No. 2020-3.

Reddit. (n.d.). What constitutes vote cheating or vote manipulation? https://www.reddithelp.com/hc/en-us/articles/360043066412

Robertson, R. E., Lazer, D., & Wilson, C. (2018, April). Auditing the personalization and composition of politically-related search engine results pages. In *Proceedings of the 2018 World Wide Web Conference* (pp. 955–965). Switzerland: International World Wide Web Conferences Steering Committee, Republic and Canton of Geneva.

Sandvig, C., Hamilton, K., Karahalios, K., & Langbort, C. (2014). Auditing algorithms: Research methods for detecting discrimination on internet platforms. In *Data and discrimination: Converting critical concerns into productive inquiry*, 22, 4349–4357.

Schultz, A. (2020, November 10). What do people actually see on Facebook in the US? Facebook. https://about.fb.com/news/2020/11/what-do-people-actually-see-on-facebook-in-the-us/

Silva, M., Santos de Oliveira, L., Andreou, A., Vaz de Melo, P. O., Goga, O., & Benevenuto, F. (2020, April). Facebook ads monitor: An independent auditing system for political ads on Facebook. In *Proceedings of the Web Conference 2020* (pp. 224–234). New York: Association for Computing Machinery.

Simon, H. (1969). Designing organizations for an information-rich world. [Lecture] Brookings Institution, Washington DC.

Statista. (2020). Number of monthly active Facebook users worldwide as of 3rd quarter 2020. Statista. https://www.statista.com/statistics/264810/number-of-monthly-active-facebook-users-worldwide

Sterman, J. D. (1994). Learning in and about complex systems. *System Dynamics Review*, *10*(2–3), 291–330. https://doi.org/10.1002/sdr.4260100214

Taneja, H., & Wu, A. X. (2014). Does the great Firewall really isolate the Chinese? Integrating access blockage with cultural factors to explain Web user behavior. *The Information Society*, *30*(5), 297–309. https://doi.org/10.1080/01972243.2014.944728

Tansley, A. G. (1935). The use and abuse of vegetational concepts and terms. *Ecology*, *16*(3), 284–307. https://doi.org/10.2307/1930070

Thornbecke, C. (2020, July 10). NAACP president calls Facebook a "threat to democracy," says ad boycott isn't dying down soon. *ABC News*. https://abcnews.go.com/Technology/naacp-president-calls-facebook-threat-democracy-ad-boycott/story?id=71695281

Tucker, I. (2020, July 26). Roger McNamee: "Facebook is a threat to whatever remains of democracy in the US". *The Guardian*. https://www.theguardian.com/technology/2020/jul/26/roger-mcnamee-facebook-is-a-threat-to-whatever-remains-of-democracy-in-the-us

Twitter. (2020). Twitter investor fact sheet. https://s22.q4cdn.com/826641620/files/doc_financials/2020/q2/Q2_20__InvestorFactSheet.pdf

Wardle, C., & Derakhshan, H. (2017). Information disorder: Toward an interdisciplinary framework for research and policy making. *Council of Europe Report*, *27*, 1–107.

Wong, J., Lewis, P., & Davies, H. (2018, April 24). How academic at centre of Facebook scandal tried – and failed – to spin personal data into gold. *The Guardian*. https://www.theguardian.com/news/2018/apr/24/aleksandr-kogan-cambridge-analytica-facebook-data-business-ventures

YouTube. (2020). *YouTube Official Blog*. https://blog.youtube/press

Zannettou, S., Caulfield, T., De Cristofaro, E., Kourtelris, N., Leontiadis, I., Sirivianos, M., Stringhini, G., & Blackburn, J. (2017, November). The web centipede: understanding how web communities influence each other through the lens of mainstream and alternative news sources. In *Proceedings of the 2017 Internet Measurement Conference* (pp. 405–417). New York: Association for Computing Machinery.

Zuckerman, E. (2019). Four problems for news and democracy. *Trust, Media and Democracy*. https://medium.com/trust-media-and-democracy/we-know-the-news-is-in-crisis-5d1c4fbf7691

Index

Note: Figures are indicated by *italics*. Tables are indicated by **bold**. Endnotes are indicated by the page number followed by 'n' and the endnote number e.g., 20n1 refers to endnote 1 on page 20.

Aam Aadmi Party (AAP) 11, 35, 36; anti-corruption 48–51; background 39–40; Dalit leaders, joining of 48, 52; degree, income, WiFi *49*; in Delhi election 40; E-governance *48*; electricity and water bills *47*; in Goa election 40; interviewee information **41**; in Punjab election 40; 2013 manifesto 43, *44*; 2015 manifesto 44, *45*, *46*; women entrepreneurs *50*
Alternative für Deutschland (AfD) party 6–8, 12, 70, 123, 128
Alternativet 4
Amusing Ourselves to Death (Postman) 170
Anning, F. 80
anti-corruption 48–51
anti-elitism 5–7, 136
Australia 75–8, 80, 86, 89
Australian Labor Party (ALP) 76, 81, 84, 86, 88
Austrian Freedom Party (FPÖ) 12, 135, 141, 145, 146

Baldwin-Philippi, J. 118
Bang, H. 98
Batten, G. 12, 57–61, 63–9
Baumgartner, J. 179
Beck, U. 98
Benjamin, C. 64
Benkler, Y. 180, 181
Bennett, W. L. 39, 88, 98
Bharatiya Janata Party (BJP) 36, 39, 44, 48, 51, 52
Black Lives Matter (BLM) 179
Blassnig, S. 153, 154, 156
Bobba, G. 153
Bolton, H. 61, 63, 65, 66
Bracciale, R. 12
Braine, R. 69
Brazilian Worker's Party 52
Brexit referendum 7, 11, 56–60, 63, 65, 67–9
Britain First 57, 69
British National Party (BNP) 63–4, 69

Campion, K. 88
Carson, R. 170

Ceccobelli, D. 153, 156
Ceron, A. 12
Coalition of the Radical Left (SYRIZA) 135, 140
Collins, K. 179, 180
communication-centric approach 152
Communication Constitutive of Organization (CCO) 3, 12
communication practices: contemporary progressive movement parties in 26–30; movement parties in 24–6; relational and dynamic perspective 23–4
Communist Party of India 52
Computer Assisted Web Interviewing (CAWI) 122
content popularity 153, 156, 163
Corbyn, J. 104
Coretti, L. 39
Covid-19 pandemic 1, 10, 52, 129, 177
Cremonesi, C. 118
Crowther, S. 61
cultural hegemony 59

Dahlgren, P. 104
Dalton, R. 98
Danish People's Party 140
Davis, M. 77
Delhi 35, 36, 39–41, 44–8, 51, 52
della Porta, D. 3, 11, 12
Derakhshan, H. 177
Deseriis, M. 21, 38
Die Linke (The Left) 123
digital activism 21, 94, 101, **102**, 105, 106, **112**; dependent variable **113**; descriptive statistics **100**; extra-institutional political behavior and 97–8; new movements parties and 96–7
Digital Influence Machine 179
'digital native' vs 'digital immigrant' parties 120–1
digital parties 20–3, 127, 128
Di Maio, L. 135, 141–3, 157, 158, 160–3
Dodds, T. 120
Downing, J. D. H. 32n1

INDEX

Earl, J. 98
Ebner, J. 179
electoral campaigns 2, 27, 84, 93, 95, 97, 104, 106, 136, 141, 162, 163; Internet, use of 10; policy proposal 135; populists' communication 139, 158; TV/Facebook Live videos on 142
electoral turnout 95–6, 98, 100, 101, 104, 105, 107, **113**
Engesser, S. 20
English Defence League (EDL) 57, 60, 64, 69
Ernst, N. 138, 154
Errejón, Í. 6
European General Data Protection Regulation 129
European Union (EU) 7, 56, 137, 143, 145, 170
Euroscepticism 6
extra-institutional political behavior 97–8

Facebook 7, 76, 77, 79, 100, 118, 119, 129, 135, 139, 140, 142, 153, 154, 156–8, 161–3, 170–2, 174, 175, 178–80, 182; AAP post *47–50*; anti-ALP framing on *86*; data **157**; fan-page network *82*; Islamophobic framing on *85*; PHON 77; UKIP page 64
Farage, N. 7, 56, 61
far-right movements 3, 7, 57, 60
Five Star Movement (M5S) 4, 6–9, 10, 12, 21, 24, 27, 38, 39, 52, 57, 135, 141, 143, 146
Fraser Anning's Conservative National Party (FACNP) 76, 78, 80–5, 87–9
Freedom Party of Austria (FPö) 12, 37, 138, 141, 145, 146
Freelon, D. 179
Front National 52, 70, 123

Gab 182
Garrett, K. 39
Gephi 79
Gerbaudo, P. 21, 96, 117, 121, 127
Germany 6, 12, 28, 104, 116–18, 122, 123, 126–9, 181
Ggplot2 65
Giglietto, F. 181
Gomez, R. 10
Google 174, 175
Great Recession 121
Greece 7, 24, 27, 28, 135, 140
Groshek, J. 97, 105

Hallin, D. 129
Hameleers, M. 118
Harmel, R. 38
Hazare, A. 37
Hindu (Hindutva) 51–2
Hoffmann, C.P. 104
Hungary 7

Iglesias, P. 135, 141, 143
India 35–7, 39, 51
India Against Corruption (IAC) 35, 37, 40, 42, 43, 45, 48, 50

Indian National Congress (INC) 36, 39
information and communication technologies (ICTs) 4, 5, 11
Islam 57, 59, 61, 64–8, 70, 76, 79, 85, 86, 88
Islamophobia 77, 85, 86
Italy 6, 9, 24, 27, 28, 57, 116, 117, 118, 122, 123, 126–9, 135, 140, 146, 157

James, D. 61, 63
Jobbik 7, 8
Johnson, D. 170
Jones, A. 64
Jungherr, A. 104
Justicialist Party in Argentina 38

Karpf 121
Kejriwal, A. 35, 37, 39, 40, 42–5, 50, 51–2
Kimport, K. 98
Kitschelt, H. 3, 22, 96
Klein, O. 11, 12
Koc-Michalska, K. 97, 105, 118
Kriesi, H. 154
Krippendorff, K. H. 164n1
Kumar, R. 48
Kumar, S. 48

La France Insoumise 4, 6, 123, 128
Lega (The League) 123
Lega Nord 12
Leichty, G. B. 40
Le Pen, M. 52
LGBTQ 69
Linguistic Inquiry and Word Count (LIWC) 135, 142, 143
List Pym Fortuyn 134
Lobera, J. 12
Lutz, C. 104

Mancini, P. 129
McCoombs, M. 174
McKibben, B. 170
McLuhan, M. 170, 171
McNamee, R. 170
McSwiney, J. 11
Media Cloud 180, 182
media ecosystem 169; attention flows *176*; invention of 169–71; pre-digital information 173; research 178–81; understanding of 182–3; vulnerabilities *176*
Meechan, M. 64
Messenger 119, 120
Miller, C. 77, 88
Mobile Instant Messaging Services (MIMS) 116; controls 124; data 122; dependent variable 123; independent variables 123–4; marginal effects of *125–7*; multinomial models 124–5; populist parties' communication 117–20
Modi, N. 36, 39, 43
Mokken scale analysis 124
Morisi, D. 118

INDEX

Mosca, L. 12
movement parties: amalgamation of 2–5; and communication 18–20; communication practices in 24–6; delineation of 3; digital parties 20–23; online populism 20–3; populist communication 5–8; quality of democracy in 8–11; relational and dynamic perspective 23–4
movement-party alliances 3
Mozilla 183
Mudde, C. 89n1, 152
multiculturalism 59, 80, 121
Muslims *see* Islam
Mutz, D. C. 106

neoliberalism 9, 24
networked communication 2–5
NodeXL Pro 79
Nuttall, P. 61, 63, 65, 66

Obama, B. 105
online populism 19–23, 31

Palmer, C. 82
Palmer United Party 81, 87
Panebianco, A. 37, 38
party institutionalization: approaches to 37–8; personalistic and movement 36–7
Party of the Democratic Revolution in Mexico 38
Pauline Hanson's One Nation (PHON) 76–8, 80–9
PEGIDA 60, 63, 64
Peucker, M. 77
Pirro, A. L. P. 11, 12
Podemos 4, 6, 8–12, 24, 27, 30, 38, 94, 145, 146; growth of 96; history of 28; Internet, use of 97; organizational structure of 29; voting for 101
populism 5, 20, 117, 118, 121, 123, 151, 152; case selection 139–42; content and style 136–9; data collection 139–42; as ideology 152–4; nature of 135; as political communication style 154–7; relevance of 134; scholarship on 97; semantic analysis 143–5; topic model analysis 142–3; *see also* online populism
populist communication 2, 20, 136, 138, 140, 141, 145, 151, 152, 154–6; digital media for 119, 122; by movement parties 5–8; style elements *159*, 160–3
Portos, M. 12
Postman, N. 170, 171
Principal Component Analysis (PCA) 100

Quanteda package 61
Quaranta, M. 12

The Rage (Ebner) 179
Rajoy, M. 140, 141
Ramiro, L. 10
Rand, A. 47
Reddit 179, 180

Reinemann, C. 121
Renzi, M. 157
Robinson, T. 57, 63, 64, 69
Rohlinger, Deana A. 40
Roncarolo, F 153
Roose, K. 179, 180

Salvini, M. 123, 135, 141–3, 145, 146, 153, 157, 158, 160–3
Sánchez, P. 141
Sanders, B. 105
Schaub, M. 118
Schumann, S. 118
Segerberg, A. 98
Shaw, D. 174
Shorten, B. 86
Siddarth, D. 11
Silent Spring (Carson) 170
Simon, H. 171, 172
Slovak National Party 140
Social Networking Sites (SNS) 116, 117, 119; controls 124; data 122; dependent variable 123; features of 120; independent variables of 123–4; marginal effects of *125–7*; multinomial models 124–5; populist parties' communication 117–20; use of 122
Sørensen, E. 98
Spain 4, 6, 9, 10, 24, 28, 57, 96, 140; digital political participation in 98–9
Strache, H.-C. 135, 141, 143, 146
Swiss People's Party 134

Taneja, H. 181
Tansley, A. 169–71, 177, 183
Telegram 119, 120, 179, 182
TikTok 173
True Blue Crew 78
Trump, D. 82, 105, 170, 177
Tucker, J. A. 104
Twitter 40, 60, 61, 64, 65, 76–9, 118, 139, 154, 157, 158, 163, 176, 178; anti-ALP framing on *86*; descriptive statistics of **62**; fan-page network 81–4; Islamophobic framing on *85*; socio-demographic features of 140; UKIP **66**; use of 84–7; WPP **66**

UK Independence Party (UKIP) 7, 8, 11, 12, 56–8; anti-Muslim discourses in 64; electoral growth 63; organisational change 64; percentage of tweets **66**, **68**; portion of tweets 65, *66*; strategy 58–60; on Twitter pages 61, **62**
UK Labour Party 3, 104
United Australia Party (UAP) 76, 78, 80, 81, 83–9
United Kingdom (UK) 7, 56
United States 104, 170, 181, 183
US Republican Party 3

Vlaams Belang 70

Wardle, C. 177
War Plan Purple (WPP) 11, 58–61, 64, 65; percentage of tweets **68**; proportion of tweets *66*; on Twitter pages **62**, **63**
Waterloo, S. F. 120
Waters, A. M. 63, 64
Watson, P. J. 64
Weston, P. 63
WhatsApp 119, 120, 123, 129, 179, 182
Wilders, G. 81, 82

Wirz, D. S. 153
Wodak, R. 136
Wu, A. X. 181

Yellow Vest Alliance (YVA) 76, 78, 80–5, 87–9
Yiannopoulos, M. 64
YouTube 64, 171, 173, 178, 179, 182, 183

Zuckerman, E. 12

Taylor & Francis eBooks

www.taylorfrancis.com

A single destination for eBooks from Taylor & Francis with increased functionality and an improved user experience to meet the needs of our customers.

90,000+ eBooks of award-winning academic content in Humanities, Social Science, Science, Technology, Engineering, and Medical written by a global network of editors and authors.

TAYLOR & FRANCIS EBOOKS OFFERS:

- A streamlined experience for our library customers
- A single point of discovery for all of our eBook content
- Improved search and discovery of content at both book and chapter level

REQUEST A FREE TRIAL
support@taylorfrancis.com